'History comes alive in this book—in the intriguing detail of a Syrian who lived it, in the depth of a scholar who studied it. Syria's brutal war changed our world—Rime Allaf helps us understand why in her page-turner of a chronicle.'
Lyse Doucet, Chief International Correspondent, BBC News

'Weaving her own story through an account of recent Syrian history, Rime Allaf provides a riveting insider's perspective. She shows in painful detail how everyday life in Syria was dominated by the Assad family, so the reader understands why the country went so quickly from jubilation to jeopardy after the overthrow of Bashar Assad in 2024.'
Lindsey Hilsum, International Editor, Channel 4 News, and author of *In Extremis: The Life of War Correspondent Marie Colvin*

'A vital portrait of a nation whose fate will shape the Middle East—and the world. A Damascene and one of the region's esteemed analysts, Allaf blends intimate, on-the-ground reportage with piercing geopolitical insight to show Syria as few outsiders ever could. In the aftermath of the Assad regime's fall, her story makes one thing clear: to understand the future of the Middle East—with all its risks and possibilities—you must first understand Syria.'
Janine di Giovanni, Executive Director of The Reckoning Project, and author of *The Morning They Came for Us: Dispatches from Syria*

'I loved this book. Rime Allaf takes you on a journey, deeply personal at times, through Syria's recent history and revolution, her vibrant writing bringing life to every page.'
David Nott, author of *War Doctor*

'One of the most important books on Syria and its revolution. Its human voice rises above the noise of military analyses, major political issues, ideology and stereotyping, placing the Syrian people at the heart of the story: their dreams and disappointments, their astonishing resilience, and their determination to live, despite

all the death that has surrounded them for decades.'
>> Dima Wannous, author of *The Frightened Ones*

'A gripping and passionate account of how Syrians were subjected to fifty years of Assadisation, and how, despite betrayal and abandonment on many fronts, the long Syrian Revolution finally succeeded in breaking through. Full of forensic detail.'
>> Diana Darke, author of *Stealing from the Saracens*; *Islamesque*; and *My House in Damascus*

IT STARTED IN DAMASCUS

RIME ALLAF

It Started in Damascus

How the Long Syrian Revolution Reshaped Our World

HURST & COMPANY, LONDON

First published in the United Kingdom in 2025 by
C. Hurst & Co. (Publishers) Ltd.,
New Wing, Somerset House, Strand, London WC2R 1LA
Copyright © Rime Allaf, 2025
All rights reserved.

The right of Rime Allaf to be identified as the author of this publication is asserted by her in accordance with the Copyright, Designs and Patents Act, 1988.

Distributed in the United States, Canada and Latin America by Oxford University Press, 198 Madison Avenue, New York, NY 10016, United States of America.

A Cataloguing in Publication data record for this book is available from the British Library.

ISBN: 9781805264118

This book is printed using paper from registered sustainable and managed sources.

www.hurstpublishers.com

EU GPSR Authorised Representative
Easy Access System Europe Oü, 16879218
Address: Mustamäe tee 50, 10621, Tallinn, Estonia
Contact Details: gpsr.requests@easproject.com, +358 40 500 3575

Printed and bound in Great Britain by Bell and Bain Ltd, Glasgow

For my mother, my eternal inspiration who taught me everything we Damascenes do, and encouraged me to write the book she always knew I had to write.

For my daughter, the light of my life whose literary and artistic sense helped guide my path, generously indulging my Syria fixation with love and empathy.

For my brothers, whose selfless support and understanding carried me through my long journey.

And in memory of my father, who always carried his love of the nation with pride, and who believed in his convivial people's resolve.

'WE ARE THE PEOPLE WHO KNOW HOW TO ADORE LIFE;
NEITHER THE RUSSIAN BOMBING NOR USA'S IGNORING
WILL TERMINATE US.

THE SYRIAN REVOLUTION—FROM KAFRANBEL 31 OCT 15'

(Protest banner)

CONTENTS

Author's Note — xi

PART ONE
THE PATRIMONIAL LEGACY

1. Clinton's Sigh — 3
2. Twenty Years of Solitude — 29
3. Banana Politics — 51
4. A Breeze from Madrid — 71

PART TWO
AN ERRATIC DECADE

5. The Cult of Hope — 95
6. Rami's Prerogative — 115
7. The Prohibition Troika — 131
8. Entertaining Dissent — 149
9. Sibling Rivalries — 167
10. The Doctor's Turn — 187

PART THREE
THE REVOLUTION FOR DIGNITY

11. Anatomy of Extermination — 209
12. Death of an Illusion — 233

CONTENTS

13. The Great Exposure   255
14. New Dominions in Greater Syria   281
15. On the Winding Road to Damascus   305

Acknowledgements   331
Index   335

AUTHOR'S NOTE

This book was supposed to have a different ending. When Bashar Assad fled Syria on 8 December 2024, I had already written nearly ninety percent of *It Started in Damascus* and was about to start work on the last two chapters; the manuscript was scheduled for submission to my publisher in the early new year, for publication in the autumn of 2025.

Naturally, the last chapter was delayed and fully changed, to reflect the events of the last weeks of Assad's rule, and the initial shock, exhilaration, and anticipation following the regime's collapse. Nothing else was changed in the rest of the book, which remained faithful to the proposal I had written in September 2023.

Despite the wide coverage Syria received during the years of revolution and war, I knew that the people's struggle could only be understood within the context of their dreams, their patience, and the disillusionment that finally led to their uprising. Outside of geopolitical parameters, theirs was not a well-known history.

That is why the book begins with the hope that permeated much of Syrian society in 2000, taking the reader through the intricacies of the transition between two Assads—Hafez, the former minister of defence who had seized power in 1970, and his son Bashar who had unexpectedly become his heir while training as an ophthalmologist.

AUTHOR'S NOTE

Part One covers the three decades that preceded that event, recounting how Assad cemented his rule with the support of a loyal army, a pervasive intelligence apparatus, and a Baath Party tasked with indoctrinating generations of Syrians from their earliest school days. After Assad's domestic repression and regional trouble led to years of isolation, Syrians found themselves daring to hope that renewed international engagement would improve their lives.

In Part Two, the book resumes from that point of transition in 2000, taking the reader through Bashar's first decade in power. It relates the Damascus Spring of 2000–01, the socioeconomic dimensions of a closed economy and enduring restrictions of civil liberties, and the impact of his actions in Lebanon and Iraq that isolated Syrians again. By the end of that decade, however, Assad's fortunes had been revived and his ties with many nations rekindled.

Part Three unravels the timeline that drove some Syrians to demonstrate in March 2011, and recounts the regime's escalations that fuelled protests all over the country. Through Assad's increasingly heavy repression, culminating in a full war on the population with help from his foreign backers, the book demonstrates the clear connection between decisions made on a global scale and the regime's growing sense of impunity, leading to a displacement crisis not seen since World War II.

In my twenty-five years of work on Syria and the region, I have generated copious amounts of articles, briefings, papers, blogs, social media posts, interviews, and piles of notes that continue to invade my shelves; I therefore did not seek the help of a research assistant for this book and worked alone. Any mistakes or omissions I may have made will be mine. Most of the events and incidents I relate are easily searchable from credible sources with a proven record of accuracy.

Every personal anecdote I have recounted in the book happened exactly as told, but a few names were changed to protect

AUTHOR'S NOTE

the privacy of friends and relatives. These stories, I hope, will help introduce the different themes broached throughout.

* * *

It was my fate to be born in Damascus because it happened in the month of August, during my parents' visit back home. A lifelong diplomat, my father had whisked his bride overseas right after their wedding, and they whisked me out too when I was one week old. Despite never having lived in Syria as a child, save for a few months between my father's postings, my connection to my Damascene roots kept amplifying over the years, as did my fascination with Syria and my attachment to its people.

My hope is that after reading this chronicle of Syrians' aspirations and struggles, after seeing how the spark of their revolution was lit long before the Arab Spring, you will appreciate the tremendous fortitude of this warm and hospitable people in their hour of rebirth. My hope is that you join the friends around the world who have tirelessly supported Syrians' right to live in dignity, standing by them and carrying their voices; they have the eternal gratitude of a nation still trying to find its way, who will welcome old and new friends with open arms in the country Syrians are determined to rebuild.

I entrust you with *It Started in Damascus*, a labour of love and of intellectual necessity, hoping that I have given the Syrian people the recognition and the respect they are due.

20 May 2025
Rime Allaf

PART ONE

THE PATRIMONIAL LEGACY

1

CLINTON'S SIGH

Damascus springs often transitioned to summers rather swiftly, heralding a change of rhythm as temperatures rose. As soon as they finished lunch, the main meal of the day in Syria, most Damascenes slipped into a languorous mood and the pleasant hum of fans lulled them into a nice afternoon nap. The city slowed down, quietly recharging before the evening commotion; that was the time I would visit George on weekends, knowing we would have the place practically to ourselves. On that mellow Saturday in June 2000, after our leisurely coffee, cigarettes, and conversation, I relaxed as he ran his fingers through my hair; had the regime not ruined it, this would have been a great hair day.

Watching our reflections in the mirror as he worked his magic, I saw his associate Sami walking towards us, his face pale and looking sombre.

'The *muallem* has died,' he said in a low, trembling voice.

I swivelled in my chair to face them both, a flippant remark on the tip of my tongue about that imposed 'master' moniker; I was, to put it mildly, not exactly devastated by the apparent news that Hafez Assad, the tyrant whose rule had tormented Syrians for three decades, was finally dead. But George's face had dropped, and even though we had known each other for years, I sensed it was inappropriate—and, more importantly, unwise—to display anything but respectful concern. Courtesy aside, I trusted George, but not Sami.

For a while, they both just stood there looking stunned. Then George turned on the TV in the corner, flicking through channels: Syrian state television was still broadcasting its regular programming, but regional media networks were already in breaking news mode.

After years of rumoured ill health, evidenced by his drawn, yellowish face, the prospect of Assad's looming demise had been entertained, on and off, by Syrians and non-Syrians alike. One of the most comical Syrian rumours doing the rounds at the time was that the Mossad had secretly analysed his urine and determined he was dying; very few dared to wonder aloud how they would have gotten the sample, and even less whether Assad had provided it willingly to the Israeli secret service.

George turned my chair to face the mirror again and mechanically made a few quick finishing touches, as I wondered what my lovely hair and I would do after this buzzkill; Saturday night plans had just been cancelled for everyone.

'Do you think I should go back to my place or to Mom's?'

George was adamant: 'You go straight to your mother's house, and you don't move from there until further notice.'

My apartment, unfortunately, was situated in a street between the Malki and Muhajireen neighbourhoods, behind the presidential compound, a stone's throw from the very building where Hafez Assad lived, worked, and had probably died. I had often regretted having chosen that place where I hardly spent any time anyway, putting me in an area where the ubiquitous, black-suited security men parading their Kalashnikovs stood every few hundred metres, their constant glares reminding us that no matter who we were, we were always at their master's mercy.

CLINTON'S SIGH

I would have loved to see what they looked like at that moment, but it was not to be, at least not yet. Reluctantly, I concurred with George that it was probably best to head straight back to my family's home in the Mezzeh neighbourhood until we knew more. Just as I was grabbing my purse and turning to leave, a lady walked in, clearly unaware of the news. She was shocked to be turned away by the always courteous George, who explained gravely but gently that the president had just died and that he would have to close the salon. No further explanation was needed.

The lady and I silently stepped outside, nodding to each other before going our separate ways. My car was parked around the corner in front of Nora, the small store known to every Damascene as a 'supermarket' despite its eclectic, dusty, and ridiculously expensive merchandise, probably much like a black-market shop in Soviet Russia would have been. I glanced across to the Pit Stop café and to Gemini's above it, the trendy restaurant owned by the son of Mohamed Khouli, one of the regime's honchos; they were practically deserted, but that was not unusual at this time. On the palm tree-lined Abou Roummaneh Avenue just behind, the light traffic was normal for a Saturday afternoon in Damascus, and there was so far very little to indicate whether or not all hell was going to break loose.

Technically, there was no reason for trouble to erupt. Hafez Assad had meticulously prepared his succession over a long time, gradually alienating and eliminating all the important figures who could have posed a danger to his dynastic plans. With the main potential inner regime competition gone, hardly anyone was left to dare dispute the legitimacy of his son's ascension to power. To seal the deal, a few weeks earlier Assad had suddenly convened the Ninth Baath Party Regional Congress, due to take place that very month of June.

While the party's meetings are mostly for show, this one was significant, coming over fifteen years after its Eighth Congress in

IT STARTED IN DAMASCUS

January 1985. During that entire time, the party supposedly governing the country had not been summoned—or summoned itself—once, despite the many changes taking place in its self-appropriated realm. Indeed, members of the Central Committee of the National Command were practically clerks compared to those of the far more important Regional Command, which had decreed itself to be the body dealing with the entire Arab world. For Baathists, Syrian politics were not just about Syria.

Of course, this congress was meant to be a pre-coronation of sorts for the heir to the throne, Bashar Assad, who would parachute to the top tier of the Regional Command. One week after the death of Hafez Assad, it would now officially bestow upon Bashar, amongst other gratuitous graces, the leadership of the party that had controlled Syria since 1963, with the catchy slogan of 'Unity, Freedom, Socialism' for the lucky Syrians. As per the constitution adopted under Assad's rule, Bashar also got his nomination as the sole candidate for the next presidential referendum in which Syrians would be asked, for the sake of appearances, whether they accepted Assad (junior, this time) as their lord and master. And they always did.

The Baath Party took itself very seriously, and while some could consider it a mere third wheel, it was an essential pillar of the triple axis from which the Assad clan drew its power: army, intelligence, and party. Assad's death on 10 June 2000, just days before the hastily announced congress was to happen, meant the axis now needed a slightly revised scenario. Still, none of us imagined just how simple, and just how blatantly dictatorial, it would turn out to be over the next hours and days.

* * *

I decided to drive around a bit before heading home, just to get a sense of the mood. The traffic policemen did not seem tense, and while I probably could have passed by my place to pick up a few personal belongings, I was worried I would get stuck there when security forces and the army inevitably took over the streets of Damascus. Driving up Abou Roummaneh Avenue and turning at the Saudi embassy, I remembered that my cousin was also going to a salon in the area that afternoon, and thought I could pick her up on my way. I grabbed my phone to call my aunts who would have the salon's number; at the time, I was one of very few people in Syria to own a mobile phone.

When my aunt Amina answered the phone, her voice sounded hoarse and weak, and I thought I heard crying in the background; unless they had guests, that meant it was my two other aunts, Aicha and Wajiha, who were crying. I felt my heart sink to the soles of my feet as I stepped on the brake to slow down, bracing myself for the tragic news I was clearly about to hear—rendered doubly more difficult by the fact that whatever it was had seemingly happened on the exact same day the dictator died. Worst timing ever, I thought.

My three aunts were an institution. They lived together in a large apartment in Mezzeh, on the same floor as my family's home where my mother now lived. My paternal grandfather had commissioned that small building after selling the family's huge traditional Damascene house in which my father had grown up in the old city. Their home had become a nucleus of sorts for the myriad cousins and assorted relatives who would come visit them regularly throughout the year, and religiously on the occasion of every Eid, wedding, and funeral. If anything happened in the larger Allaf family, this was the place to be. And whoever had just died, judging from my aunt's voice, was a big deal.

'What is going on, *Ammeh*?'

My aunt blurted out in a weepy, high-pitched voice: 'The president died.'

'Yes, I heard the news, but what is happening with you? Are you all okay?'

IT STARTED IN DAMASCUS

This was serious crying, after all, not the woe-is-us kind of sorrowful tones and contrived tears, occasionally turned on to extract something—usually guilt—from one of us. We could tell the difference.

'Nothing happened to us, we are fine.'

'So why are you crying?' I asked, raising my voice slightly.

'We are sad about the president,' explained my aunt, as if talking to a very slow, clueless person.

As the years went by, and on the many occasions I have recounted this story, I have regretted every time a little more my enraged reaction to the sudden madness of these elderly ladies so dear to me. But as I screamed 'Have you all gone insane?' at my aunt, so loud that my throat hurt, I felt no sympathy for their strange, alleged pain, nor even relief at hearing that nobody in the family had died, today of all days. It took the sight of a traffic policeman to bring me back to my senses and to roll up the window.

Through her tears and despite my shouting, my desolate aunt and I managed to establish that my cousin had called and was already on her way home. I was confident that she, like me, would not be crying; as far as I knew, there were no regime fans among us.

I drove straight to Mezzeh and stormed into my aunts' apartment, finding them and a couple of cousins solemnly gathered, looking glum as they watched the main Syrian television channel. For once, they were not happy to see me, rightly expecting an epic rant following our surreal phone conversation. As I fired shocked questions about their behaviour, insisting they should be relieved Assad was finally gone, one of my cousins jumped up and closed the windows, beseeching me to lower my voice lest the neighbours—or worse—hear me.

As the daughter of their favourite late brother, I certainly had leeway in how I spoke with my aunts, to the annoyance of most cousins. I tended to be treated differently not only because of my presumed preferred niece status, but also because of my perceived foreignness given my lifelong Western upbringing and education. But my incensed outburst was indeed dangerous, and they wisely chose to ignore my provocations, waiting until I ran out of steam and shushing me as official media finally jumped into action.

The madness was just beginning, and compared to what we witnessed over the next days in Syria, my family's reaction turned out to be rather mild.

* * *

I had been trying to reach my mother or one of her friends since hearing the news. The entire Damascus Bridge Club, where she played several times a week, had gone to Aleppo for a tournament the day before, and I knew they would have just been starting a session when Assad's death had been announced. At least she would be safe, considering the elitist nature of the club; everyone there was someone, in Syrian terms, and the club was headed by a very close Assad relative who happened to love the game. When she finally managed to call me an hour or so later, she was brief and used her distinct 'don't say anything stupid over the phone' voice (not imagining I had already done that with crying relatives), saying she was driving back to Damascus with friends and would be home by midnight.

Meanwhile, in true Arab dictatorship fashion, official Syrian state television had nose-dived into full tragedy mode, broadcasting glorious Assad military moments (well, one really) in a loop, interspersed with replays of the announcement of his death. Thankfully, in those pre-YouTube and social media days, few outside the Arab world would have seen this bizarre Syrian spectacle. Think North Korea, but not as organised or decorous. And considering the forty-day mourning period the Assad regime had imposed on the entire population in 1994 after the death of heir number one, Bassel Assad, I was dreading what awaited us.

IT STARTED IN DAMASCUS

Brevity had not been required from Marwan Sheikho, the television presenter tasked with breaking the news we had already heard. In a long soliloquy fit for a holy prophet, voice trembling and sobs barely contained, wearing a suit as grey as his Baathist moustache, he enumerated Assad's heroic attributes. Hafez Assad, Sheikho reminded the nation, 'was the one who loved the people the most' and had been 'the star who lit the sky of Syria and the Arabs for more than three decades.' Not content with lighting our skies, if not always our streets and homes, Assad was also 'a lion who devoted his brain, body, and heart for the sake of hoisting the banner of the nation. He struggled, was patient, and endured for the sake of a safe, prosperous, proud, and strong homeland.'

This extraordinary eulogy did not refer to Assad as our immortal leader, even though this had been his standard appellation for years. Instead, Syrians were reminded that he was 'a father in his love for his citizens, sharing with them their sorrow and joy.' The presenter then concluded the mother of all obituaries, saying: 'My brothers, today, we lost a brother, a comrade, a friend, a father, a leader, and a teacher. Today is a day of sorrow and pain in every house, in every school, university, factory, farm, and shop.' No wonder my aunts were crying.

After telling Syrians how they should feel, live television coverage switched to the Syrian parliament where an extraordinary session—extraordinary in every sense of the word—was about to start. All the parliamentarians had been found and reported for duty within the hour, sitting elbow-to-elbow in the crowded assembly hall as the Speaker began the session with his own homage to Assad. As if on cue, most members of parliament, in unison with every member of the Syrian government seated in the front row, began crying, weeping, and making an absolute spectacle of themselves. As the nation's first official mourners, they embraced their roles with reckless abandon, some even hitting themselves in melodramatic grief in scenes we usually correlate with the theatrics of Arab soap operas. Only a select few retained a modicum of dignity in grave silence; for the camera-aware majority, the more distraught, the better.

Possibly for the first time in decades, Syrians the world over were paying attention to a session in parliament, assuming the technicality of transition was about to be resolved. The grapevine had been in overdrive with a question everyone had: with Bashar Assad guaranteed to succeed his father, how would the regime explain its flouting of the Syrian constitution, adopted by the regime itself nearly three decades earlier, requiring the Syrian president to be at least forty years of age? It was common knowledge that the heir was only thirty-four, and Syrians had been noting during the last year or two that the likelihood of his father kicking the bucket before Bashar reached the required age was increasing. Prayers for God to extend Hafez Assad's life had evidently not been heard, so what would the regime do now to maintain face?

Opinions on the matter had differed. Some thought we would be told deadpan that Bashar was actually already forty, silly us, and his birth certificate would simply be edited accordingly in the unlikely event anyone ever asked for it; after all, who were we to argue? Some believed the age requirement would be quietly lowered to thirty, a nice round number that catered to the regime's sudden need without unnecessary precision. Still others thought that the regime would simply ignore the age requirement altogether, since only a suicidal fool would dare to bring it up publicly. But I do not recall anyone correctly predicting what we saw unfold that day in parliament, because nobody thought they could be so shameless with the world's attention turned to Damascus.

In that small, crowded chamber, in the building dating back to the French Mandate where democracy had begun to sprout in Syria after independence, the Syrian constitution was changed right there and then, in mere minutes, without even the pretence

IT STARTED IN DAMASCUS

of a debate. In the midst of a humiliating display of exaggerated grief, the official representatives of the Syrian people (who, granted, did not have much choice in the matter) unanimously passed a change to the constitution, altering the required age for a president from forty to, lo and behold, thirty-four. They might as well have voted to require that the Syrian president be named Bashar Assad.

As Syrian jaws dropped despite the certainty we already had about the country's fate in the post-Hafez era, the Assad regime turned Syria into a hereditary republic where absolute power is bequeathed from father to son. And Hafez Assad had not even been buried yet.

* * *

With the derisory formalities of changing the constitution over, there was a funeral to organise. And if there's one thing Hafez Assad had always wanted, it was a funeral resembling that of the late Egyptian president Gamal Abdel Nasser, with the added glitz and glam of international representation. This required three components: a massive display of popular grief, à la Nasser, dedicated and extensive coverage by the world's leading media, and a respectable turnout of foreign dignitaries. The first component was easy, the second turned out to be a piece of cake, but the third was rather tricky.

Since the advent of the Baath Party to power and its imposition of the Emergency Law on 8 March 1963, civil liberties had been severely limited for Syrian citizens, foremost among which was the right to meet and to congregate freely. Groups of more than a few individuals theoretically had to obtain the authorisation of the security services before meeting anywhere outside a private home. Since the regime itself organised all the marches, rallies, and spontaneous protests in support of a given cause (such as Palestine) or in opposition to another (such as Western imperialism or Danish cartoons), it was necessary for the authorities to pre-approve the wished-for hordes of mourners flooding the streets. With rare exceptions, such as the massive funeral in 1998 of our beloved national poet, Nizar Qabbani, Syrians had rarely dared to take to the streets in groups of any size, let alone en masse.

On that Saturday night of 10 June 2000, most people were glued to their television sets, anxiously watching Syria take breaking news status everywhere. Those who carefully ventured outside would have noticed that only a few grocery stores had dared open that evening, after receiving assurances that it was allowed and that shopping for food was not deemed a serious threat to national security. This was an unprecedented situation, and few people wanted to be trailblazers.

When my mother finally arrived home that night, she told me they had all been seated at their bridge tables when someone arrived to inform the Club's manager, who then relayed the news of Assad's death to the entire hall. Without a word, she said, without needing to be told what to do, they all put their cards down and stood up for a minute of silence; they then rushed to their hotel rooms, packed precipitately, and were on their way back within the hour. The streets that usually bustled on Saturday nights were emptying out gradually, and little noise could be heard; everyone was on auto-pilot, trying to look inconspicuous and erring on the side of caution.

Thirty years of Assadism had trained Syrians well, I thought as I watched from our living room window the comings and goings at the Military Hospital, a few hundred metres from our building. I could have never imagined that just over a decade later, that same hospital would become the last station for thousands of dead Syrians who dared to defy the Assad dynasty by demanding the dignity for which they yearned, young Syrians who had become emaciated corpses in savage torture dungeons.

* * *

IT STARTED IN DAMASCUS

The next morning, unable to contain my curiosity any longer, I got into my car and made my way to my own apartment despite my family's protestations. I had never seen Damascus as I did that day, silent and eerily empty at a time when traffic is usually maddening. Gone were the cacophony of cars, the constant honking, the bicycles ringing their bells as they zigzag through congestion, the vendors banging on their carts or—worse—their gas canisters, shouting diverse offers in ear-piercing shrieks, the drivers blaring music in a never-ending competition to be louder than the others.

Soldiers and armed security were everywhere, at every corner, and along every main artery. On practically every car I saw that day and over the next weeks, a black ribbon had been tied to the antenna or hung on car windows. In the safety of my car, I had defiantly turned on my music, just loud enough to make me feel I had stood my ground and not followed the protocol, but my pointless pseudo bravery began to falter as I approached Umayyad Square and found military checkpoints stopping the few cars ahead of me. I quickly turned off the music and lowered my window as I stopped by the soldier, who looked down at me and simply stated the supreme Assad regime directive: *Mamnou* (it is forbidden).

Trying to sound adequately mournful, I told him where I lived and said I just needed to pick up some personal items to last me a few days. 'It is forbidden,' he repeated, annoyed by my petty request in this time of national tragedy, surprised I still had not turned the car around and driven obediently out of his sight. Of course, I had more than enough clothes at my mother's place, but I was itching to look around the area so I dared to insist.

As he considered how he should handle me, I saw my first march of popular mourners advancing onto Umayyad Square, filing in from Shukri Quwatli Street—which we all called Exhibition Street because of the International Damascus Fair that used to be held there. And an exhibition this certainly was: dressed in black from head to toe, sporting black bandanas and black shirts and black trousers, a group of youngsters carrying several black banners and identical portraits of the dead immortal leader were chanting for Assad and marching our way in unison.

I looked at my soldier again who finally took my name and instructed me to drive through the square to the next checkpoint by Assad Library, where his superior was posted. I had to drive at a snail's pace as the mourners passed around my car, bellowing odes to the president which, to me, sounded like battle cries. For the first time since Assad's death, I became apprehensive and suddenly felt I was sticking out like a sore thumb in my noticeable car with no black ribbon in sight, in my non-mournful attire of jeans and a blue t-shirt. For a moment, I regretted my empty bravado and wondered what I would do if they noticed I was not being respectful enough, but the youngsters were so entranced by their mourning mantras that they loudly marched past me, oblivious to the heathen in their midst.

When I reached the next checkpoint, I was distinctly more apologetic to the soldier's commanding officer, who easily let me through saying 'but quickly.' I drove up Adnan Al Malki Avenue and turned left on Ibrahim Hanano Street, approaching my building with trepidation, wanting to see something that would indicate the regime's mood. My field trip was disappointing, however, because apart from seeing many more men in black hugging their AK-47s, I found nothing to report but a magnified sense of heaviness. I hurriedly picked up a few things from my place and headed back a different way, passing Shami Hospital where even more fully armed men in black glared at me as I drove by slowly in the deserted street.

It was only Sunday morning so the marches still had to pick up speed; however, I already had no doubt that the regime would end up getting its multitude of mourners, and then some.

IT STARTED IN DAMASCUS

Indeed, over the next couple of days, the Baathist machine was in full grind as the biggest squares and the main streets of every Syrian city were overtaken by people hoisting banners and flags, spreading blackness everywhere. And for the first time, with the immortal leader out of the way, the country resonated with chants of 'God, Syria, and Bashar only,' with mourners pledging to sacrifice their soul and their blood for him, as they had for his father for the better part of thirty years.

We were treated to an impressive succession of marches, planned and executed by every committee, department, and section of the humongous Baathist machine. When the television announcer had said there was sorrow in every house, school, university, factory, farm, and shop, it was expected indeed that every house, school, university, factory, farm, and shop would demonstrate this sorrow one way or another. Those who organised, managed, and participated in the marches were checking 'present' on the obedience list. Just like their compatriots in the People's Assembly, many Syrians were making sure their allegiance was beyond doubt and their behaviour beyond reproach.

In every shop, in every office, in every school, and on most cars, photos of Hafez Assad were displayed either with a black ribbon or in a black frame. Posters and banners bearing eulogies and expressing sadness sprouted everywhere, as did condolence tents in various neighbourhood streets and squares. Bigger shopping areas dared to open again, discreetly, without the usual Syrian market hustle and bustle. Women avoided going out in full makeup, lest they be seen as disrespectful—not that there was anywhere to go, really.

Meanwhile, the regime had already demonstrated its strength and unity by broadcasting the visit of the country's top generals to the Assad home. Shown seated next to Bashar Assad on a blue sofa with a bright pink cushion between them, Minister of Defence Mustafa Tlass and other senior military officers were officially on a condolence call, but they were jovial and relaxed, in contrast to the vast officialdom which displayed only affected doom and gloom. The main message from that blue sofa and that pink cushion, a short walk from my own apartment, was simple: the army, the intelligence, and the party were in charge, and so was Bashar Assad.

These images were much more significant domestically than they were abroad, especially to media that thought Rifat Assad's statement, two days after his older brother's death, could amount to anything. Bashar's now insignificant uncle, once the second most powerful Syrian man, had been banished from the country since his failed coup attempt of 1984. From his Parisian mansion on Avenue Foch, from where he claimed he was the rightful heir of Hafez, he had become, as Syrians say, a zero on the left. In fact, every potential troublemaker had already been retired, demoted, or worse by Hafez Assad (the feared officials of the eighties and nineties like Ali Douba, Ali Haidar, and Hikmat Shehabi, for instance, were already out of the picture).

Not only was the regime fully in control, but it also found a way to skim off more money from Syrians over the next days, in ways no casual observer of Syria could even begin to guess. The three official Syrian newspapers, *Tishreen* (named for the month of October 1973, in what the regime has always marketed as a Syrian military victory in the war with Israel), *Al Baath*, and *Al Thawrah* (The Revolution), started publishing citizens' condolence messages, raking in millions. Most made do with two or three lines, the length of classified ads, but those who could afford it went bigger and bolder. The messages were read by television presenters, documenting the nation's grief in the absence of other programming, and subtly egging on people who had forgotten to pay—literally—tribute to Assad to do it promptly. The show-offs and the sycophants bought billboard space around the big cities and hung ugly banners on trees and buildings, advertising their bereavement and allegiance to Assad 2.0 for all to see.

To my immense frustration, my family did so too after my mother's well-placed friends advised her in no uncertain terms that she had to publish a message and include all our names. The last thing we wanted, the friends insisted, was to stand out with our silence, especially as my father had been an important Syrian official at one point. She paid the few thousand Syrian pounds necessary and arranged for the message to be published, as I fumed about our impotence and the little regard our friends had for my principles. Realpolitik started at home.

The marchers carried on, undeterred by the increasingly uncomfortable June temperatures. Whether because of the heat or because of their grief, a number of women began to faint on Syria's streets; as luck would have it, there was always a television camera or a photographer to catch their distress, bearing witness to the effect of Assad's death on his beloved people. Media networks large and small descended avidly on Damascus from around the world, jumping on the golden opportunity to look around after the regime, for once, had promptly granted visas to all those who wanted them. Many journalists crossed over from Beirut, and others flew into Damascus Airport for the first time, delighted to freely roam the streets of our beloved ancient capital and to capture the sights and sounds of a Syria that nobody—Syrians included—had seen before.

The result was superficial reporting laden with clichés, accompanied by simplistic analysis and some outright nonsense. This included news networks like CNN, whose correspondent explained with a straight face that 'everybody knows that Syria is going through a transition period, a transition period regarding the economy. There has been a campaign against corruption. Very high officials have been targeted. Some of them were kicked out. Some of them have committed suicide after they have been pursued by the law.' The claims that reform was underway, and that corruption was on top of the agenda, were as old as the Assad regime itself—neither new, nor factual.

'Hafez Assad is perceived here in Syria as the last Arab champion,' the reporter continued, elaborating that 'Dr Bashar has a vision, he wants Syria to be part of this new world.' Explaining what Syrians supposedly believed, the reporter concluded: 'They have known Dr Bashar through his campaign against corruption. So, their perception of Dr Bashar is that he's a pure man. He is clean. He is honest. He is trying to modernise Syria. He's trying to take Syria on a new course into globalisation, into opening up.'

This report would not have been out of place in Baathist state media, as was another in the *Los Angeles Times* explaining that 'to many people here, Assad was the man who made them proud to be Syrians.'

CNN also suggested that 'US officials right now are bracing themselves for what is likely going to be a behind-the-scenes power struggle in Damascus.' Not likely at all, actually, as anyone who knew anything about Syria could have told them. But foreign reporters were not entirely to blame for this debacle: having only ever reported about Syria from a foreign affairs perspective, usually within the limited contexts of Israel or Lebanon, most journalists for non-Arab media were unprepared to comment in depth on the situation, let alone to analyse the potential succession of events. For most foreign media, the situation in Syria was reduced to Bashar Assad's acceptance (smooth or otherwise) by the regime at large, and to his allegedly amazing qualities.

Adding to this scarce insight was the fact that at the time, the only Syria analysts known in academic circles, and very slightly in the media, were the scholarly, historian type, most of whom knew little about Syrian society. For the most part, they indulged in platitudes on macro-politics that had not been updated for years, viewing the Syrian regime through a regional prism, and evaluating it according to the relations it entertained with different powers. While this handful of experts may have understood the minutiae of regime actions on the basis of its relations with the US and the Soviet Union, they were ignorant of most Syrian socio-cultural and economic considerations, let alone of the travails of a population exhausted by decades of repression of free speech and civil liberties.

One of those scholars, whose body of work on Syria included one of the most flattering and forgiving biographies a tyrant could hope for, summarised the entire Syrian predicament and this monarchical transfer of powers to Bashar thus: 'He will not deviate from his father's political legacy. Now, the most important elements of that political legacy are the independence of Syria, its refusal to accept dictates from the United States or from Israel, the importance of recovering every inch of territory lost in 1967, but of course, at the same time, the readiness to make peace, as long as it's an honourable peace.' Syrian people and society were absent from Patrick Seale's considerations.

The consequences of the preceding thirty years for Syrians either signified little or were unknown to academics or journalists, and those in Damascus who could have told them a few truths about the real Assad legacy would not have even dared to whisper them.

* * *

With such unprecedented coverage massaging the biggest Syrian regime egos, the Assad dynasty had only the foreign dignitaries to fret about. That was far from a done deal, especially with the recent competition; thirty years having passed since the funeral of Gamal Abdel Nasser, there were two more recent state funerals against which to be measured and appraised.

When King Hussein of Jordan died in February 1999, his state funeral was attended by an international Who's Who, including the sitting US president accompanied by three former US presidents, the presidents of Russia and France, the secretary general of the United Nations, the British prime minister, and numerous other leaders—including Hafez Assad himself who showed up in Amman at the eleventh hour, having realised he could not miss a golden opportunity to appear reasonable and rub shoulders with other leaders. Likewise, for King Hassan of Morocco's funeral in July 1999, practically every other president and world leader made the trip to Rabat, except Assad who did not even bother to turn up, sending his vice-president, Zouheir Masharqa, instead.

As is customary in the Muslim tradition of prompt burial, King Hussein was buried the day following his death in Amman, while the funeral of King Hassan, who died on a Friday at 16:30, was held on Sunday in Rabat. For Hafez Assad, the regime gave itself a full three days to prepare for the funeral on Tuesday 13 June (and that is assuming that he indeed died on 10 June, and not earlier). It was perhaps hoped that more time would help beef up attendance, but no reason was given for this delay.

Official Syrian media had regularly lambasted both late kings and other Arab leaders indirectly as being 'puppets of the West' because of their good relations with the latter; nevertheless, it was clear the latter would be very welcome in Damascus for such an occasion should they decide to come. Nobody in Syria imagined for a moment that the US president would deign to attend the funeral, even though some probably wished for a miracle. It was announced early on that President Jacques Chirac would be making the trip, France having become increasingly involved in the region under his presidency. Chirac had even welcomed Bashar Assad to the Elysée Palace a few months earlier and honoured him by greeting him on the steps outside, in his capacity purely as son (and expected heir) of Assad.

For the rest, it was open to speculation, but it gradually became clear that the highest level the Syrians could hope for,

IT STARTED IN DAMASCUS

from most Western democracies at least, would be that of prime minister or foreign minister. The presidents of Turkey and Bulgaria showed up, but UN Secretary General Kofi Annan, who had rushed to the funerals of King Hussein and King Hassan, only sent his chief of staff to Damascus. Britain sent its foreign secretary, Robin Cook, and European Union countries joined forces by sending Romano Prodi, EU Commission president.

More surprising was the relatively low-level representation of Russia, where Vladimir Putin had become president a few months before. After having initially announced that Putin would attend the funeral, Russia was represented instead by Duma Speaker Gennady Seleznyov and former foreign minister Yevgeny Primakov. Considering the decades-long alliance between the former Soviet Union and Baathist Syria, this had been neither anticipated nor appreciated by Syrians, and Putin at the time would never have imagined that Assad would one day become his most problematic but also most useful protégé, giving Russia the foothold it needed in the region with a port and an airbase on the Mediterranean.

In the Arab world, reactions to Assad's death were, as expected, gracious and respectful, as by this time he was considered an unavoidable player in the region. Saudi Arabia, Egypt, and Syria had become a regional political troika in Assad's last years, agreeing to agree on most of the area's pressing issues while accepting that each country would deal with its immediate surroundings as it saw fit. The big Arab names all came to pay their respects, and even Palestinian leader Yasser Arafat hitched a ride with Egyptian president Hosni Mubarak, not wishing to tempt fate by showing up alone after a particularly rough patch with the Syrian regime. The biggest and loudest mourning sounds came from Lebanon, of course, which after twenty-five years of Syrian occupation knew on which side its bread was buttered; it announced seven days of official mourning as Lebanese leaders and businessmen flocked to Damascus, looking suitably solemn and forlorn. Not to be outdone, North Korea—Assad's source of inspiration for an unrestrained cult of personality that turned the country into 'Assad's Syria'—declared its own week of mourning as well.

* * *

Those following Syrian affairs would never have expected that President Bill Clinton, who had attended both King Hussein and King Hassan's funerals, would make the trip to Damascus for Assad's. Although relations with the Clinton administration were relatively cordial at the time, Syria was still considered a sponsor of terrorism by the US and was very far from having the type of relations countries like Jordan or Morocco enjoyed with America. Moreover, the last Clinton–Assad encounter, a summit in Geneva a few months prior to discuss the ever-stalled peace process between Syria and Israel—a summit initiated by Assad himself—had infuriated Clinton after he was subjected to the notoriously lengthy Assad lectures and a pointless meeting. Although Israel had not given any concessions either, Clinton was embarrassed to have been put in this position by Assad and felt he had given him a free PR stunt.

On that Saturday 10 June, President Bill Clinton had been sitting on a stage in Minnesota, waiting to address a graduating class and about to become an instant hit on Syrian screens. In a short scene caught on camera, an aide passed him a slip of paper with the news of Assad's death; Clinton read it and, in his characteristic expressive manner, pressed his lips in what could possibly—very liberally and creatively—have been interpreted as a resigned sigh. It was not an expression of sadness or shock, but likely a quick mental calculation of what he would soon have to say about it. These few seconds ended up on Syrian national television on repeat. Clinton's decent statement was aired repeatedly, of course, but Syrian TV presenters outdid themselves with an emotive description of what they decided, for lack of a better offer, best conveyed the importance of Assad's life and death to the United States. 'And he sighed,' they said, over and over, pausing dramatically each time President Clinton was shown reading the note, and then, well, sighing. '*Wa tanahhada*' would repeat the grave voice-over, willing people to believe that Clinton's sigh encapsulated Assad's status, regardless of who showed up for the funeral.

Even casual students of Assadology at the time would have understood that stuck, as ever, between hating the US and wishing it could be admired by it, the Assad regime was pretending it did not care that it had to settle for a ministerial-level representation from Washington. After he was done sighing, Clinton had dispatched Secretary of State Madeleine Albright and civil rights leader Jesse Jackson to the funeral, both of whom were kept waiting to meet Bashar while he chatted at length with Iran's president, Mohammad Khatami. This first meeting of the Bashar era had set the pace for a new level of relations that would grant the Iranian Islamic regime unprecedented influence and access to Syrian resources, land, and political and military power, years before the revolution.

Other Arab states may have had the fancy packed funerals, but the Assad regime had Clinton's sigh. Remarkably, many Syrians also felt they had Clinton's sigh, and in the days and weeks that followed, I began to understand just how much they, too, were hungry for recognition from the world, and how much the period following Assad's death had demonstrated their need to stand and be counted.

Official mourners were of course putting on an act expected of them, but there were undoubtedly other factors responsible for these overly dramatic, exaggerated displays of patriotic grief. Syrians from the older generation had gotten used to the quiet status quo; my aunts, like many others, had accepted the presidency-equals-country equation, and were shaken when something happened to either of them after thirty years of history between them. Others, having invested years of obedient acquiescence in order to eke out a living, were hoping their sacrifice would pay off; they had reached a modus vivendi that was the best they could get, and therefore did not want to jeopardise it by rocking the boat, even if they were not truly mourning Assad's passing. The vast majority stayed home, indifferent at best, with unknown numbers skilfully masking their schadenfreude.

But what about all these young people who rendered such convincing performances in front of the media, and who so loudly, so resoundingly mourned the only president they had ever known? Were these seemingly indoctrinated Baath scouts really that grief-stricken, even though they knew full well, despite their young age, that theirs was a country like no other? Why were the ones who watched foreign channels and craved all things Western, who dreamed of unattainable social and civil liberties, who fantasised they would one day achieve a semblance of a normal life—why did they care, or at least pretend to care, that Assad was dead? Why did they declare their allegiance to the appointed heir so persuasively?

Were they all afflicted by Stockholm Syndrome? Partly, perhaps, and this would be a terribly expedient explanation if it were that simple. As the following months and years would prove to me, however, there were more layers of reason to this apparent dichotomy.

These young people, and all those they indirectly represented, simply had a visceral need to matter to the world. They needed to count, to be seen and heard, to be considered, to be part of something big as others started to watch them. After years of isolation, after this long journey alone, they yearned for meaning, for a place in the universe. That June of 2000, they—and their parents—thought that they had reached a bend in the road, and that a smooth stretch to normality was about to start.

IT STARTED IN DAMASCUS

I have no doubt that they thought Bashar Assad's rite of passage was theirs too, a realisation I often remembered with sadness as I watched them evolve and then regress over the next decade, slowly reaching the point of implosion.

Most people I spoke to over the next weeks seemed upbeat about the smooth succession of events, about the imperceptible feeling of change they swore was in the air. It was frighteningly simplistic, as if anything less drastic than the doomsday scenario was a reason to rejoice and be grateful. Even the forty-day mourning period turned out to be less stifling than the one Assad had imposed in 1994, following the death of his original heir, Bassel; this time, regular living was allowed, as long as it was quiet, orderly, and clearly respectful.

As media, regions, and world watched Syria and Syrians with interest, for once with genuine curiosity instead of the distrustful glare of yore, a sense of calm and relative order reigned around me, and hope seemed to spring eternal as people started showing visible signs of relief that life could, just maybe, get a little better. I remained in the sceptical camp, not expecting worse, but also not expecting much better ahead save for cosmetic makeovers. Above all, I was taken aback by how deliriously optimistic so many seemed to be.

A single friend, a known stubborn critic of the regime who exactly two years later would pay dearly for his defiance with a ten-year jail sentence, joined me in viewing this hype with concern. A few days after Assad's burial, as we met to browse the net for coverage about Syria, he told me in confidence: 'The day might come when we will regret Hafez Assad and have mercy on him.' As one of the least enthusiastic Syrians about the potential of Bashar, I thought my friend was surely exaggerating; no matter how bad Bashar was, and even if he was just as bad as his father had been, he could not possibly be worse. Or could he?

In the early morning of 13 June, I opened the front door after hearing unusual noises outside: one of the men in black stood on the landing, clutching his Kalashnikov to his chest, waiting for my aunt next door to bring the key that would open the door to the roof of the building. Neither of us even bothered to mutter a simple hello as we glared at each other until he climbed the stairs to the top, mutual resentment unexpressed but nearly palpable. Of course, no one would have dreamed of requesting his ID or refusing to comply, but I was surprised that snipers would be placed so far off the funeral route, and irritated by the regime's unnecessary display of absolute power to civilians everywhere.

A few hours later, we all watched an impassive, unflustered Bashar Assad walking towards Umayyad Square behind his father's coffin, smiling faintly as he waved to people who were shouting the slogan that years later would gain a truly morbid meaning: God, Syria, and Bashar only. This was by no means a reluctant heir. Even before he officially sat on the throne a month later and was anointed president in a referendum that gave him 99.7% of the votes, a humble figure compared to his father's 100% the year before, Bashar Assad had been hastily promoted to the rank of Field Marshal and named Commander-in-Chief of the Syrian Armed Forces.

The Ninth Baath Party Congress, which Hafez Assad missed by a week, had obediently come out of its fifteen-year slumber to consecrate Bashar as the head of the party and as the sole presidential candidate, courtesy of the amendment to the Syrian constitution days earlier. And Bashar Assad, in the first of what would be many long, rambling speeches, inaugurated his reign calmly with a televised address at the People's Assembly, only interrupted by parliamentarians shouting odes to his glory and virtually throwing themselves at his feet. Just as he had wanted since his brother's death, after years as the alternate heir while his more powerful relatives ruled, Bashar was finally king of the realm.

As things settled after this nominally transitional period that changed Syria, and that would eventually change so much in the world, the Assad regime was extremely pleased with itself: it got the popular homage it demanded, it received the attention of the world's most important media, and it bagged crowds of mourners, Chirac's presence, and Clinton's sigh.

The popular clamour was considered an entitlement and went unacknowledged as business got back to usual. But the regime should have been paying closer attention to the resigned and relieved sighs of millions of Syrians who, having spent the previous thirty years paying their dues, were waiting for an escape route from their virtual enclosure. They believed that Bashar's direct and implied promises on every possible matter, domestic and international, meant that their lives were slowly but surely going to change for the better over the next years.

It was supposed to be a modern story of survival and rebirth, of strength and radiance emanating from the oldest capital in the world. With each of the regime's missed opportunities and delusions of grandeur, however, it turned gradually into a tale of shattered dreams that had started, that fateful month, in beautiful Damascus.

2

TWENTY YEARS OF SOLITUDE

The airport road ran a good thirty kilometres in a straight, deserted stretch before hitting the city. With unshakable confidence that behind everything lay a nefarious reason, the Syrian grapevine argued that the Assad regime had built the airport as far away as possible from the centre to hinder a coup or a military takeover, giving the regime time to activate its reinforcements in Damascus. It made total sense to us, even when reminded that the French had started building the airport in 1965—post-Baath, but pre-Assad.

For this first family trip back to Syria in over eight years, my parents had drilled my brothers and me about what to do, and even more about what not to do: we were to see nothing, hear nothing, and above all say nothing—especially in public. In the shabby airport's cavernous arrival hall barely illuminated with dim neon lights, we had remained quiet, intimidated by gigantic portraits of Hafez Assad and the glare of scattered armed men eyeing us as we walked from the baggage belt. Unlike the rest of the equally tired passengers on our flight, who braced themselves for the infamously petty, invasive search of their luggage, we breezed through customs as my father's status and our diplomatic passports opened invisible doors; most other Syrians could not get through without enduring a humiliating search and paying a hefty bribe if they happened to have a non-authorised item.

As my father was whisked away by one group of waiting family members, one of our well-to-do relatives handed my mother the key to a car he generously offered for our stay, and we piled in as she reluctantly took the wheel. At a stop on a major road crossing, the car stalled, and it took my flustered Mom a few tries to get it started and moving again; used to her smaller automatic car, she was uncomfortable driving this large manual transmission Mercedes on roads she had not seen for years. Finally home, where more relatives welcomed us, she mentioned how pleasantly surprised she had been by the considerate behaviour of other drivers stuck behind us for a while.

'Imagine, nobody honked!' she said. A couple of cousins exchanged glances, nodding knowingly as she continued: 'In most other cities in the world, they would have at least flashed their lights after a few seconds.'

My uncle chuckled: 'It's not because they're civil or nice; they didn't honk because they were afraid.' Afraid of what? 'Not of what, but of who they assumed your husband could be,' he explained, 'because only someone high up could have a car such as this one. They wouldn't dare honk no matter how long it took you to get the car started again'.

We had been in Damascus less than an hour and had already learned that the rich and powerful here were not like the rich and powerful elsewhere. During the dark, stifling 1980s in Assad's Syria, owning any car—let alone a luxurious one—had become an unattainable dream for the overwhelming majority of Syrians. For the normal people to whom laws actually applied, car imports were only possible through the government after years on a long waiting list and the payment of an import tax of nearly 300%. Like Cubans who lovingly pampered their vintage American cars, Syrians who already owned a car before Assad's Baathist era thanked their lucky stars and treated their treasured, battered old cars with the utmost care and devotion.

The laws of the land did not apply to the flashy cars of the top percentile that made their appearance on the streets of Damascus, often at breakneck speed because they could, or in menacingly slow motion as they patrolled the few areas where young women would take a stroll in the evenings. These cars were the quasi-unique privilege of regime officials and insiders, a few government officials, and some wealthy personalities (such as the uncle who lent us his car) who had good ties with them and whose businesses were regime-sanctioned.

My grandmother had been preparing for our visit for months, stocking up on the things she knew we would expect to find. That first night, she had opened a closet in the hallway and proudly pointed to the loot she had been stashing for us: rolls of toilet paper, packs of paper tissues, odd assortments of soap, all smuggled from Lebanon or bought at exorbitant prices around the city when word got around that a delivery of things Syrians craved had arrived in some shops. These were luxuries in Assad's Syria, and my grandmother seemed a bit disappointed that we were not more impressed by her prowess. 'Use them sparingly,' she advised, seeing we had not grasped the value of these supplies, 'we might not be able to get more while you are here.' That certainly got our attention.

It did not take us long to realise that what my parents had been told during our extended years in the US and Switzerland was only the tip of the iceberg. Even the oppressive summer heat, which we later discovered was practically inescapable save for scattered hours when the regime magnanimously allowed homes access to electricity, was not as palpably heavy as the weight of the omnipresent air of Big Brother. Except there was no pretence that it was brotherly at all.

IT STARTED IN DAMASCUS

Life had become a struggle for Syrians following the Hama massacre of 1982, itself a culmination of the regime's battle with the Muslim Brotherhood that had instigated an armed insurrection in the late 1970s. To secure his regime and prevent other threats, Assad had imposed draconian measures on the population, leading to conditions so extreme that other Arab dictatorships looked mild in comparison. The few civil liberties that had miraculously survived the Baathist coup of 1963 had become relics of the past, especially when things soured outside Syrian borders as well. In the blink of an eye, this sociable, generous, convivial society found itself a prisoner of conditions it could not have foreseen, taking away its ability to move or breathe without the scrutiny of the regime's security forces who controlled every action and monitored every word. For years after Hama, survival of the quietest was the only strategy to follow.

* * *

Nothing in Hafez Assad's first years in power had prepared them for any of this. In fact, there had even been a common high on a national level following the joint Syrian-Egyptian war of October 1973, an attempt to regain the Syrian and Egyptian lands invaded and occupied by Israel in the 1967 Six Day War. Although the war did not achieve its declared goals, a patriotic wave had carried Assad through that period, the first instance of a demonstrable point of agreement between regime and people on an issue of true national interest, a mere three years into his presidency.

Syrians the world over had supported government and army in a rightful cause they held dear—the return of the Golan Heights to Syria. Most were filled with a sense of national pride, no different to any other population's attitude when combating an enemy. Moreover, the sudden comings and goings of the US Secretary of State and other international figures to Damascus gave Syrians a sense of regional importance and belonging. For

Assad, this genuine popular support and international spotlight was doubly rewarding, somewhat effacing his 1967 failure to defend the Golan as Syrian minister of defence.

In the aftermath of these 1973 events, the notion of an Assad regime as we then got to know it was inconceivable, despite being yet another military governance. The country's short-lived democratic era and the free speech it had enjoyed when the French Mandate ended in 1946 were by now a fading memory, and Syrians were used to having successive leaders for relatively short periods in power, following the first military coup of 1949 (with the blessing of the CIA) that overthrew Syria's democratically-elected president, Shukri Quwatli.

Assad's own coup of 1970, ousting President Nureddin Atassi and Baath leader Salah Jadid, seemed to be gaining in stability and acceptability: he was seen as the military dictator he was, for sure, but not yet a sinister tyrant. Nobody could have predicted that the imprisonment of President Atassi, liberated because of ailing health only a few months before his death in 1992, and that of Salah Jadid, thrown into and left in a jail cell until his death in 1993, were going to be a leitmotif of the Assad dynasty with anyone who stood in its way.

Naturally, the 1973 war also got the full attention of the US, not only in the obvious context of its support of Israel, but in the consequent one of the pan-Arab support of Syria and Egypt. As Israelis counterattacked on the Golan, troops from Iraq, Jordan, Morocco, Kuwait, and Saudi Arabia had supported Syrian forces' operations. But in response to Israel's request for $850 million worth of weapons, President Richard Nixon had offered it a $2.2 billion package instead and triggered King Faisal of Saudi Arabia to respond with the Gulf-led OPEC oil embargo. This drove oil prices to unprecedented heights, decreased production, and spread panic around the world until it was lifted in March 1974.

Henry Kissinger, the newly appointed American Secretary of State, travelled tirelessly between various influential countries

IT STARTED IN DAMASCUS

after the October War, developing shuttle diplomacy and paving the way for a regional entente that would guarantee disengagement with Israel and the all-important security the US sought. This opened the door to a first in the history of modern Syria: a visit by a US president that would highlight Syria's and Assad's stature in the region. In June 1974, President Nixon and his wife Pat found temporary respite from the Watergate scandal in the friendly Middle East, travelling to several welcoming capitals and delighting Damascus with a visit that seemed to herald a new era of cordial relations.

The Nixons stayed at the government's official Guest Palace at the bottom of Abou Roummaneh Avenue, from whose balcony President Gamal Abdel Nasser had greeted tens of thousands of enthusiastic supporters in 1958 celebrating the creation of the United Arab Republic, the union between Syria and Egypt that would only last until 1961. As the official motorcade passed crowds of genuinely interested Syrians waving at them throughout the city, the Nixons were also greeted by a big sign with the message 'Revolutionary Damascus Welcomes President Nixon'.

Just before the state dinner at the famous Orient Club where Nixon and Assad said all the right things to one another, the Nixons had even met the Assad children, the occasion recorded for posterity with a photograph that could have been mistaken for a memento from a pleasant reunion between long-time friends. When the return of ambassadors was agreed between the two presidents, it seemed that the years of hostility following the closure of the US embassy in 1967 were starting to fade away.

* * *

In that summer of 1974, Hafez Assad was standing at a crossroads. Syria's population was just over seven million, growing steadily in an environment that could have delivered great potential for the country. Even before the oil and phosphate production sectors took off, agriculture was already a leading Syrian cash cow (with crops like cotton accounting for roughly a third of exports in the mid-seventies) and manufacturing was developing. The loss of Syrian productivity resulting from the 1963 Baathist takeover and its detested nationalisations, à la Nasser, was now being offset by money flowing copiously from the Arab Gulf countries, eminently familiar with the commercial mindset of Syrian merchants and entrepreneurs who had brought their mercantile vitality to Lebanon, Egypt, and elsewhere in the Arab world. There was every reason, then, for lucrative economic stability and industrial growth to become key indices of Syrian development.

Less than two months after the Nixon visit, on 9 August, a new American ambassador was appointed to Damascus; fate dictated that it was on the same day that President Nixon resigned and that President Gerald Ford took office. While Kissinger retained his position of Secretary of State, he had already managed to get the Agreement of Disengagement signed between Syria and Israel before Nixon's visit; his shuttle diplomacy had achieved its purpose in the twenty-eight visits he had made to Damascus since the October War. From Kissinger's perspective, there was no need for him to maintain this kind of engagement at such a high level when the problem, as seen by the US, had been resolved: the Syrian–Israeli border was to remain quiet for decades, even as Israel continued to illegally occupy the Golan.

Even though President Jimmy Carter would travel to Geneva in May 1977 specifically to meet with Assad, interpreted as a gesture of esteem for Syria's position while other important Arab leaders like President Anwar Sadat and King Hussein would go to Washington, and though President George H. W. Bush would meet Assad in Geneva in 1990 as the world dealt with the Iraqi invasion of Kuwait, it would be twenty years before another US president visited Damascus again, for just a few hours.

IT STARTED IN DAMASCUS

Assad was already heading in an entirely different direction in the cultivation of other foreign ties and, unfortunately for Syrians, he liked what he saw on his new ventures and decided to bring it home. The steady ascension into full-fledged authoritarianism was about to begin in earnest.

* * *

In September 1974, still on a high from his auspicious start and popular action to retrieve occupied Syrian land, and from being courted by important partners, including Arab leaders, Hafez Assad travelled to two of the most closed countries in the world. These visits would have a lasting and terribly detrimental effect on his regime's approach to governance. The first was a trip to Bucharest to visit Romanian president Nicolae Ceaușescu, and the second was to Pyongyang to meet with North Korean leader Kim Il Sung, both dictators heading extreme authoritarian regimes that controlled their populations with an iron fist. It was the latter, in particular, who triggered in Assad the inspiration for a giant personality cult—just as he had done for Ceaușescu following his own visit to North Korea three years prior.

Coming so soon after the welcome attention it had received from world leaders and fellow Arab states, the Syrian population would find this unexpected development much less palatable. Assad could hardly wait to apply this tried and tested method for total control, whose results he had witnessed first-hand and now openly craved; with the ruling Baath Party and the army under his belt, and a growing network of intelligence and security services, the mechanism needed for Assad to make Syria his—in name and in deed—was ready.

No sooner had he returned to Damascus than he began to develop the paraphernalia to propel this cult of adulation to extraordinary levels. Creeping Assadisation was just beginning to show its tentacles throughout Syria, and domestic and foreign mayhem was merely going to help the regime cement this aggressive personalisation drive over the next years. Syrians witnessed, speechless and powerless, how anything relating to the state became directly associated with Assad, the nation's identity becoming inseparable from his own.

Soon after, we got Assad's National Library, Assad's Dam, and Lake Assad on the majestic Euphrates river, which he would have probably appropriated as well in this renaming frenzy if he thought he could get away with it. Syria became Assad's Syria, a national identity theft that preceded and far outdid any other regional dictator's delusions of grandeur, an identity posted in literal claim of every Syrian border and in every area of the realm. Some began to wonder whether the Golan Heights, should they return to Syrian sovereignty under this regime, would also become Assad's Golan.

The Eternal Leader, as he eventually started promoting himself so that people understood he was not going anywhere, saw to it that this spiritual eternity rested on physical dimensions as well. Posters of the leader in various settings were multiplying like wild mushrooms all over the country, a permanent benevolent smile always there to seemingly refute notions of force or authoritarianism, whether he was shown dressed in military fatigues and dark sunglasses or a business suit. As the years passed, it seemed that Assad was on every wall and every shop and car window, his face and his name inescapable in Syrian public space.

Murals copied from North Korea, themselves replicas of material from the golden years of Soviet and Maoist propaganda, began spreading all over Syrian towns; the Leader was always surrounded by his adoring population of workers, farmers, and students, all enthralled by Assad's benevolence, wisdom, and vision, ecstatic to be in his presence. These assorted frescoes and images were supplemented by larger-than-life statues of Hafez that sprouted liberally, keeping an eye on Syrians throughout the dominion. You could not forget about Assad if you tried: his giant likeness on paper, in bronze, or in stone, and above all his name, had overtaken Syria's public space while his intelligence services invaded the limited remaining private space.

Hafez Assad's pearls of wisdom and pronouncements on matters of state were published every day, splashed in the headlines of the three official newspapers. The execrable *Syria Times* newspaper, a worse version of the worst Assad-era publications translated into what can only be called a semblance of English, was born a few years into the evolution of the Assadisation drive. A bad copy of its muse, the *Pyongyang Times*, it brought the regime's Baathist and cultist drivel to wider non-Syrian audiences so they could bask in Assad's glory as well—and many of them did, as we discovered decades later to our great surprise.

Was there something in the celebrated water of Damascus, from the lovely springs of Fijeh, that pushed Syrian men to get too big for their military boots as they clutched the reins of power in post-independence Syria? After all, Adib Shishakli's few years in command in the 1950s had already shown us how men at the top inflated their own importance to the country, relying on modern, albeit rudimentary public relations gimmicks and communication offensives (including a caricature of Shishakli as the Statue of Liberty, raising a torch of freedom). This was true of many world leaders of the post-colonial era though, not just limited to Syria or even the Arab world. Appropriating a nation's entire cultural heritage and identity, however, was a purely Assadist audacity of a different level altogether in the region, and it used a lot more than imagery, slogans, and crude propaganda without the slightest attempt at subtlety.

* * *

Syrian circumstances were to change irreversibly with the start of the civil war in Lebanon in April 1975, presenting Assad with an opportunity to grant himself the Levantine leadership role he believed was his to take. In his capacity as head of the Arab Socialist Baath Party and all that entailed in pan-Arabist ideals, the geographical limitations of the modern Syrian state were not enough to contain his wider aspirations.

By 1976, Assad had dragged the Syrian army, and the entire country with it, into the heart of Lebanese and Palestinian affairs with an occupation that would last three decades. Formally acting as the Arab Deterrent Force, sanctioned by the League of Arab States to pacify Lebanon as it faced mounting challenges to its state authority from Palestinian militias, the Syrian army's first goal was to contain the Palestine Liberation Organisation (PLO) and various leftist guerrillas opposed to Maronite Christian groups—in effect putting Syria and Israel on the same side.

Lebanon had become the PLO's main base following its expulsion from Jordan. In 1970, during a period that became known as Black September, King Hussein had reclaimed control of Palestinian militias' strongholds in Jordanian territory, from where they had been launching attacks on Israel in their quest to liberate Palestine. By the summer of 1971, the Palestinian militants and leaders had relocated to Lebanon and recreated the mini state within a state that the Syrian army, as the Jordanian army had before it, would try to subdue.

In August 1976, shortly after Syrian troops entered Lebanon as its civil war intensified, the self-proclaimed defender of the Palestinian cause tasked his army with helping enforce the long siege started by militias from the Lebanese Front, a coalition of nationalist parties, and then with leading the assault that massacred up to 3,000 Palestinians in the UNRWA-administered refugee camp of Tal Al Zaatar in East Beirut. Nearly four decades later, his son Bashar would enforce another siege and a massacre of Palestinians in Damascus, with Hezbollah helping the Syrian army's assault on the camp of Yarmouk.

IT STARTED IN DAMASCUS

While the Arab League had sanctioned Syria's entry into Lebanon, the Tal Al Zaatar massacre was not well received by most Arab rulers, for whom the appeal of Assad was beginning to dampen. Following a few years of Gulf money pouring into Syrian coffers, especially following the 1973 October War, the easy liquidity began to slow down with Assad's actions in Lebanon. When Israel invaded southern Lebanon in 1978, and then Beirut in 1982 where its three-month siege and war killed some 18,000 people, it ended with the expulsion of the PLO from Lebanon and with the massacre by the Lebanese Forces of up to 3,500 Palestinians in the camps of Sabra and Shatila, this time with the assistance of the Israeli army.

There was little Syrian involvement as these cataclysmic events shook Lebanon and the region in the summer of 1982. Assad was trying to recover from the devastating loss of nearly one hundred fighter jets in a single day in June, following Israel's attack on Syria's Soviet SAM (surface to air missile) batteries that had been moved to the Beqaa Valley after Israel's earlier downing of two Syrian helicopters. He was already stuck in a quagmire that showed no signs of abating. In parallel with Syria's encroachment in the Lebanese imbroglio, terrible things were happening back home; they had escalated over the years, and reached a horrific climax even before Israel's devastating siege of Beirut.

* * *

Not everyone in Syria had been as relatively positive, or even impassive, about Assad's early performance, notwithstanding his military and diplomatic feat that placed the country back on the map even without the recovery of the Golan. In 1973, he had proposed a new constitution that would have removed the stipulation that the president must be Muslim. For the Muslim Brothers, a political organisation with a Sunni Muslim composition whose impact on regional politics was beginning to grow, this was a step too far and they considered this attempted constitutional amendment as evidence that Alawis, the sect from which Assad hailed, were not real Muslims.

The Syrian branch of the Muslim Brothers (MB) was formed in 1946 by Mustafa Sibai, a friend of the Egyptian founder Hassan Al Banna, and had been outlawed by the Baath in 1963. While they could no longer partake in Syrian politics, the MB were well connected and influential in some social circles; this helped spread opposition to the 1973 constitutional amendment proposal, which was met with protests and strikes in a number of Syrian cities.

Assad had quickly retreated and chosen not to fight that battle, reverting to the traditional clauses of the Syrian constitution. At the same time, he benefitted from a timely statement from Imam Mousa Sadr, a charismatic, erudite Iranian-born Shia cleric in Lebanon, whose *fatwa* (religious ruling) declared that Alawis were a sect of Shia Islam. Before the advent of Iran's Islamic revolution of 1979, Sadr had been one of the most recognised and respected Shia religious figures, the first leader of the Supreme Islamic Shia Council, and the founder of the Amal Movement which became a strong political party whose militia was an important player in Lebanon's civil war.

It was certainly through Sadr that initial relations between the Assad regime and what would become the Islamic regime in Iran began to blossom during the Shah's last years in power. Sadr's disappearance on a visit to Libya in 1978, at the invitation of Muammar Qaddafi, remains unexplained to this day, giving way to numerous theories about allies and foes who could have arranged for the popular Sadr's elimination from the scene. For Assad, it barely mattered: the Baath's marriage of convenience with the Islamic Shia political movement was already consummated, even as he prepared to fight the Islamic Sunni political movement that was one of those challenging his rule in Syria.

IT STARTED IN DAMASCUS

As matters deteriorated in Lebanon, with the Syrian army's exploits against Palestinian groups clashing head on with the regime's alleged Arabist credentials, the MB was also ramping up its battle against the regime all over Syria with a spate of bombs and assassinations to which the regime would retaliate with equal, and then greater ferocity. It was one of the most violent periods Syrians had lived before 2011, one when people knew few details about what was happening, but also one when they understood that events would have lasting repercussions on the whole population.

* * *

It was around then that different armed factions of the Syrian regime became more openly active, brazenly showing their might to an increasingly apprehensive population. The most powerful of these were the Defence Brigades who acted like an independent militia and pledged absolute allegiance to their commander to whom they simply referred as The Leader, Rifat Assad, the president's brother. Part of Rifat's 55,000-strong elite force had been deployed to Lebanon for some of the regime's first actions against the PLO, but its biggest impact was inside Syria itself, where it led much of the campaign against Muslim Brothers and their alleged sympathisers. Eventually, it got so powerful that it would even pose a threat to Hafez Assad himself.

Most of the events of the late seventies and eighties were relayed among Syrians through word of mouth and furtive, coded phone calls in the era before satellite television news. When rumours would begin to spread about potential trouble brewing, family members alerted one another to take extra caution and pray for the best as news seeped through about events. One major incident, however, was experienced by thousands of Damascenes and witnessed by many more; among these were several of our close relatives and friends who saw these scenes in person, later giving us a detailed account and corroborating others that had emerged.

On 29 September 1981, hundreds of soldiers from the Defence Brigades, accompanied by girls and young women in military uniforms from the Baath's Vanguards (the party's student wing) who had just completed parachute training (one of Rifat Assad's pet projects). They were dropped off by military vehicles in the neighbourhood of Muhajireen. From there, they were deployed around Damascus and took up positions in several of the city's main streets, as people went about their day assuming it was a training exercise in preparation for an operation against regime opponents.

Without warning, the troops spread out in groups and the parachutists proceeded to stop every headscarf-wearing woman on the streets or even in cars, harassing them, insulting them, and ordering them to remove the hijab covering their hair. Those who refused were grabbed roughly and had it yanked off their heads. Terrified women in cars, some with crying children next to them, had tried to refuse to roll down their windows, pleading with the girls harassing them; they had to comply when threatened with guns pointed at their heads through the windshields, and the female parachutists would violently grab the hijabs and wave them triumphantly in the air, like pitiful spoils of battle, adding to the humiliation of their victims before proceeding to the next car. Drunk on their own temporary authority, some shouted scornfully that they were here to teach these Damascene women how to be civilised.

Men who happened to be alongside some of these women naturally tried to intervene, only to be beaten and overpowered by the armed militia members swarming the area. One man walking with his wife in the Salhieh shopping street turned out to be an army officer in civilian clothes on his day off; when she was insulted and physically attacked, he pulled out his gun and shot the Defence Brigade assailant, whose comrades in arms promptly avenged him by shooting and killing the officer.

As mayhem spread amidst the sound of shouted orders, screaming, and gunshots, shopkeepers ushered women into their shops and closed the door, standing guard in front of them, while people in the streets shouted for everyone to run home or hide in residential buildings offering refuge. The merchants and shopkeepers of the Hamidiyeh Souk had been alerted too; armed with nothing but batons, they gathered at the entrance of the famous 200-year-old market and waited for the Defence Brigades to arrive, hoping their number would dissuade the troops from entering the area. The troops never got there: by then, Hafez Assad had ordered his brother to withdraw his militia from the streets of Damascus.

Assad was conscious of how ugly and violent things could still become; this had been an unprecedented physical assault on Syrian society, an immense affront to women, and to their and their families' dignity by the state's own armed forces. While this would have been unacceptable and terrifying anywhere in the world, it was even more offensive in a conservative society.

That evening, as Damascus boiled with fury, as the news spread around the country, the Syrian president addressed the population in an unplanned televised speech. While he never uttered words of regret, it was for all intents and purposes an indirect apology that sought to avoid a further escalation. 'These are our mothers, our sisters, our daughters, and we respect them,' he said in an attempt to distance himself from these actions, adding the culprits were overzealous youngsters who were sad to see Syrian women sidelined—an additional slight in itself.

The next day, those same young female parachutists were ordered back on the streets of Damascus, distributing white carnations to any women they came across, an empty gesture that in no way diminished resentment of the regime. As always in

TWENTY YEARS OF SOLITUDE

Assad's Syria, justice and accountability for the heinous actions of 29 September never came.

That ugly day is engrained in the memory of many Syrians who experienced the Assads' brutality. In later years, as I delved ever deeper into the modus operandi of this regime, I gathered that Hafez would not have been upset by Rifat's actions, assuming it had been Rifat's decision alone, even though his pseudo apology appeared to show some attempt at damage control. This provocation had been well calculated, a good cop, bad cop signal to the population that things could get so bad that even the government would not be able to stop certain groups if pushed too far. The survival of the Assad regime relied on continuing to sow fear and hatred between different segments of Syrian society. In that vein, the parachutists were encouraged, even directed to be bellicose and nasty, to treat regular people with scorn and push them to the brink. Thirty years later, a new generation of regular people and their children would be treated with the same contempt, by the same regime, as they finally reached that point of no return.

* * *

With every passing day, the regime proved how willing and able it was to stifle dissent, and how its response to violent insurgency would be anything but proportional. As the MB escalated its attacks, the regime's retaliations became more violent, culminating in collective punishments on an innocent population. In June 1979, over eighty cadets at the Aleppo Artillery School (all of them Alawis) were massacred by MB members, although the organisation denied any involvement or prior knowledge. The regime responded by killing a dozen political prisoners accused of affiliation with MB, and the cycle picked up in intensity from that date onwards, including sieges and army assaults on parts of Aleppo in 1980 during which the regime killed some 2,000 people, arrested over 8,000, and disappeared many more.

IT STARTED IN DAMASCUS

On 27 June 1980, the day after a failed assassination attempt on Hafez Assad in Damascus, Rifat Assad and some of his Defence Brigades helicoptered to the notorious Palmyra Prison. In a few hours, they killed up to 1,000 prisoners at close range, moving from cell to cell at first, then lining up groups of prisoners for mass executions. With every MB attack on regime and government officials and armed forces, retaliations would often target uninvolved Syrians.

On 2 February 1982, the MB's insurgency in Hama led to the regime's first mass-scale attack on its own civilian population. For the first few days, army tank shells and airstrikes hit Hama indiscriminately, destroying the city's historic centre before several elite regiments and the Defence Brigades entered to sweep the streets, conducting house to house searches, arrests, and executions. The full horror of what happened in Hama emerged bit by bit, widely exposed and documented in later years, although no inquiry was ever demanded by the UN. It is believed that up to 40,000 Syrians were massacred in Hama in less than a month, with thousands more disappeared, and thousands fleeing as the regime razed the city to the ground, terrorising Syrians into submission for decades afterwards.

Even with complete obedience, people were increasingly afraid of the regime's omnipotence as the eighties dragged on, and of the strong factions showing their might. Heart problems had forced Hafez Assad to a prolonged hospital stay in November 1983 and a long recuperation, during which time he entrusted the country's governance to some of his closest subordinates, sidelining his brother Rifat who began to plot his takeover. In March 1984, Rifat's Defence Brigades took control of key points in Damascus, as Ali Haidar's Special Forces, loyal to the president, prepared to confront Rifat. It is said that Hafez immediately headed to Rifat's house and established dominance, forcing the younger brother to retreat and desist, and to agree to leave

Syria after being named Vice-President to save face. The Defence Brigades were dissolved and integrated into the Republican Guards of which Bassel Assad was named Commander, and from where he began his path as his father's heir.

* * *

The army and intelligence had by then become a fixture in daily life, dominating public space. For most people, this was no longer the feted national army of 1973. Regardless of their grade, officers and operatives stormed around like masters and drove their cars, jeeps, and trucks like rules did not apply to them—and indeed, they did not. Uniformed junior officers bullied people waiting in line for hours for fuel, or even for mediocre bread at the government's bakeries as economic hardships grew.

Men in civilian clothes, the subordinates of powerful officials, barked orders or spoke with disdain and insulting language that few dared to counter, knowing they had the power to hurt them—especially if speaking with a coastal accent that would indicate to many Syrians that they could be Alawi, and therefore potentially powerful or connected to the top echelons of the regime. Regime officials' residences would commandeer half of the street space for their numerous cars, armed guards keeping watch from rudimentary shacks that mushroomed all over Damascus and other cities, becoming one of many hated symbols of the regime's entitlement and excesses. While such overindulgences paled in comparison to what would emerge under Bashar, the great chasms were already blatant and visible to all.

The young Syrian men who spent nearly three miserable years doing their mandatory military service were often forced to serve as part of the personal home staff of officials' wives. As all Syrian families have heard in detail from their sons, actual military training was meant to break their spirit and remind them of their place, not prepare them to be strong defenders of the homeland.

IT STARTED IN DAMASCUS

Young men from every single family would be subject to humiliations they would remember their whole lives. They would be cold, hungry, and mistreated. This was not the kind of army training seen in films, building character and proverbially making men out of boys in places like Sandhurst or West Point. In Assad's Syria, military service was now designed to degrade conscripts while showing them who ruled over them; it included physical abuse, but also psychological mind games that left young men constantly afraid of their superiors. Only families with strong connections were able to spare their sons the worst treatment, and officer training was reserved for a chosen few whose job would be defending the regime, not the homeland.

In such a security-obsessed regime, informants soon proliferated, eager to find a channel that improved their status in life. Denunciations became a way to prove loyalty to the regime, but quickly also became a way to settle scores with unsavoury neighbours, unpleasant coworkers, or even uncaring love interests. It soon became difficult to trust new people in unfamiliar environments outside of close circles, especially if rumours circulated that they had 'nice handwriting'—Syrian code for snoops writing copious reports about others' activities and opinions.

University students launching into intellectual discussions and idealistic political activism, yearning like young people everywhere to voice their dreams and help form their destiny, were grabbed from their homes and their classrooms and thrown into jails for years, even decades, accused of every affiliation possible from Islamism to communism.

It seemed that instead of going slowly forward like most other countries, Syria had stopped dead in its tracks and become petrified in a dark, gloomy era, having submitted to a repressive force that had a strangling hold on the entire country. Those dreadful eighties were stifling in every way; long electricity cuts and water shortages had become the norm, the streets became dark as soon as the sun came down, as did the shops with their sparse shelves and dim lights. Everywhere, the glare of black-suited security men followed people. The Syrian population became increasingly anxious and pessimistic about its prospects, retreating further into the relative safety of home—even though everyone had learned that walls had ears.

With everything in the public realm belonging to the rulers, the sense of national heritage was weakening as people focused on survival. Even worse, the understanding of civil society was getting lost. At first, I had been shocked to discover that garbage was liberally thrown in the streets, even in nice areas of Damascus. How could this happen when every Syrian home I had ever entered was clean and orderly, the pride of the lady of the house? As with many other issues in Syria, it took me time to understand that this faded sense of civic duty had happened gradually, by necessity, as people retreated to protect the only thing they could still control: their own homes. Anything outside of their front door had become someone else's problem and responsibility.

In many buildings, even the weekly cleaning of the common staircase became the subject of legendary arguments easily heard from the street—and becoming the butt of jokes—as neighbours shouted at each other about whose turn it was to clean. Those who could afford it employed someone for this task, but even then, arguments would erupt about whose water would be used at which stage.

Such were the preoccupations of people as the world outside had cut them off, as they struggled to survive the hazards of crossing this now well-established dictatorship. This was unfamiliar terrain they had no choice but to navigate. While they were not in a banana republic, for sure, they had to use their inimitable Syrian flair to play by the rules of the banana politics of Assad's Syria.

3

BANANA POLITICS

The initial shock factor of our first trip gradually abated, giving way to an odd sense of resignation that this was just the way things were, that there was no choice but to accept the weird, the frustrating, the unjust. With every subsequent trip, idiosyncrasies of Syrian life seemed less daunting, and absurdities were becoming normalised; the more we went there, the more depth and scope I gained on the strange layers of Assad's Syria.

During one of our stays, some of our distant relatives from Denmark came to visit Damascus for the first time. We took them to the usual tourist sites as well as the city gems best known to locals, and my uncle invited us all to the Sheraton Hotel nightclub, one of the rare places back then where a lucky few could enjoy a nice meal while watching popular regional singers. In the eighties, even modest entertainment options were out of reach for most Syrians in Assad's Baathist habitat, so this was considered a treat.

After the club had filled up and people were well into their dinners, a table by the dance floor remained empty. One of our guests asked why the best place in the club was still available if the singer, as he had been told, was so popular. As designated interpreter, I matter-of-factly explained to him what I'd already gathered by then: it was probably reserved for General Mustafa Tlass, who tended to show up a bit later. He laughed and leaned back with his drink as the lights dimmed and the singer started his set.

In the middle of the third or fourth song, the commotion started. Chairs were moved aside as waiters swarmed around a newly arrived party, and every single man in the nightclub—my uncle included—rose slightly from his chair to give that quintessential Syrian half-wave, half-salute to the cheerful figure in a white suit who waved back at everyone, flashing bright smiles as he escorted his wife to the vacant table.

Our puzzled Danish guest looked at me with raised eyebrows, edging closer to ask who this clearly famous individual was that we all seemed to know. 'It's General Tlass, the minister of defence,' I responded in an I-told-you-so tone, very pleased to have been proven right. I had learned a thing or two about Syria, but the look on his face made me realise that what had become customary for us was still bizarre and even outlandish for others. His jaw dropped as he stared at the Tlass party: 'That's impossible,' he said, 'this must be a double'. My brain was on Syrian mode, and I scoffed: 'Why on earth would he even need that?' Nobody was out to get Tlass or any regime official by then, and he could—and did—parade around in public whenever he wanted. Nevertheless, it was hard to argue with the logic of our Danish guest: it was not conceivable or reasonable that the minister of defence of a socialist country, of a state that was technically at war—officially with Israel, and unofficially with several other countries—would appear in public at this late hour, in this flamboyant manner, at a nightclub to boot.

Although I smiled at his scepticism and explicit disapproval if this really turned out to be the minister in question despite his strong doubts, it dawned on me that perhaps I had quickly gone a tad soft in my country of birth, finding this admittedly distinctive scene to be nothing too unusual. Given the restrictions imposed on everyone else, we should not have become indifferent to the flashy behaviour of some regime officials and the deference they all expected. I had to concede that the equality, free speech and women's lib monologues that I regularly delivered to my parents in Europe, in sustained advocacy for my own freedoms, sounded a bit hollow when I so casually, uncritically enjoyed such privileges on our Syrian escapades. The dictated mantra of 'that's just the way it is here' used to justify everything was clashing with the young idealist identity I had fancied for myself.

I felt the evening was beginning to drag, but unfortunately the Tlass show was not over. A newly married couple, celebrating with their friends at the back of the club, got up and made their way to the General's table as the singer congratulated them. It was the first time I would witness a gesture I had heard of: as she was known to do, Mrs Tlass stood up and removed the gold necklace she was wearing, putting it around the bride's neck as everyone applauded this public display of generosity. My dinner companion did not ask for an explanation, nor did I offer one, silently questioning how Syrian society had reached this point of submission to the absurd.

Tlass was merely the most visible—and the least lethal—of the regime's top officials in the reign of Hafez. Much more powerful and feared figures like Ali Douba, the head of Military Intelligence, or Special Forces Leader Ali Haidar, were less known physically to the general public, but their sons and grandsons moved in similar public circles in the Bashar years, considering everything from accolades to a piece of the pie in many businesses to be their due.

The Arabic word for regime, *nizam*, also means system, a perfect concurrence in the case of the Assad regime being both a regime in the political sense and a system in every other dimension. It could function only in that way because it had been designed as such, a pyramid with a broad obedient base and gradually smaller levels that worked for, and were also at the mercy of, the omnipotent peak. What worked for the top of the Assad pyramid was the real law of the land, and Syrians had to be trained to live by the system and accept their place—or at least to pretend they did. They had learned to speak 'Baathese,' that uniquely Syrian lingo that merged the wooden institutional language with the sycophantic praise. Flattery often did get you somewhere if you knew the right people and could recite the right slogans.

* * *

Since the Baath Party's coup of 1963, Syria had been subject to a continuous state of emergency that remained in place with the 1970 coup that brought Hafez Assad to power and gave him full control of the party—a state of emergency that prevailed, ironically, until mass protests began in 2011. While Syrians had to keep a low profile as the regime's violent authoritarianism rose, the Assad regime did not rely on their obedience alone: the Baath, a perfect tool, pushed and reinforced a Machiavellian process of indoctrination applicable to everyone.

The initial Baath coup was marketed to Syrians as the Revolution whose anniversary was observed every year as a public holiday. While hardcore Baathists of the Hafez era did not necessarily wear their hearts on their sleeves, they did so on their upper lips: most of them proudly sported what we called 8 March moustaches, grown to be bushy and groomed to look like the number eight (which in Arabic looks like an upside-down letter V) to celebrate the glorious 8 March 1963 that brought them to power.

Assad's follow-up coup was claimed as the Corrective Movement. That, too, was commemorated every 16 November in tribute to Hafez's power grab on that day in 1970 to correct, as he said, his own party's mistakes and reset it on the straight path. The Preamble of the new Syrian constitution he had parliament pass in 1973 claimed that his Corrective Movement had 'responded to our people's demands and aspirations' and was an important qualitative development and a faithful reflection of the party's spirit, principles, and objectives. That said, he busily continued to correct for nearly three decades.

That constitution also gave the Baath Party the starring role through Article 8: 'The leading party in the society and the state is the Socialist Arab Baath Party. It leads a patriotic and progressive front seeking to unify the resources of the people's masses and place them at the service of the Arab nation's goals.' Evidently, such lofty objectives required a rigorous preparation of the masses.

The Syrian educational system made every Syrian child a Baathist scout by default. At each stage of their school life, and until their graduation at the age of eighteen, children gradually went up the various levels and echelons, from Baath Vanguards in primary school, to Revolutionary Youth in secondary. From an early age, they were already taught different aspects of conformity, including the precise manners of saluting and of clapping rhythmically in unison, skills that Baathists would later continue to display abundantly in their roles as officials, parliamentarians, and assorted governmental employees.

The ruling party had also imposed military-style school uniforms for all grades (in a sandy beige colour at the elementary level, and a military khaki one as of secondary) and included mandatory military-style camps and trainings throughout the educational years. Pan-Arabism, at that period in history, was a cause for which one had to fight, and it remained interlocked with militarism.

Regardless of their area of academic focus, students could only graduate and receive their Baccalaureate if they achieved a passing grade on the two subjects the party considered to be the most important: Arabic, an important foundation of the Baath's credo of Arabism, and Nationalism (*Qawmieh*), undoubtedly the most detested course of the curriculum for nearly every student. Memorising an ample selection of quotes from President Assad, whose image graced the cover of schoolbooks and classroom walls, was part and parcel of this Syrian educational milestone.

Many secondary school students learned that it paid to go the extra Baathist mile by volunteering for extra-curricular activities, such as military training or participation in festivals under the wing of the Revolutionary Youth. This guaranteed them additional marks that would count in their final Baccalaureate score, increasing their chances of entering their university faculty of choice. In exceptional cases, students could even be given an exemption from exams, meaning they could enter any faculty they wanted regardless of the grades they received—just like the exemptions that children of important officials routinely received because no teachers in their right mind would dare to fail them.

In theory, Syrian education under Assad's Baath was meant to produce the pan-Arab nationalist socialist citizens—or the comrades, as they had to refer to one another—who would support the aspirations of modern Syria and technically also historic Greater Syria, or however far the Baath Party felt its influence was justified. In practice, it was a comprehensive indoctrination process—or at least an attempted one—that mechanically drilled empty slogans and ridiculously grandiose and unrealistic concepts, training Syrians to obediently and automatically repeat what they were told. Through *Qawmieh* and its likes, Assad was nipping the hazards of independent thought in the bud.

Every school morning before they entered their classrooms, students of all ages would stand in orderly rows in their school yards to pledge allegiance to party and country, loudly chanting its slogans and saluting the Eternal Leader. Teachers would supervise, ensuring conformity in dress and behaviour as cries of 'Unity, Freedom, Socialism' and 'One Arab nation with a single message' resonated from the mouths of babes. While the repetition of these slogans may not have proved useful for dealing with practicalities of life after school, familiarity with the Baath's countless rules and regulations was crucial to passing university exams, to surviving the traumas of dealing with the authorities in every aspect of personal and professional life, and even to understanding the intricacies of the political process—for process there was indeed at some levels of the pyramid.

* * *

While political and economic circumstances had worsened in Syria during the seventies and the dark eighties, people found ways for Baathism to work in their favour and practiced speaking the regime's jargon. Above all, awareness of the Baath dogma helped people who wanted to find employment in the public service sector; in a country whose private enterprise had been severely limited, with a lack of opportunity elsewhere, the position of civil servant became a highly desirable one that made continued affiliation with the Baath Party necessary.

Working for the government was a means to an end: it guaranteed a steady (albeit modest) wage, a pension, and countless fringe benefits—especially job security. For people of meagre means, connections were vital to securing such positions. Moreover, good relations with influential Baathists also made a great difference for promotions and job referrals, as only active party members could be recommended for promotions in the public sector. The Baath had an intricate system of branches and geographical areas at a horizontal level, and a clear hierarchy structure within those branches and above them; this meant that even relatively junior Baathists were given enough leeway and enjoyed a certain level of influence on their own little turfs.

IT STARTED IN DAMASCUS

Like every Syrian, I had several relatives employed at various ministries and governmental institutions around the city. They all related tales about 'the way things were' that ranged from the ridiculous to the infuriating, of how certain bosses had gotten their positions, of colleagues who got away with marked incompetence because of who they were related to, of informants who took liberties and came to work whenever they wanted, of powerful managers' relatives with fictitious jobs who only appeared once a month to take home their pay check.

One of my cousins had been working for years at the Central Bank of Syria, a place I assumed followed a more rigid recruitment process and a serious workflow. On one of my visits, she asked me if I would like to join her one day for a late breakfast at the office, to look around and meet some of the colleagues; I could hardly wait for this occasion to visit the imposing building that dominated the Seven Fountains Square in Damascus, and to see the staff cafeteria where I imagined that bankers, economists, policymakers, and their support teams would grab coffee in one of the state's most essential institutions. In retrospect, I may have been influenced by one or two movies that showed a different world.

My vision of order and efficiency did not prepare me for what I saw when my relative escorted me to her section. She took me into the office that she shared with several of her colleagues, where introductions were made and we spent an appropriate amount of time enquiring about the health of our respective families, the obligatory first step in any Syrian conversation, and discussing how I was finding Damascus lately. One of them noted it was getting late and we were probably all hungry by now, so they jumped into action—not by leading the way to the cafeteria or canteen to which I had assumed we would head, but by opening bags and setting up a prep station right there, on one of the desks. Pushing files aside, they lined up a couple of chopping boards and plates, and unpacked the ingredients for the tabbouleh we would be having. Of all the delicious Syrian treats we could have had, this was not what—or where—I had been expecting.

Our Danish guest had been shocked to see a minister of defence at a night club, but it was nothing compared to my own astonishment as I witnessed finely chopped parsley, spring onions, and tomatoes being tossed on a desk in the heart of the Syrian Central Bank, before being mixed with pre-soaked fine burghul, seasoned, and drizzled with virgin olive oil and lemon juice. My hosts were amused by my surprise and insisted that while this was not a regular occurrence, it was neither unusual nor a big deal.

As we ate, their supervisor walked in to ask about something. They introduced him to me as I swallowed awkwardly, worried he might reprimand them in my presence, but he seemed to find nothing wrong with the situation. Besides, they had already offered him a nice plate and he happily joined along. They sure made a nice tabbouleh and a lovely glass of sweet tea, but I never got around to finding out specifics about all their jobs.

Low productivity in the Syrian public sector may not have mattered much if these had been isolated cases, but seeing government employees so detached from the goals of their institutions was all too common. It was the modus operandi of the Syrian regime's employment pyramid, with its connected officials and their cohorts of minions presiding over lower-rank employees who had no stake in the impact of their work, through no fault of their own.

Certainly, there should be a degree of personal responsibility in every place of work, but in Assad's Syria all fingers pointed in the same direction. The regime and the system rewarded loyalty and subservience, not qualifications and competence, making no effort to place the right people in the right places either in government or in the civil service. This created a monstrous public sector machine that existed for its own sake, that dragged productivity and efficiency to the ground, that frustrated and drained citizens who had to deal with the hell that was Baathist bureaucracy. Its numerous rubber stampers, those who, unlike my cousin, interacted with the public, took out their own frustrations on the regular citizens needing a document and being dragged through several desks, as they were made to buy several stamps, paying bribes along the way. So who was to blame for this general dereliction of duty with important state assets?

After Assad's Corrective Movement and the restriction of economic freedom, the public sector was the only reliable desk job provider in town for many people who lacked technical, artisanal, or manufacturing skills. The nation with a long history of trading and entrepreneurship was now shifting gears, making way for an increasingly large contingent of newly graduated Syrians; having initially dreamt of big things, they found themselves praying they would find a way of working for the government in the absence of other opportunities. They often supplemented their small incomes with afternoon and evening work, driving taxis, giving private lessons, working odd jobs to make ends meet and to help deal with numerous regime-caused aggravations.

Potential for success in any given field depended very much on 'belonging' to one or more regime cronies, and on the extent of the praise lavished on self-styled leaders, an archaic method leaving little room for achievement-based progress or decent work ethics. With its emphasis on compliance, it resulted in the pervasive glorification of third-rate higher-ups who themselves continually extolled the virtues of those above them, and so on until the top of the pyramid.

* * *

People had focused on survival in the wider sense with a closed economy and some international sanctions, and the regime severely limited access to some consumer goods as a way of controlling the population. It was difficult for most people to acquire the most basic commodities without going through official channels, and waiting for the government to announce the rare imports of fresh produce, electronics, or other consumer goods. When these were allowed in, on random occasions, word got around quickly and people rushed to secure what they could, often standing in line for hours at state distribution centres. The only other way was to pay higher prices for goods smuggled from Lebanon, mostly by regime-sanctioned parties and the shabiha (Assad family-affiliated militia) that initially controlled the lucrative smuggling routes around the Mediterranean coast.

Those were the days when Syrian parents dreamed of obtaining the bananas that their children craved, that they had rarely—if ever—tasted, and that were generally impossible to find. That basic, inexpensive fruit had become an end goal, even a status symbol, a sign of clout. On more occasions than I can count during those years of import restrictions, teas and lunches at the houses of relatives and acquaintances would eventually be crowned by the bananas they offered us. I remember politely refusing this fruit I was never crazy about as I reached for the local watermelon or desserts I much preferred, not understanding fully at the time how generously, how earnestly they were trying to honour my family's visits in true Syrian hospitality fashion.

Those who could afford it and knew someone who went there would have bananas brought in from Lebanon. The rest had to wait for Assad's entourage to exclaim, on a whim, 'let them eat bananas!' Even when that happened, the first batches would inevitably be too expensive for most people as the regime's little helpers set their prices to include hefty profits. It would take a while for prices to decrease slightly and for measly bananas to become barely affordable for the ordinary people whose children could finally taste them.

IT STARTED IN DAMASCUS

The banana shortage, or rather its arbitrary limitation, became symbolic of everything Syrians craved but could not have, and gave way to the term that defined the eighties: banana politics (*siyassat al mawz*) made the population dependent on the regime's largesse, forced to show obedience and flattery to superiors in anticipation of random paltry rewards for good behaviour. Navigating these banana politics was the name of the game: you did what you had to do and praised who you had to praise in order to bring home the bananas.

With this constant state of pressure on procuring basics of daily life, big purchases remained in the realm of dreams. Cars, if they were at all allowed on occasion for normal people, could only be attained via irregular government orders. Not only did they carry an import duty and a luxury tax of up to 300% of their value, but they were brought over in batches. People had to sign up for these cars, be put on extensive waiting lists, pay the bill in advance, and wait a long time again before finally receiving a car they had not even chosen themselves from a regime-sanctioned make that would suddenly flood the market in the same dull colour.

In these conditions, Syrian streets became an open-air museum of classic old American and European cars dating back a few decades. In every neighbourhood, you would see men lovingly washing and buffing huge cars with shiny fenders, chrome bumpers, and flashy tail fins. They would wax the leather seats, polish the smooth wood panels that used to be the norm, and carefully clean the giant steering wheels with the gear stick at the side. The brightly coloured Buicks, Chevrolets, Dodges, Oldsmobiles, GMCs, even the odd Cadillacs, were perfectly at home on wide avenues such as Abou Roummaneh, but they seemed out of place in the narrow streets and alleys of old Damascus, barely squeezing through neighbourhoods that long predated cars.

BANANA POLITICS

Owners took great care of them, certainly growing an emotional attachment to some vehicles that were true beauties, but mainly because that would probably be the only car they could ever own if nothing changed. Many would readily admit they would have loved to drive a newer car with modern options, but as long as adept mechanics managed to keep the old-timers running, despite their high petrol consumption, the cars were a blessing. Over the years, we took many trips to Beirut, Amman, or to other Syrian cities in one of those comfortable cars that had become taxis running the long-distance treks, easily accommodating five passengers and a generous luggage allowance per journey.

Syrians also owned a variety of classic European cars, mostly from Germany and France, that were popular before the Baathist economy blocked imports. The sleek Mercedes of the sixties and seventies, the cute Volkswagen Beetles that bounced around the tightest streets, and the old Opels and Peugeots were as common as the American cars, and highly appreciated because they were generally smaller and slightly more suited to the older city roads. But whether they preferred American or European cars, whether they were happy to cherish their old cars forever or yearned for a modern car with nice options, all Syrians agreed on one thing: they hated the white Peugeot 504 station wagons, seen around the country in their hundreds as the car of choice of the intelligence services, the despised *mukhabarat*. Even the youngest Syrian children knew it was never good news when one of those dreaded vehicles came your way.

* * *

Destined to repeat the cycle of survival over and over, people were busy dealing with the hassles of daily life. They had to contend with the maddening electricity and water cuts for hours on end, leaving limited time to fill their water tanks, shower or bathe, or do their laundry. They waited for weeks as cold days approached to secure heating oil, that poor quality sulphuric *mazout* whose pervasive smell lingered in homes with *sobia* stoves, liberally spreading soot on the walls. They kept an ear out for the sellers of cooking gas cylinders, who announced their presence by banging on their battered load with a metal rod as their carts moved around neighbourhoods. They roamed depressingly bare government shops and scattered grocers in search of basic hygiene products, whose usual scarcity was as inexplicable as their sudden brief appearances on Syrian markets.

Even within the banana politics context, there was no rhyme or reason to the regime's decisions on why certain products were allowed, and others were not. The first time I accompanied my mother to a convenience store near my grandmother's house in Abou Roummaneh, we had looked in vain on a few shelves for products that were so basic she assumed they would be found. She asked the grocer for a certain brand of cheese: 'Sorry, we don't have that.' How about this other type, she asked? 'We don't have that either.' She remembered a brand of tea they used to drink at home: 'We don't have any, unfortunately.' Even though she already knew it was highly unlikely she would find paper tissues, she requested some, just in case. The grocer smiled apologetically and asked, despite having heard her Damascene accent: 'Excuse me, Madame, but you are not from here, are you?' It was a question we would be asked repeatedly for some time, until we learned to stop wanting things the regime had decided nobody should have.

Ironically, perhaps, or wickedly, rather, anything the Syrians had or could access began to be framed as being 'given' by Assad—an offering, a present, or even charity for which the people needed to show appreciation. Anything new, or anything good, or even anything that was suddenly slightly better than before was said to be a gift from the Eternal Leader. The notion that normal services were a privilege, not a right for average citizens, was drilled into the Syrian subconscious for years, so much so that it survived well into later decades when regime loyalists vilified the 2011 protesters for being ungrateful 'after everything the country has done for you'. Free education and the presence of rudimentary hospitals, for example, was supposed to have been enough to warrant eternal gratitude and submission, went this peculiar logic, as if this did not exist in the vast majority of countries in the world.

* * *

By the end of the exhausting eighties, the subjugation of any type of popular discontent rested comfortably on a complex mesh of encouragement and containment, with regular reminders that things could get a lot worse for those who failed to toe the line. The Baath had laid out the parameters of compliance through its extensive infrastructure and hierarchy; the more than a dozen intelligence services, each reporting on the people, on officials, and on each other, took care of the rest. Together, they made sure that people would be too stressed and too afraid to even think of objecting.

Overseeing all this observance of the regime's rigid rules were the officials at the top of the various regime divisions with their respective portfolios. Each was a *mass'oul* (responsible), both an adjective and a noun in Arabic, denoting those of a certain rank. A high *mass'oul* could be envied or reviled, but he was always feared, and his influence was generally extensive. The higher his position, the more strings he could pull, the more superior his fleet of cars, the bigger his group of accompanying bodyguards, the grander his homes, the better his guard shacks, the more entitled his children, the more flamboyant his wife.

Under these responsible officials sprouted a symmetry of social contamination. The control of a civil society through force and indoctrination was but one of the steps towards thorough compliance, but to make a society truly submissive, it was necessary to turn citizens against each other, even if they were doing it subconsciously. The corrupt state corrupted society by encouraging citizens to carry out their own oppression, taking their frustrations out on fellow citizens, breaking the bond of trust with the ever-present threat of stool pigeons. While some snooped willingly, many others did not, having been forced to report on their friends and neighbours. This simple psychology of domination pyramids and of communal control was not unique to Syria, but it had become pervasive by the mid-eighties.

The state also oversaw the slide into an equilibrium of corruption. At first, the regime had enticed its cronies with riches in order to ensure their support, the way countless regimes have done over the ages. Now, wealth was becoming an end in itself, making corruption rampant at every level of the state and of society. With minor exceptions, officials freely demanded and received cuts in deals they facilitated, taking money away from public investment. Others accepted direct bribes to facilitate specific deals, as middlemen in their own sector of responsibility, their own ministries.

This corrupt mindset spread through the lower echelons of the public sector as well. Policemen were routinely bribed to overlook a speeding ticket, some professors accepted or expected bribes to give students passing grades (sometimes having withheld them even though the student had achieved good marks), and even nurses sometimes waited for a small incentive to admit patients to see a doctor, not just in the public sector but also in the private one, as my mother unexpectedly discovered.

My grandmother had fallen ill during one of our stays, so my mother accompanied her to the doctor and sat her down in a crowded waiting room. Feeling antsy, she instructed my mother to go slip the doctor's assistant some money to let them in before their turn. My stunned mother refused, saying she would not even know how to go about it. 'This is how it is here, go do it,' insisted my grandmother. After a few minutes of dithering, my mother discreetly offered the assistant a folded bill with a self-conscious smile, half expecting to be indignantly rejected. Most of all, she was embarrassed to do this in front of other patients who had waited their turn. My grandmother was the next patient to be seen, of course, but my mother remained uncomfortable in these situations for a long time, even though this had technically been a tip and not a bribe to a government employee.

My own first time was much worse, and it was most definitely an illegal bribe. I had driven to the Meridien Hotel with my cousin who was in town at the same time I was. Lamia now lived in the US, but unlike me had been raised in Damascus and was no stranger to the unofficial conventions in the country. As we got out of the car, a policeman approached me and said I had driven in the wrong direction on a one-way street—something I would never do. I told him he was mistaken, this was not a one-way street; he insisted there was a new sign, that was maybe hidden, but 'everyone knew' it was now a one-way street. Lamia watched this back and forth for a bit, and then softly told me, in English: 'Give him one hundred' (the equivalent of two US dollars). I was horrified and silently screamed 'What?' She rolled her eyes and repeated the advice, knowing that this was the only way this exchange was going to end.

I remember my hands shaking as I fumbled inside my purse, trying not to make it obvious I was trying to extract a bill; the cop knew exactly what I was doing and hardly seemed offended. I clumsily placed the hundred-pound bill in his easily accessible hand, and asked that he make the sign visible so other drivers would not make the same mistake. He nodded and walked away, just like that, leaving me overwhelmed with the enormity of what I had just done. My cousin was gracious enough not to laugh at my ridiculous apprehension; we all knew how things functioned here, after all. Still, this first bribe troubled me for a long time and I often relived the moment, wishing our traffic policemen and all those in the public sector had wages that made tips or bribes superfluous.

Despite their frustrations with the bribery epidemic, most Syrians had accepted that this was part of the system indeed, rationalising that it would otherwise be impossible for most people to make ends meet. They had convinced themselves that it was equivalent to giving charity to civil servants whose monthly salary did not even reach one hundred dollars at the time. It had become practically impossible to get even the most insignificant governmental procedure done without paying a bribe, but it was easier to slip the bills inside the paperwork being handed to the civil servant. Refusing or forgetting to do so merely guaranteed long waiting times and several comings and goings at the very least—and even possible bureaucratic complications in the worst-case scenarios. Besides, there was no independent authority to turn to when facing the walls of institutionalised corruption, of rampant governmental incompetence, or of the dismal state of the public sector's delivery of goods and services.

* * *

The state's violence and its banana politics had subdued and exhausted Syrians during that difficult decade. The 1984 clash between Hafez Assad and his brother Rifat had terrified everyone, even though the outcome would probably not have changed much in Syrian lives regardless of who won; people had already seen the ruthlessness of both brothers and that of the armed brigades that obeyed different commanders. Already prisoners of the regime, of regional circumstances, and of the closed political and economic life imposed on them, they would be delivered yet more blows with some of Assad's actions in the region and beyond.

BANANA POLITICS

In 1986, an attempt to blow up an El Al flight from London's Heathrow Airport implicated the Assad regime. A bomb was discovered in the bag of a pregnant Irish woman, who stated it had been given to her by the father of her baby, her Jordanian boyfriend Nizar Hindawi. After he had dropped her off at the airport early in the morning and returned to central London, Hindawi had boarded a Syrian Arab Airlines bus a few hours later to catch a flight to Damascus. Informed that the bomb had been discovered, he got off the bus and headed straight to the Syrian Embassy, which helped him change his appearance by dyeing and cutting his hair. The next day, however, Hindawi handed himself over to British Police.

A British court found him guilty of planting the bomb in his girlfriend's luggage, leading Prime Minister Margaret Thatcher to break off diplomatic relations with Syria immediately, followed by the US and Canada, who promptly withdrew their ambassadors from Damascus. Syria's hosting and political support of the Kurdish separatist leader Abdullah Ocalan, allowing him to plan and launch attacks on Turkish soil from northern Syria, ensured that relations with the northern neighbour remained tense as well, adding to the disagreements between the two countries on a fair share of the Euphrates' waters.

As for the leaders in the Arab world who had embraced Assad after 1973 and then distanced themselves following the Syrian actions in Lebanon, which would still see a denouement in 1990, they had been unpleasantly surprised to see Assad take the side of Iran during its eight-year war with Iraq, started in 1980 by the latter's Baathist leader, Saddam Hussein. For most Arabs observing this position, Assad's claimed pan-Arabism seemed rather shallow, and he lost all the goodwill he had managed to amass less than a decade before.

As this gruelling decade was ending, Assad had managed to isolate Syria on all fronts, and Syrians had little reason to believe that their solitary struggle was ever going to ease, or to imagine that changes elsewhere could impact their lives. Yet, the miscalculations of one of Assad's archenemies would soon have a butterfly effect on Syrian lives in the most unforeseen manner.

4

A BREEZE FROM MADRID

The renowned Al Rawda Café on Abed Street, a few metres from Salhieh's boutiques and shops and the Syrian parliament on the opposite side, was rarely empty, regardless of the time of day. Men whiled away their free hours in its cordial atmosphere, drinking coffee or sipping the notably strong Syrian tea in small glasses; under clouds of smoke, some would play backgammon, others would read the papers and have agitated discussions about the state of the world. I had often passed its large windowpanes while trying to hail a taxi if I had run errands in Salhieh, or on my way to the shop owned by one of my relatives a bit further up on Abed Street. Occasionally, I would peek inside and entertain the idea of just walking in one day, finding a table, and waiting to be served.

I never dared, though, and no man in my social circle volunteered to accompany me; neither my curiosity nor my capricious impulses for provocation were satisfied. In that era when Syria seemed frozen in time, when people tried to keep their heads above water and held their tongues on nearly everything, traditional popular cafés like Al Rawda or the equally famous Havana were still mostly male territory. What if they decided to stop me at the door, telling me there were no women there? My plan to barge in uninvited could have embarrassed me and definitely would have embarrassed Ziad as well, my cousin who was one of its many regulars and would surely hear about my breach of social etiquette even before the coffee cup touched my table.

Syrians were not exactly shy when enquiring about one's name or background, often asking point blank to what family—literally, to what house—one belonged; '*Min bayt meen?*' was a question I would hear repeatedly over the years from total strangers who sensed I was not fully from there, even though my accent seemed to prove otherwise. You would think one could ignore or evade questions like these, but at the time it was harder than it seems. Although I liked to imagine I was tough, the truth is that I was still rather intimidated by this kind of blunt insistence that most Syrians had perfected to an art form.

I did want to bring my personalised women's liberation feats to a wider audience, having exhausted the patience of many acquaintances with my interrogations on why men and women had different degrees of liberty in this society, but I was also well past the initial culture shock and felt more at home with each visit. I was getting to know these people—my people—on a deeper level, becoming privy to Syrians' thoughts and feelings beyond the superficial niceties, or the rigid customs that I had at first found overbearing. As I matured, I focused less on fighting their social norms and more on understanding their aspirations, their perspectives on the world, their daily life challenges. I was beginning to appreciate them, even to love them.

What did the men talk about in these cafés I could not visit, I asked my cousin Ziad? He told me the Syrianised joke about a man describing the equitable decision-making process in his household. His wife would rule on minor, routine matters such as the children and their education, large purchases for the home,

A BREEZE FROM MADRID

when to visit in-laws and invite friends, or where to go on holiday; as for him, the man of the house, he would be in charge of all the important matters such as what to do about the Arab–Israeli conflict, how countries should vote at the Security Council, which of the US or the Soviet Union was more powerful, and other issues of that magnitude. Like everyone, everywhere, they talked about big ideas and events that technically had no immediate impact on their own lives but still mattered to them.

As long as the politics they discussed did not include direct or veiled criticism of the regime, it was safe to chat about news that seeped into the country despite the walls of censorship and repression. Try as they might, the regime's minions could not stop Syrians from regularly tuning in to the crackling shortwave radio broadcasts that carried the news they wanted. Among others, they would listen regularly to Radio Monte Carlo (France's popular Arabic-language station directed at Middle East and North African audiences) for news about the Arab world and beyond. And every day, they would make time to catch '*Houna London*' (Here is London), announced by the BBC World Service's Arabic news readers at the top of every hour, to get information about regional and global events they might not have heard of. These radio broadcasts were trusted sources that connected people to the outside, making the world seem more accessible long before the advent of satellite television. More closely followed than Voice of America, the BBC was legendary in the region; even if they did not listen to it themselves, people would eventually hear what it had announced through word of mouth.

I heard *Houna London* on my father's radio every morning on our Damascus trips, and even remember it from my childhood in Geneva or New York as it had simply become part of his morning routine, even when every other media was readily available. Decades later, as I walked into the iconic Bush House in central London for the first time to give an interview at the headquarters of the BBC World Service, awe and nostalgia simultaneously overtook my senses. Pausing at its majestic entrance, I thought of the multitude of people whose days had regularly started with the dependable Here is London greeting that gave them a sense of belonging, that link to others who were listening to the same news about their same world.

Occasionally, Syrians would also seek neighbouring countries' stations on their short-wave transistors, constantly fiddling with the dial to limit the static when listening to the news from the other side. Residents close to the borders could sometimes even watch something other than Syria's rigid Channel One and, after 1985, Channel Two. Accessing Jordanian, Lebanese, and even Israeli channels allowed them to see more foreign shows at the time, and, undoubtedly, more informative programmes despite the grainy reception.

Many families would wrap up the evening back on Channel One and gather around the programme '*Ghadan Naltaki*' (We Meet Tomorrow), one of the cultural symbols of that pre-satellite TV era before twenty-four-hour television arrived. Always presented by a smooth-voiced woman, it was a strangely comforting overview of what the channel would broadcast the following day, a visual TV guide of sorts, mixed with snippets from popular songs, a few stanzas from well-known poets, scenes from funny Egyptian plays, and short extracts from drama series. Every night, just before the national anthem was played, the presenter would end the day's programming with 'Syrian Arab Television greets you from Damascus'—our very own dependable daily salutation, the local *Houna London*.

* * *

Through their various sources of information, and the occasional Lebanese newspapers that escaped the censor's zealous page tearing and survived the crossing intact, there was a lot to talk about in the late eighties. Granted, Syrians' lives were at a standstill, but they were drawn to events near and far that were about to drastically change the world—not their own world, alas, but that of equally-deserving others. In every corner of Eastern Europe, a region attached to the Soviet Union's hip since the end of World War II, common popular goals such as liberation, breaking the shackles of authoritarian oppression, freedom of speech, open economies, and free trade had suddenly emerged.

They were countries Syrians knew relatively well; thanks to the regime's relations with their ruling comrades in arms, many had gone to various places there for their university studies, and for professional or military training. Because of this connection and the yearning for civil rights they shared with Eastern European people, many in Syria closely followed the momentous developments that shook the Soviet Bloc in the late eighties after Soviet leader Mikhail Gorbachev introduced perestroika, the move to restructure and reform the state's political and economic system, and the concept of glasnost that called for transparency during the process.

The opening salvo took place in 1988, when unrest in Poland gave Lech Wałęsa, an electrician at the Gdansk shipyard, and his Solidarność movement victory at the 1989 elections that removed Polish ruler General Wojciech Jaruzelski from power and made Wałęsa president a year later. 1989 also saw the dismantling of Hungary's symbolic Iron Curtain (in effect, the fence on its border with Austria) and the abandonment of the country's Stalinist constitution. In November 1989, the world watched the infamous wall dividing Berlin come down, at first figuratively when a crossing opened to allow thousands of East Germans through to West Berlin, and later physically, ushering German reunification and leading to the creation of the European Union, as mandated in the 1992 Treaty of Maastricht.

IT STARTED IN DAMASCUS

On 29 December 1989, Czechoslovakia's Velvet Revolution ended the decade on a high note when writer and dissident Václav Havel was elected president. A few days prior, on Christmas Day, Romania had experienced one of the biggest political earthquakes when demonstrations escalated and ended with the execution by firing squad of Nicolae Ceaușescu and his wife. The communist dictator who, like Assad, had built a massive cult of personality along the lines of the North Korean model, was gone a mere two weeks after a flash revolution had pushed Romanians into action.

The unimaginable was happening in countries supported by the Soviet Union, the same power that armed and supported the Assad regime. Even though the gradual weakening of the Soviet state had begun to affect its financial support of his regime, none of these events came even close to worrying the Baathist dictator that he would suffer the same fate as his communist counterparts. With the Hama massacre still fresh in their minds, Syrians were in self-preservation mode, not even thinking about taking action. They seemed destined to remain an insignificant oppressed mass in an isolated country, as the world's political and economic order moved ahead and went through its biggest post-war shift.

Then, on 2 August 1990, they woke up to the news that Iraq had invaded Kuwait in the middle of the night. They did not know it yet, but Saddam Hussein, the Iraqi dictator, had just brought them a different kind of change that nobody had expected, least of all the Syrians.

* * *

It would have killed them both to admit it, but it was Saddam Hussein who saved Assad from the isolated hole he had dug for himself over the previous decade or so. By doing something so much worse, the Iraqi dictator had made the Syrian one look like the lesser evil; in the global context, invading a sovereign state

A BREEZE FROM MADRID

(at least one allied with the US) was a greater sin than committing a massacre of tens of thousands, and arbitrarily jailing thousands more. At the very least, it was a punishable crime.

Ironically, Hafez Assad's Syria and Saddam Hussein's Iraq closely resembled each other in ways that annoyed both leaders. The two countries espoused Baathism, each claiming they were the true centre of the original Arabist movement (with the Syrians arguing they led because the founders of the Baath, Michel Aflaq and Salah Al Din Al Bitar, were Syrian). The two rulers were both ruthless autocrats who had never hesitated to bring their people to their knees when necessary, or to purge their own ranks of dangerous competitors or alleged traitors. Iraq had supported the Syrian war effort of October 1973 to regain the Golan Heights occupied by Israel, when Saddam was vice-president, sending an armoured division to the front and around one hundred fighter jets. When the Islamic revolution toppled the Shah and transformed Iran's domestic and foreign politics in 1979, however, the potential warmth these two pan-Arabists could have maintained greatly dampened, mostly because of Assad's supportive position on Iran, whose new regime was considered a threat by its Arab neighbours.

Saddam Hussein launched his war on Iran in 1980, leading to an eight-year conflict that claimed over a million lives according to most accounts. Most Arab states actively supported Iraq, leaving only Hafez Assad and Libya's Muammar Qaddafi to take the side of Iran. The enmity between Assad and Hussein had reached its apex then: for years afterwards, Syrian passports were stamped with the advisory that they were not valid for travel to Iraq, a rule that was still in place when Saddam decided to invade Kuwait that summer of 1990.

In one fell swoop, without changing a single thing in Syria or compromising on any issue vis-à-vis his foreign critics, Hafez Assad went from being a tyrant with whom one could not deal to being an unavoidable regional partner with whom the US and its allies needed to talk while planning the next steps in the Middle East—the liberation of Kuwait, and the containment of Iraq.

President George H. W. Bush had begun his term in January 1989, as events in Eastern Europe were about to end the Cold War and bring American diplomacy to the forefront of international affairs. He understood the need for a common Arab position to make the liberation of Kuwait a success, to invalidate the criticisms associated with a US-led intervention, and avoid the complications that rejectionists could cause. He knew Syria needed to be brought back into the club to achieve this consensus and a new long-term stability.

His diplomatic outreach to Syria quickly yielded fruit as both parties had much to gain: Bush was eager to handle Iraq with maximum political support, and Assad was eager to rekindle relations with nearly everyone. Having agreed on entering a new stage of mutually beneficial relations, the two presidents met in Geneva in November 1990, breaking Assad's stringent isolation at the highest global level possible.

The containment of Iraq barely took a few months and happened in two stages. The first, Operation Desert Shield, saw the build-up of an international military presence in the region: 500,000 US combat troops, over 50,000 British troops, and tens of thousands more from a total of forty-two countries in the coalition were rapidly deployed to Saudi Arabia, an astonishing number in any context. It sent a clear message that this new global coalition would not tolerate opposition, as the US navigated the sensitivities of maintaining such a massive force so close to Mecca, the most sacred Muslim site in the world.

Syria contributed some 20,000 troops to the international coalition to liberate Kuwait; they joined Operation Desert Storm, the second stage of the process to expel the Iraqi army that began in mid-January 1991 and was over by the end of February. Assad

A BREEZE FROM MADRID

included one wise caveat to his acceptance of US terms: from their base in Saudi Arabia, Syrian troops would enter Kuwait, but they would not step on Iraqi soil.

* * *

The news that Syria was being invited once more into the international fold felt like a breath of fresh air for Syrians, who sensed that being noticed by world governments and media was going to be much better than being out of sight and out of mind. For the first time in nearly two decades, regime and population seemed to be on the same wavelength, at least on the surface. Britain re-established the diplomatic relations it had cut with Assad following the Hindawi Affair and promptly sent a new ambassador to Damascus. At the same time, Arab Gulf money and limited investments tentatively began to make their way to Syria once more, as ties with the rest of the Arab world began to warm again. After a long period of estrangement between Syria and Egypt, following the 1978 Camp David Accords that established peace with Israel, and after the Iran–Iraq war that had put them on different sides of that conflict, cordial relations were back on track.

Under this unexpected spotlight and a new state of affairs with the neighbours, Assad took Syrians by surprise when he introduced Law No. 10 in January 1991, legislating the investment of funds in the country. While limited in scope and made unnecessarily difficult by the maddening complexities of Baathist bureaucracy, as always, it nevertheless improved conditions for private investment in several sectors (including tourism), lifted restrictions on some imports, and allowed for new exemptions from custom duties and taxes. Many Syrians, my father included, had welcomed the announcement of this law as a positive and overdue development, a light that shone at the end of a long tunnel of socio-economic deprivation that, they hoped, would gradually brighten more areas.

IT STARTED IN DAMASCUS

Assad's good mood was also helped by the two important rewards that his role and engagement in the liberation of Kuwait would bring him, now that his punishing isolation was a thing of the past. The first reward was a de facto carte blanche in Lebanon that allowed Assad the guardianship of the Taif Accord that had ended the Lebanese civil war a few months before the invasion of Kuwait; there would be no more pressure regarding Syria's presence in Lebanon. The second reward was the establishment of a serious US-sponsored peace process that would put real pressure on Israel for the return of Syrian and other Arab lands to their pre-1967 status, as per the relevant Security Council Resolutions 242 and 338.

Days after Kuwait's liberation, President Bush addressed Congress on 6 March 1991 and delivered on his pledge to Assad and other leaders, declaring: 'The time has come to put an end to the Arab-Israeli conflict.' This speech marked the beginning of a new era of shuttle diplomacy for another US Secretary of State, James Baker, who would spend the next eight months making sure the peace conference would happen even though Israel, under the leadership of then-prime minister Yitzhak Shamir, was the least favourable to the initiative and tried to hinder his efforts.

* * *

In August 1991, my father received a one-sentence fax from the Syrian Ministry of Foreign Affairs, requesting his urgent presence in Damascus with the earliest flight available. In typical Syrian regime mode, there was not even a hint as to the reason for this sudden convocation, and my parents spent that evening discussing the situation. Why was he being summoned in this manner when he had left the Syrian government over a decade earlier? Had he written or said something that had displeased the regime in one of his recent articles published in pan-Arab papers, extensively analysing and commenting on the region? Could he even consider not responding to this summons? Not a man to shirk responsibilities or challenges, he faxed back his arrival details and flew to Damascus two days later, leaving my anxious mother waiting in Vienna by the phone.

His last posting as a Syrian diplomat had been as Ambassador to New York, a post he had left—with great difficulty—to accept a high-ranking position that was unexpectedly offered to him at the United Nations. He had been working with the Syrian diplomatic service since the fifties, starting there immediately following his law studies, one of several distinguished career diplomats who were already well established before the arrival of the Baath, and of Assad. They were from a dwindling generation of educated and widely travelled patriots and polyglots, who had never become partisans and who prided themselves on representing their nation, not on endearing themselves to its rulers. To his dying day, my father remained politically independent, refusing to join the ruling party—or any other, for that matter—even though it could have brought him significant benefits.

Assad had initially rejected his request to leave his post of Ambassador, relenting after weeks of refusal only after the intervention of the-then Secretary General of the United Nations, Kurt Waldheim, who convinced him by pointing out that my father would be the first Syrian—and indeed the first Arab—Under-Secretary-General. This was a prospect Assad liked. From New York, we had moved back to Geneva (where his previous ambassadorial posting had been), and then to Vienna a few years later when my father was appointed by the next Secretary General, Javier Pérez de Cuéllar, as the first Director General of the United Nations headquarters there, a post he had left by the time the convocation came. It had been nearly fourteen years since he had plunged into the heart of Syrian politics in person.

He was picked up from Damascus Airport and taken straight to the ministry, where the foreign minister at the time, Farouk

Sharaa, asked him to manage preparations for the Syrian negotiation dossier, and to then lead the Syrian delegation that was to attend the Madrid Peace Conference launched by President Bush. After that, he was to personally conduct the negotiations.

My father was told that this request, if one could call it such, had stemmed from Assad himself, whom he would see again during that short trip and subsequent ones over the next years. In his first meeting with the Syrian president after all this time, he had formally accepted the brief, even though his genuine patriotism (and his former official status) never really gave him a choice. He asked Assad what minimum Syria would accept for the negotiations to be successful. Assad had laughed and replied to my father, whose reputation clearly still preceded him: 'If you had not insisted on knowing that, I might have begun to doubt that you were really Mowaffak Allaf.' The minimum was the Golan, all of it, Assad said. On this, Assad and my father, and the overwhelming majority of Syrians, were in agreement.

The Syrian grapevine circulated the rumours that several big shots at the top of the intelligence pyramid had tried to object to Assad's choice of chief negotiator, arguing that it was more logical to choose one of their own trusted men instead of my father, a known independent in word and in deed. This was one of the times the head of the regime had privileged competence over personal loyalty. They then allegedly proposed other senior diplomats who had remained in the service or in the country, on whom they would have more personal sway; they reasoned that it would look odd that they could not find anybody in the entire country for that position, we were told by people in the know.

The truth is that nobody really knew, least of all my father, why Assad insisted on him for the role. He certainly had wide experience as a seasoned diplomat and was a well-read intellectual with a legal background; he was also a gifted writer and orator, and was known among his colleagues as a walking encyclopaedia of the Arab–Israeli conflict. Moreover, he had never shown the slightest interest in rising up the regime ranks. They could have asked him in a different way, with less drama, but it was clear to all those who knew him that he would try to support his country at this historic event.

With his appointment as chief Syrian negotiator in the peace talks with Israel, yet another chapter in our family's deep connection to Syria started. It also expanded my own horizons even more, fuelling my growing interest in its politics and in the Syrian psyche that still had so much to reveal to me.

* * *

The Madrid Peace Conference launched to great fanfare on 30 October 1991, with Arab and Israeli delegations facing each other in one room for the first time, under the patronage of President Bush and Soviet Union Leader Mikhail Gorbachev, and under the watchful eye of the world's media. It would be Gorbachev's—and the Soviet Union's—last appearance on the world stage.

Most international affairs observers have become blasé about similar events that served mainly as photo ops, but the new peace process was a huge deal and a 'first' on many levels. Because of the centrality of the Palestinian cause when considering the greater picture in the region, collectively we have often neglected to consider the effects of seminal milestones on populations whose voices had been subdued, absent from the conversation. We may remember some of the antics seen at Madrid's Palacio de Oriente, where leaders and officials gave their opening speeches. We may recall the intense scrutiny and attention that renowned journalists gave to the peace process. With the passage of time, we may even take a wider perspective on the consequences that the invasion and liberation of Kuwait brought to the Middle East and beyond.

IT STARTED IN DAMASCUS

I did all of that as well. What I also did was come to realise how much the lives of Syrians could and should have changed as their country entered the world's field of vision once again. Everything we observed during that period demonstrated how much interest Syrians placed in the peace process that followed Madrid, how much hope they held in this sudden emergence from their isolated misery, and how much they wanted to have government officials who respected them and listened to them.

As the regular negotiation sessions began in Washington, D.C., people in Syria were probably following the news more closely than others in the region, and certainly more than they themselves had ever done before on their own channels, as well as the ever-trusted *Houna London*. The negotiations became the focus of Syrian news over the next years, and there is no doubt that the talks were extremely popular with the population. It was not the same level of excitement that events in Eastern Europe had provoked in their people who began to realise that their communist system was collapsing. Rather, in Syria, it was an enthusiasm that seemed to herald a slow and steady road to normality, and a more relaxed regime that was not worried anymore about uprisings or being shunned by important foreign powers. If there was no incoming threat, people deduced, why would the regime continue to restrain the population?

* * *

For the next few years, my father was constantly flying between Vienna, Washington, and Damascus, spending much time there before and after every new round of negotiations. Even before I had seen with my own eyes the effect these talks were having on Syrians, we were hearing from relatives and friends that my dad had become very popular. Fair enough, we thought, he was constantly on the news and would be recognised by many. It was only when speaking to my mother on the phone, the first time she had accompanied him on one of those trips, that I began to get a better idea of what was happening: 'You're not going to believe it,' she said, 'your father is a bit like a celebrity now.' Really? So much so, in fact, that their social outings together now took much longer than usual, because everyone wanted to greet him and speak with him wherever they went.

Before my own next trip to Damascus while my parents were there, I had assumed he was being treated like any official in the public eye: spotted, greeted, given some praise as Syrians tend to do, and thanked for his service. I was so wrong; it was much deeper than that.

Over the next months and years, on numerous occasions on the street, in shops, in restaurants, I saw Syrians of all ages, even teens, greeting him effusively, telling him how happy they were to have him represent the country, and how right it was that 'we' were being treated respectfully by the world. They felt they were a part of this big development, and his own warm and friendly demeanour, his absolute humility in talking to everyone on an equal footing, only encouraged more people to approach him. I saw him being hugged, being kissed, being blessed, being invited into shops and homes. I saw people telling him how much they wanted peace and getting our land back, so we could build a great future. I saw how he listened to Syrians who shared their own dreams and ideas hurriedly, excitedly, a little shocked that he gave them time and let them speak their mind.

Like anyone would be, I was immensely proud that my father was the way he was, even though those of us who knew him well were not surprised to see how approachable and patient he was with so many. More than that, I was moved by the reactions of this Syrian street that had never seen, heard, or met anyone like him in a position like his before. Most officials they were used to seeing in Syria came across as pretentious, entitled, intimidating, uninterested in people's spontaneous outreach. The man who for a few years represented their nation under the spotlight, a nation they wanted to see thrive, was not like these officials: he was the exact opposite of the notorious *mass'oul* archetype of the regime. And, perhaps just as importantly, he was the first official they had come across in such a position who did not parrot Baathist and regime slogans and vapid statements, and who did not refer with exaggerated deference to the president. He spoke like they wanted to be heard by the world.

I did not realise then the huge significance of these wholesome moments I was so lucky to witness, moments that were representative of people who wanted to count, to matter to their country and to the world. It was that same hope that would be revealed again when Hafez Assad died, that hope that kept Syrians waiting for yet another decade until they could wait no more.

How telling this Syrian outpouring of appreciation and anticipation had been in my father's negotiating years. How little it would have taken for this patient population to feel seen, respected, and treated with dignity by its rulers. How easy it would have been for the regime to give Syrians the right to live simply, to improve their lives and give them prospects.

Some changes started coming, drop by drop. The bananas that Syrian children craved in the eighties did seem to have become less rare as the mood lightened during that period. Smuggling from Lebanon expanded ever so slightly at first, as did Syrian manufacturing, allowing shops to stock more basic items—from hygiene products to a multitude of snacks—that thrilled Syrian consumers. Satellite dishes, although still banned, began to make discreet appearances on Syrian roofs, hidden under blankets during the day and unveiled in the dark of night to beam the series and shows that people outside Syria already enjoyed. Investments in the millions began pouring into the country again from the Gulf, in gratitude for Syria's place in the coalition that liberated Kuwait. Assad released a few political prisoners here and there, though thousands more remained incarcerated. Under US pressure, he finally allowed Syrian Jews to leave the country if they wished, without the restrictions they had endured for years—a welcome human right for them, a sad loss for Syrians with whom they had always lived.

Softly, slowly, the extreme solitude of the eighties was beginning to dissipate, and Syrians were daring to hope again. What could possibly go wrong this time?

* * *

On 21 January 1994, days after the Syrian president had gone to Geneva to meet with President Bill Clinton for the first time to discuss the peace process, Assad's eldest son Bassel, whose name and portraits had been appearing for years on Syrian roads and buildings, was killed in a car accident at the age of thirty-one. He had been driving himself at high speed when he crashed at a bend near Damascus Airport, and it is said that Syria's highest officials, and those closest to Assad, were tasked with breaking the news to the president, whose first question was whether Bassel had been assassinated.

The heir apparent, nicknamed 'The Golden Knight' by state media because of his equestrian skills, had come to some prominence soon after his uncle Rifat's exit from Syria in 1984. Even back then, everyone knew he was next in line to succeed his father. This was even more the case after he was named a commander in the Republican Guard and Head of Presidential Security, and launched the Syrian Computer Society in 1989.

Immediately, Syria plunged back into its darkest mode as the regime imposed an official state of mourning on the entire country, even though the deceased had no official capacity apart from his military position. Following the funeral and a significant public demonstration of grief by tens of thousands, Bassel was buried in Qardaha, the Assad family's hometown. Several Arab dignitaries were in attendance, most importantly Egyptian President Hosni Mubarak and Jordanian Crown Prince Hassan, and, as

IT STARTED IN DAMASCUS

expected, the highest-ranked Lebanese leaders—President Elias Hrawi, Prime Minister Rafic Hariri, and Speaker of Parliament Nabih Berri.

Syrians mostly found the mourning protocols to be excessive by any standard. Everything closed, television programmes changed, even alcoholic drinks were withdrawn from sale as a measure of respect. People were expected not just to be respectful, but also to be grieving to a degree that began to exasperate many. Far from abating, the practical deification of the senior Assad—and the beatification of Bassel—sharply increased. Bassel was now referred to as a martyr of the nation, his image even more prominent in death than it had been in his short life. Latakia Airport was named after him, statues appeared, and events and places began to carry his name as well. The Assad portraits eventually included the trinity of Hafez, Bassel, and Bashar, all watching over the Syrian realm.

Assad was said to be devastated by the loss of his son, certainly on a personal level, but also on a political one. To whom would he now bequeath the country he had so blatantly made his, now that his heir was gone? After everything he had done over the years to prepare Bassel, he found himself with no Plan B, so he turned to his second oldest son, the spare, in royal parlance. Bashar was brought in from London where he was a year and a half into his ophthalmology training, following his medicine studies in Syria. His brother had been considered by many to be charismatic, dashing, cavalier, and he certainly had a lot more familiarity with the inner workings of the regime and sway with most officials, but this was a moot point. There was no question in any Syrian's mind that Assad's second son would now take the leadership of the country after his death. Few imagined he would have only six years to prepare for the inheritance that would have otherwise gone to his brother Bassel.

* * *

A BREEZE FROM MADRID

Some things changed outside Syria as well, as Israel had succeeded in breaking up the peace process into several smaller ones. Syrians, like most people, were surprised to hear about the secret negotiations held in Norway between Israel and the PLO that had started in 1992. A year earlier, in advance of Madrid, Israel had insisted that Palestinians would not have their own delegation but rather be part of a joint one with Jordan, without the PLO's participation. PLO leader Yasser Arafat's disastrous decision to support Iraq, following its invasion of Kuwait, had left him with few allies in the Arab world who would have wanted to counter this stipulation, least of all Syria.

These secret negotiations produced the Oslo Accords that were signed on the White House lawn in September 1993, as a smiling President Bill Clinton, in his first year in office, watched over the famous handshake between Israeli prime minister Yitzhak Rabin and PLO leader Yasser Arafat. This was quickly followed by a peace treaty between Israel and Jordan in 1994, leaving only two Arab delegations—Syria and Lebanon—still technically at war and negotiating. Successive frameworks would be attempted by the Clinton administration to push through a Syrian–Israeli peace treaty, with different iterations that resulted, by the end of 1999, with the Israeli prime minister (by then, Ehud Barak) and the Syrian foreign minister Farouk Sharaa meeting face to face for the first time.

In November 1995, Prime Minister Rabin was assassinated by a right-wing Israeli extremist during a public rally in support of Oslo. The qualitative advances made between Syria and Israel, including with the 'Rabin Deposit' premise made through US Secretary of State Warren Christopher (whereby he considered the basis of a full withdrawal from the Golan for a full peace), would never bear fruit.

Post-Kuwait, and with the ongoing containment of Iraq that followed, a new modus vivendi had been reached between three

IT STARTED IN DAMASCUS

important regional actors: Saudi Arabia, Egypt, and Syria. There was a clear understanding by then of the need for mutual support and refrained meddling on others' turf, the different states having specific zones of influence that did not infringe on others.

This became an important balance when Assad found himself entangled yet again in a thorny situation with Turkey, with whom relations had always gone up and down. The Euphrates and the shares of water each country should receive was always a point of contention for both sides, as was the lasting Syrian complaint about the loss of the territory of Alexandretta to Turkey that had been facilitated by France in the 1930s. More recently, Assad's support to Abdullah Ocalan, leader of the Kurdistan Workers' Party (PKK) that launched countless terror attacks from Syrian soil resulting in thousands of Turkish deaths, nearly pushed the two countries into war.

Having had enough of Assad's dismissal of Turkish concerns, the Turkish government issued an ultimatum to Syria in 1998: if Ocalan was not expelled, there would be war. As the Turkish army began mobilising along the Syrian border, President Mubarak of Egypt was instrumental in conducting mediation between Assad and Turkish President Suleiman Demirel. Assad had no other option than to finally expel Ocalan after over a decade, avoiding further escalation and possible war with Turkey. With that, the immediate pressure was now off from every neighbour.

* * *

My father's sudden passing in 1996, and my mother's move back to Damascus after a lifetime abroad, had only increased my attachment to Syria and my desire to spend more time there. Encouraged by family and friends, I took the plunge in 1999 and moved to Damascus, not imagining I would witness the expected transition so soon, nor that I would spend the following twenty-five years researching, writing, and speaking about Syria.

A BREEZE FROM MADRID

Few issues still shook the Eternal Leader who was by then delegating more portfolios to his highly visible son Bashar. Unsatisfactory officials had already been moved around or aside, like pawns, to help prepare the clean slate he would inherit. None of us thought the inheritance would happen that quickly, but it was clear that Bashar would have an unopposed start.

The breeze that had come to Damascus from Madrid had aired out quarters that had remained closed for years. Syrians had felt this gust of hope that Hafez would now feel secure enough to loosen some of the draconian measures under which the population had lived for so long, now that the isolation of the terrible eighties was over, and that the global exposure of the nineties had diminished the animosity of most previous opponents.

It was now up to Bashar to turn this breeze into the winds of change for which the Syrian people had so patiently waited.

PART TWO

AN ERRATIC DECADE

5

THE CULT OF HOPE

Damascus wasn't called the City of Jasmine for nothing. The clichés practically wrote themselves when a gently intoxicating smell would start wafting through at dawn, rising from jasmine shrubs in small gardens and jasmine vines that adorned so many Damascene walls. As the scent started to seep into our awareness, a neighbour's radio in an adjacent building would inevitably rouse us from sleep with the sweet voice of Fairuz, the Lebanese diva who serenaded the mornings of every great Levantine city. Only a cup of freshly made Arabic coffee would make such an ideal morning complete.

Many Syrians themselves might claim this was a romanticised tale that disregarded the other, more irritating morning noises and smells of this busy city. Those of us blessed to live in less congested areas might partly agree, while lamenting their lesser fortune. The Damask Rose was world-famous, but jasmine was our daily emotional sustenance, a fragrant comfort that could momentarily alleviate the frustrations that often weighed us down. It was hard to walk around Damascus without stopping repeatedly to smell the jasmine; we were ridiculous that way, probably addicted.

IT STARTED IN DAMASCUS

In a country like ours, of course, there were ample instances of less pleasant ways to be awakened. One day, as the month of Ramadan was ending, it was my turn to experience what I had only seen in dramatisations.

Urgent banging on the front door woke me from a deep sleep, sending me into immediate panic mode. I sat up quickly, like a character in a movie waking up from a nightmare, and tried to find my bearings in the dark. Could it be my aunts from next door with an emergency? Not likely, they usually called. As I stumbled towards the entrance in a t-shirt that barely covered the top of my thighs, I thought of running back to the closet to grab some jeans first; the increasingly imperious banging insisted I didn't. The sound of incomprehensible words, hollered through a loudspeaker, came through a window I had cracked open before going to bed. I tried to make out the time from the big clock on the sideboard: it was just about 4:00 am.

Heart pounding, I opened the door to find a senior police officer barking as if he were reprimanding cadets in a military academy. I barely had time to think of what I or anyone in our family could have possibly done, because this seemed to be bigger than just us. He asked: 'Do you have a car parked in front of the building?' Yes, we did. 'Take it away immediately before we tow it,' he growled. 'But why?' I asked. *Awamer*, he snarked, orders. 'But where should I take it?' I continued idiotically. He just scoffed and turned to his various subordinates rushing down the stairs as they confirmed mission accomplished; everyone had been informed, and they could not care less where we went with our cars.

My mother had by then come to the door as well, startled but not as frightened as I thought she would be. It turned out this was not her first rodeo; she told me to hurry and to head to my uncle's house if I couldn't park the car close enough to home. Thinking there was a bit of time to decide, I went to the window

THE CULT OF HOPE

and was dismayed to see security men roaming around the square while several neighbours rushed to their cars. A couple of tow trucks waited, motors running and headlights flooding our street where just a few vehicles remained, my mother's included. That fully woke me up.

I dressed quickly and ran downstairs just in time to find our car was the last one. Driving away in a daze, I looked for streets where cars were still parked normally, so that I could walk back home if it was not too far. There was not a single car in sight.

I later found out that what I thought must be a major incident was merely the preparation of a security perimeter for Assad. Every Eid, the Syrian president would pray at a different mosque worthy of his presence, and at least two or three of the larger and grander ones would be secured hours before. These always included the Great Umayyad Mosque, and, often, the fancy President Hafez Assad Mosque in whose vicinity we happened to live. Several neighbourhoods would be unceremoniously emptied of cars at ungodly hours that way, as it was never announced in advance where the beloved leader would make an appearance. This presidential mosque was not even visible from our building, however; for a regime that claimed immense popularity and for a president who later boasted he needed no security as he drove around Damascus alone, this excessively large secure perimeter seemed to argue the opposite.

The only fringe benefit to living close to where Assad might pray was the complimentary street cleaning. As soon as we had all scurried away with our bothersome, suspicious cars, the heavy-duty street-washing trucks would arrive, gushing more water out of their jets than most Syrians had seen for weeks. Only clean streets for presidential feet—and vice versa if they could—in Assad's Syria.

We would be taken by surprise again the next Eid, but remembered to park far away the following one. As the mosque in our area was always one of the possible choices, my mother and most neighbours eventually took that precaution every time to be spared the prospect of being towed. They would still be woken up like wanted suspects, presumed guilty until proven innocent of having a car in a radius too close to the leader, but at least they would not be forced to drive off to nowhere in the middle of the night.

That night had been my first encounter with the special Assad Eid production. Having found a parking spot in the Sheikh Saad market street, a market area at the other side of the Military Hospital, I had walked back home in streets barely illuminated by faint streetlights. I felt uneasy and irate, ruminating along the way about this needless disdain for people, regardless of why we were forced to move our cars. Nobody was going to argue about the government's right to take such measures, a small matter in the scheme of things; the way they still went about them mattered, however, and should not have remained the norm after thirty years of Assadism.

Could they not simply put up temporary no-parking signs, ahead of time, as they did in most other countries? Could Syrians not be treated with more respect and addressed politely as citizens, as people who had a right not to be harassed? Did alleged security considerations require this constant muscle flex, driven by an omnipresent strongman complex to remind people their only right was to obey? These were rhetorical questions; despite the hope that many people felt in the early days of the Bashar era, I doubted that a behavioural change was possible in such an entrenched and entitled regime.

Under Hafez and under Bashar, the primary script was the same, with slight differences in personal style, and aspirations. Hafez had been more aloof, feeling too important to be seen up close regularly, especially in his last years of poor health. Bashar, in contrast, liked to project a different image, that of a

THE CULT OF HOPE

cool, involved and above all admired leader, a man who understood his people and would be close to them, security provisions notwithstanding.

The publicity worked, at first. Haroun Al Rashid, the legendary fifth Caliph of the Abbasid Dynasty, could have not dreamt of a better reputation than Bashar's at the beginning of his official reign. Like the Caliph who, legend has it, walked the streets of Baghdad undercover to check on his people and attend to their needs, Bashar Assad's first months in power generated copious tales of modesty, chivalry, and personal ethics befitting a modern-day saint.

Rumours about sightings of 'The Doctor' abounded. Some swore seeing him in the most random areas of Damascus, inconspicuously walking alone or queuing to buy a sandwich from a humble eatery, casually, modestly, without bodyguards. Imagine, not even lowly regime officials would do that, they said. Others, quoting friends of relatives of reliable sources who themselves had heard from someone at the presidential palace, declared he slept only four hours a night and was always up by dawn, at his desk, working all day (except for his brief sandwich runs), so strong was his commitment to serve the Syrian people.

Stories like these were all the rage in the summer and autumn of 2000. Bashar Assad's alleged feats and his stellar character were part of the reform bubble and the modernisation dream Syrians were being sold. This had been robotically echoed by foreign media around the time of Hafez's death, and they continued to describe his agenda as such repeatedly, even as reality began to disprove these claims time and time again over the next ten years.

In those early days after the presidency was bequeathed to him, Bashar got the kind of PR that money simply cannot buy; it turned an audience that had become indifferent to the regime's empty slogans into a friendly and engaged one. People wanted to believe in this modern fairy-tale of the saviour, of a reign of promise, of sunny days after so much proverbial rain. After thirty years of endurance, fate had good things in store for the patient Syrians, it seemed to many, with the arrival of The Doctor who would start fixing the problems.

* * *

Not even four months into this hope-induced fantasy, I was at a dinner at the house of some close friends when a special treat was brought out: our host had received a copy of the 'Statement of the 99' that had been issued that day and passed it around. I was not the only one who felt a rush of adrenaline as our small party read it together: it was the first Syrian public manifesto calling for the liberation of political prisoners, free speech, the restoration of basic civil liberties, and lifting the state of emergency in place since 1963. Published that day in *Al Hayat*, a Lebanese newspaper, it would circulate in Damascus and beyond over the next days and make a lot of noise, even though the paper had been banned from entering Syria.

I skimmed the list of ninety-nine signatories with interest: some I already knew, others I was discovering before they became household names in the years ahead. This was the most significant civil society initiative we had seen in Syria, and it challenged Bashar Assad to demonstrate his goodwill and prove his promises were not empty talk. And while these demands, energising the period of political activism that became known as the Damascus Spring, were bold for a country that had gone through three decades of violent dictatorship, they barely scraped the surface of what Syrians needed and deserved, beginning with the most rudimentary of human rights.

Our small dinner group marvelled at the courage of these activists and reviewed the current conditions at length; none of us believed Syria could carry on this way for long, and all of us cheered those who called for civic freedoms and democracy.

THE CULT OF HOPE

One of the guests was a London-based surgeon with whom I would become much better acquainted when I moved to the UK the following year. On that balmy late September evening, based on the extensive political conversation at our dinner table that continued until late, none of us could have guessed he would soon become Assad's father-in-law, and one of his most vocal public defenders.

The Damascus Spring had been waiting to bloom even before the death of Hafez. What we called intellectual salons and discussion forums had become bolder at the end of his reign—and not just in Damascus but all over the country—as they addressed economic and administrative reform while trying to avoid discussing domestic politics head-on. That is partly why the expectation for change was so strong then: if Hafez had allowed those to surface, albeit cautiously and watching them like a hawk, then Bashar—'The Hope' as the PR machine was now marketing him—would surely do likewise and even respond in kind.

The initiatives to bring Syrians' civic involvement back to life were diverse and continued to spread in the country, even though a bigger count was found in the capital. They included the Committees for the Revival of Civil Society, the National Dialogue Forum, the Jamal Atassi Forum for Democratic Dialogue, the Tartous Forum for National Democratic Dialogue, and the Al Kawakibi Forum in Aleppo, to name but a few. Through their activities and advocacy, the names of their main organisers, such as Michel Kilo, Riad Seif, Habib Saleh, Michal Tammo, Suheir Atassi—and a long list of other names that the revolution would introduce—became known to a wider public. Hundreds of forums sprouted in many cities and towns, in living rooms, in enclosed domestic courtyards, in offices; Syrians were bursting with energy, eager to discuss their perspectives with others, longing to see movement in a real political sense at the grassroots level.

IT STARTED IN DAMASCUS

While most Syrians had no internet access or mobile phones in that period, nor would they for several years to come, the reach of pan-Arab satellite television had begun to change the spread of news, especially in Assad's Syria. Al Jazeera, the Arabic channel that revolutionised the Arab world's news and brought restriction-free politics to every home, had started broadcasting in 1996. Its interviews and political talk shows soon became must-watch TV for millions of people who had never seen Arab writers, journalists, economists, and various thinkers address regimes in such an open, defiant, progressive manner on live television. Although physical copies of the civil society and opposition's statements and articles would only be seen by a limited circle within Syria, the pan-Arab media would report on them and host people who became recognised names around the Arab world and beyond.

Interest about Syria was growing in the Arab world, after decades being one of the most closed and least known countries at the time. Everyone knew that Hafez Assad had ruled with an iron fist, and that Syrian troops and intelligence in Lebanon were the real rulers there as well. Arabs were also watching because of Syria's status as the first hereditary republic in the Arab world, a region where several other dictators' sons were making a name for themselves and studying how easy—or not—it would be to follow in the footsteps of the Syrian trailblazer. If Bashar was so popular and if his legitimacy had not been contested, then why was he not allowing people to enter the new century with more leeway, with more economic and social prospects? What would happen if he did?

The Doctor had responded to the Statement of the 99, indirectly, by releasing a few hundred political prisoners from Mezzeh prison (amnesties were declared randomly by the Assad regime for years, liberating people the regime did not consider significant threats). He also closed that overly visible ugly structure in

THE CULT OF HOPE

November (leaving thousands of others in many more jails). He thought that would be enough. A few articles about economic reform made their appearance in state media to propose ways to modernise the state's institutions and give the country an economic boost; they did not digress much from the well-established Economic Tuesday lectures that I had often attended even before the death of Hafez, and where I met several of the 'dissidents' and 'foreign agents' whom the regime would be targeting for years. They also did not veer far from the talk about reform in the salons that had been creating a buzz in recent months.

These discussion forums had flourished, bringing together intellectuals, economists, writers, artists, and activists who wanted to motivate civil society to participate in guiding its future, to reform the political and economic system, to increase personal liberties. As word spread about them, regime supporters would give the typical knee-jerk reaction to any criticism of the state and of the regime. They would argue that these intellectuals (so named to infer a distance from society at large) did not speak for the majority of Syrians, even though they touched on all aspects of economic, social, and indeed political life. Despite all evidence to the contrary, and despite the clear discrepancies between the promises Bashar had made and the reality he imposed, most of the usual naysayers would repeat these same canards through the entire first decade of his rule.

In January 2001, four months after the Statement of the 99, one thousand intellectuals, writers, and artists issued a new manifesto in the same manner, publishing a much stronger and more detailed 'Statement of the 1,000' in Lebanese and pan-Arab newspapers. They reiterated the same basic demands: liberate political prisoners, allow free speech, restore basic civil liberties, and lift the state of emergency in place since 1963. Boldly, they dared to add more: the need for a multiparty democratic system and all that entailed.

IT STARTED IN DAMASCUS

This time, The Doctor responded with a temper tantrum. On 8 February, he told pan-Arab newspaper *Asharq Alawsat* what he thought of these Syrians seeking freedom and reform, these perpetrators: 'When the consequences of an action affect the stability of the homeland, there are two possibilities: either the perpetrator is a foreign agent acting on behalf of an outside power, or else he is a simple person acting unintentionally.' In other words, the signatories were either traitors or idiots.

On 18 February, Vice-President Abdul Halim Khaddam gave a speech at Damascus University to explain democracy and freedom to an auditorium full of professors and deans. 'Freedom is a fundamental pillar of the Baath Party,' he said, but it was not an absolute freedom: 'Is it freedom to stand and say or launch slogans and ideas that lead to the dismantling of national unity in the country?' Apparently not. The regime's crackdown proceeded.

The accusation of weakening national sentiment and unity had always been the most convenient charge brandished by the regime to silence anyone it wanted, and it was used liberally over the next weeks and months. Less than a year into his presidency, Assad closed the salons and arrested several signatories and civil society leaders, jailing them for periods of up to ten years, crushing Syrians' hopeful Damascus Spring a full decade before the Arab Spring erupted in other countries in the region.

Syrians heard the message loud and clear: lower your expectations and remember the red lines. After all, when explaining democracy to the people in his inauguration speech on 17 July 2000, Bashar had inserted the caveat that 'we cannot apply the democracy of others to ourselves.'

This first wave of arrests under his watch also immediately created a new version of the justifications we had heard for decades under Hafez. With Assad Senior, Syrians were told repeatedly that while generic mistakes could have been made, perhaps, it was only because the President was so busy defending the nation and focusing on foreign affairs, and was therefore unaware of the bad things some officials were doing domestically. When Bashar arrived, it was still always 'the others' who were bad, because while he was trying to reform the system and fight corruption, these others were standing in his way and causing all the trouble.

Every time something was openly or indirectly criticised in the country, regime loyalists brought out the ridiculous 'old guard' myth, the idea that Bashar first had to fight this alleged remnant of his father's rule, the old figures who were trying to rein in Bashar's 'new guard' of reformers. Many Syrians bought it at first. Soon enough, however, they realised that there had only ever been one guard in Assad's Syria, whose sole ambition was its own survival and the maintenance of its unlimited privileges—regardless of which Assad ruled.

* * *

Assad barely had time to take a breather after silencing and imprisoning Syrian civil society: important guests were coming to town. In May 2001, Pope John Paul II's visit to Damascus delighted millions of Christian and Muslim Syrians who came out in droves to welcome him. For the first time, a pope entered a mosque, one of the most beautiful and important in the Islamic world, spending over an hour and a half inside the Great Umayyad Mosque, and reflecting by the shrine of Saint John the Baptist in its midst.

His visit to Quneitra, some sixty kilometres from Damascus, generated much interest as well. Israel had occupied Syria's Golan Heights in 1967, withdrawing from parts of it in 1974 in compliance with the Disengagement Agreement that Nixon and Kissinger had brokered. Before returning it to Syrian sovereignty, Israel had destroyed Quneitra, rendering the town uninhabitable for the 55,000 people who had fled in 1967. It has remained in ruins since then, because of a decision by the regime to keep this macabre reminder of Israeli actions and not rebuild it until the entire Golan was returned. The Pope prayed in a damaged Greek Orthodox church and watered an olive tree planted in honour of his visit.

The most reported part of the trip, however, was Bashar's welcoming speech mentioning those 'who try to kill the principles of all religions with the same mentality with which they betrayed Jesus Christ.' I remember being irritated and frustrated by the choice of this coarse comment that was meant to take a dig at Israel, but that could and would only be interpreted as an antisemitic remark. It was the first time that Bashar had the attention of world media after his father's funeral, and he could have found many ways to insert himself into the headlines, especially with ample available facts about Israeli actions in the region. It should have been enough to let the light shine on the historic event of a pope entering a mosque for the first time in history, let alone the mosque in the world's oldest capital from where the Umayyad Empire had spread to Spain.

In the big picture, this may not have mattered much; four months later, seismic events were going to wipe all other matters from the headlines anyway.

* * *

Bashar Assad was at the start of his second year in power when the terror attack of 11 September 2001 shook the world during President George W. Bush's first year in office. Assad was of little significance to the new administration at the time, as US attention was on the second Palestinian Intifada that had started in September 2000 when Ariel Sharon, leader of the opposition, had visited the Temple Mount in Jerusalem. The peace process was not on the table any longer.

When Bush announced his administration's 'war on terror' would neutralise and punish the attackers of 11 September,

THE CULT OF HOPE

Assad thought this was an opportunity to cosy up to the American President's team; he spontaneously offered the US extensive intelligence on a number of regional Islamist groups, calculating this would buy him leverage on other fronts. This was to be one of several superficial and erroneous Syrian analyses of American posture: Washington expected such cooperation after the attacks, never considering it a favour. Moreover, Bush was not about to make exceptions in the US definition of terrorist groups: Israeli lobbying helped ensure that Syria's backing of Palestinian and Lebanese militant groups, a central pillar in its claimed support for a common Arab cause—and a useful control tool—would no longer be tolerated by Washington.

Assad decided to be helpful another way when the US deported a Canadian citizen of Syrian origin while on a stopover in New York in 2002. Maher Arar was sent to Syria, where he was interrogated and tortured for a year before being let go, innocent of all terror charges. That bought Syria some time, Assad thought, but events proved that diplomatic acumen was not his forte.

Syria had been elected to a two-year stint on the United Nations' Security Council in October 2001. From January 2002 until December 2004, Syria was—or should have been—an influential voice as the invasion of Iraq was being planned by the US, justified, it claimed, by Saddam Hussein's weapons of mass destruction. While history was not exactly repeating itself, Iraq not having invaded a country this time around, there was nevertheless another President Bush seeking unanimous support and a Security Council resolution that would justify an armed intervention in the Middle East. As it had been in 1990, Syria was in a position to make decisions that would help its relations beyond the region.

Syria's long-standing hatred of the Iraqi regime had softened slightly in the last years of Hafez's lifetime. There was now less reason to see Iraq under attack, especially when Bashar Assad would already have had a lingering fear that the US could, potentially, succeed in improving Iraq as it claimed it would bring democracy to the country. What if it really did, and what if it triggered the dreaded regime change domino effect on neighbouring countries?

It was thus logical for Bashar to align himself with the European countries challenging the US and the UK on the issue of Iraq, such as France, and even moving closer to Turkey as both countries attempted to minimise potential consequences, not least vis-à-vis the dormant Kurdish issue both faced. With so many in the world opposing this invasion, it should have been easier for Assad to navigate the storm.

* * *

In 2002, after my move to London as the world was reeling from the 11 September attacks and hearing the drums of war, I had accepted the invitation by Assad's father-in-law, Dr Fawaz Akhras, to join the founding board of directors of the British Syrian Society he was creating. On this board would sit fourteen members, seven British and seven Syrian, known and respected personalities in their fields. There were MPs, bankers, businessmen, academics; I was probably the most junior board member, professionally, at the time.

As my first meeting with Akhras had shown me we had similar opinions on the regime and the opposition at the time of the Damascus Spring, I thought the Society could benefit Syrian people as much as it would the regime. I should have known my assumptions would be rather misplaced; as we say in Syria, the chair (one's position of power) changes people.

British prime minister Tony Blair had included Damascus in his regional tour following the September attack, to gather support for military action in Afghanistan, and later in Iraq. Assad's return visit took place in December 2002, and the first item on

THE CULT OF HOPE

his agenda was a meeting with the British Syrian Society. It was my and several board members' first time meeting him, and we all showed up at the Dorchester for our early morning appointment. The room was set up in the usual Syrian manner, his chair and that of the most senior board member by his side at the head, with the rest of us split on either side in a circle.

As Syrian television cameras filmed us watching him, Assad lectured us on the world, economics, international relations, banking, media, democracy, and other macro concepts. I believe everyone was a bit stunned, and literally speechless since nobody was asked for an opinion, an exchange of views, for an answer to a question on a subject Assad may have not known, if only about Britain. No, he knew everything and had nothing to learn from these established, competent, powerful personalities with decades of experience at the highest levels of the British political establishment and London's financial and media circles.

I found this to be a telling experience that confirmed perceptions many of us had gained over the previous couple of years of observation: Assad's self-image was already rather inflated, and the decisions he would make as time passed demonstrated that he relied on nothing but his own thoughts, unfounded and tenuous as they might be. This was a man who only gave instructions and never asked for, let alone heeded, advice.

A month before that London trip, the only Arab nation on the Security Council had voted in favour of Resolution 1441 giving Saddam Hussein his ultimatum. Syria argued, like France and Russia did at the time, that this resolution in no way approved resorting to force. Did Bashar not even have the guts to abstain? When the invasion proceeded anyway in March 2003, as American and British tanks swept across the Iraqi desert, Syria declared it stood with the Iraqi people and wished for the defeat of the invaders. The crescendo in rhetoric infuriated the US, whose response was to accuse Syria of smuggling night-vision goggles, possibly harbouring Iraqi officials, and allowing insurgents to infiltrate the porous Syrian–Iraqi border. While information about the goggles and their impact remains unclear, many Syrians did see the buses in central Damascus full of men newly released from jail heading to the Iraqi border on a regular basis.

The ambiguities of Syria's position became increasingly marked, as did its contradictions over time, a clear indication that Bashar Assad was indecisive, wavering between strong opposition and meek acquiescence. In May 2003, as the Security Council voted on UNSC Resolution 1483 that recognised the occupation of Iraq and the responsibilities of the occupying powers, namely the US and the UK, the Syrian ambassador did not even attend the session, and Syria's absence was counted as an abstention. Embarrassingly, Syria later claimed it would have supported the resolution had it not been for the seven-hour difference between New York and Damascus, and for the time diplomats needed to confer with the Foreign Ministry.

Assad had even failed to promote a discussion on a draft resolution condemning Israel's violation of Syrian sovereignty in a controversial October 2003 strike—a unique situation for a member of the Security Council. A few days later, Syria quietly voted in favour of Security Council Resolution 1511 that authorised a multinational force to stabilise Iraq, bowing to the US and trying to limit further damage. It didn't help much: in November 2003, the US Congress passed the Syria Accountability and Lebanese Sovereignty Restoration Act (SALSA), turning the attention of the Bush administration to the Syrian meddling and military presence that was still in Lebanon. Assad's needlessly chaotic official stance on Iraq had made Bush notice him.

It was clear that the invasion of Iraq, regardless of the eventual success or failure in achieving its declared goals, was one of the most worrying developments the Syrian regime had ever experienced. This time, in addition to targeting the regime of Saddam

THE CULT OF HOPE

Hussein, the US and its allies were eyeing the entire Baath Party itself, introducing the concept of de-Baathification in Iraq while its Syrian neighbour was still very much committed to its ongoing Baathification. Since he had no intention of abandoning his own Baath which had always served the regime so well, perhaps a shrewd idea was needed to differentiate the Assad Baath from the one Hussein led.

A month into Iraq's occupation, Assad decreed that school uniforms that had always been in military colours (sand beige for primary school, dark khaki for secondary school) would change the following school year; all Syrian students would henceforth wear blue in primary, and grey and pink (girls) and blue (boys) in secondary. As poorer families scrambled for extra money to buy these new uniforms, he was just camouflaging the continued Baathification of children by cancelling the original camouflage clothing.

* * *

This two-year stint on the United Nations Security Council proved unproductive. Assad neither managed to cultivate better relations with key powers, nor did he recover the status Syria had enjoyed in the nineties after the liberation of Kuwait. With the unwise meddling in Lebanon that had begun to escalate, Syria had given itself little room for movement. Intelligent manoeuvring, instead of blind defiance that delivered few benefits, might have circumvented the quick temper of the neocon American administration, determined to impose new designs on the Middle East. Assad did not play his cards well with the invasion of Iraq, especially as numerous countries equally opposed it; a better strategy might have prevented the unnecessary descent into additional sanctions and diplomatic isolation. Assad should have also nurtured the goodwill of the European Union, whose patience ran out during negotiations over the Association

IT STARTED IN DAMASCUS

Agreement that nearly every other country in the region had already signed, establishing industrial free trade facilitations and fostering economic growth in Mediterranean countries. That said, no amount of bargaining on Iraq and agreement with the EU would have diminished the backlash of his subsequent actions in Lebanon.

Over time, as my work on Syria became better known through my Associate Fellow position at Chatham House and increased media appearances, I was often asked about the early Bashar years and the Damascus Spring that had been so quickly repressed and forgotten when huge events rocked the world; the freshness and the boldness of that spring had caught the attention of many, especially around the Arab world.

In October 2004, speaking on the BBC's first ever Doha Debates programme to argue for the motion that 'This House believes that Arab Governments are not interested in genuine reform,' I spoke at length with Dr Saad Eddin Ibrahim, renowned Egyptian sociologist and human rights advocate, who had been sentenced to seven years in prison in 2000 for his activism, managing to have all charges dropped in 2003. He asked for my perspective on Assad, his decision-making style, the state of the opposition, and the apparent popular acceptance of the inherited position. With Egyptian President Mubarak's eldest son Gamal having an increasingly large presence on the political and economic scene, many Egyptians were beginning to fear the Syrian model would be tempting to others. Of all the things in which Syria could have been a leader, I thought, did it have to be in validating the hereditary republic?

I described Bashar Assad as a mansplainer, a hobby he maintained by pontificating regularly on global affairs, giving rambling interviews to journalists, and displaying alarming levels of hubris as time passed. He soon felt comfortable enough to slip into his speeches what he thought were clever insults to Arab leaders, as he praised his own logic.

THE CULT OF HOPE

He expected and demanded the respect that he felt his father had achieved. But unlike Hafez, he also wanted to be liked, loved, admired, because he was young and cool—as were his wife, his taste in music, his love of technology, his driving around the city (that fans insisted he did without a security detail), his casual dinners in the cool restaurants in Old Damascus with cool guests that would drop into town. And he was loved, we were told constantly, as deserved and as proven by the enormous portraits of his face with the word *menhebbak* (we love you) in colloquial Syrian Arabic that were soon plastered all over the realm.

While he played statesman abroad, Bashar chanted the modernisation and reform refrains domestically, claiming to fight the corruption that his own regime had pushed to new heights. In reality, he was establishing a disastrous crony capitalist system that completely ignored the demands of a growing population, and the necessity for a solid infrastructure worthy of twenty-first-century economic and logistic needs. The first beneficiaries of this very selective liberalism were the Assad clan and their closest allies, and that velvet society whose fortunes grew at dizzying rates under his reign. To manage this vast wealth blurring the lines between public funds and the Assad piggybank, Bashar entrusted the family's portfolio management to his maternal cousin, Rami Makhlouf.

6

RAMI'S PREROGATIVE

One hectic afternoon as I searched for some medication prescribed for my ailing aunt, I came upon a most endearing Syrian peculiarity that, I later realised, symbolised the sense of fairness in a people treated so unjustly. At the time, the quality of nationally produced drugs was yet to improve before the rise of the Syrian pharmaceutical industry throughout the 2000s, and the foreign drugs recommended by doctors were difficult to find. I got lucky at my fourth pharmacy and handed over two 500-pound bills; in return, I received a couple of small bills and a few individually wrapped plasters. 'I don't need these,' I said, perplexed. The pharmacist smiled apologetically: 'As usual, we don't have any small change.' I thought this was odd but understood it was her way of not shortchanging me for even a tiny amount, so I pocketed my rather distinctive return on this transaction and thanked her.

While piastres were no longer in circulation and credit and debit cards were not yet available, you could sometimes find the coins of five and ten pounds that still existed, but even that was rare. Change was often difficult to return in full, and unless one had the exact amount to pay for something, pharmacists and shopkeepers would always try to give back something of a similar monetary value, no matter how small. Through many subsequent visits to pharmacies in Damascus, our plaster collection grew, and I never failed to be touched by this simple gesture that revealed the authenticity and inner generosity of the perpetually change-free Syrians.

They did not have change at Syriatel either, even though it was the leading (and at first the only) Syrian telecommunications firm. Paying mobile phone bills could only be done in cash for years, and people would have to queue in long lines once a month to settle their bills, and then some. Unlike the shopkeepers who went out of their way to show customers they were not trying to cheat them out of a few pounds, time and time again, Syriatel not only did not return the change, but did not give them anything instead either. Those Syrian pounds, even in single digits, could have been added as credit to the subscriber's account, but they were not. The amount could have been accumulated quarterly or yearly and returned as a corresponding number of minutes or data, for instance, but it was not. No, Syriatel just rounded up, always up, and pocketed the small change of thousands and then millions of people, every single month.

That was not the Syrian way; it was the Rami way, and Rami's way had its own rules and even its own terminology. Like his maternal cousin Bashar Assad, Rami Makhlouf was often referred to by his first name only, because who else could we be talking about for anything relating to the economy of the country and the finances of the regime? A man with no official designation nor formal capacity in any governmental setting, Rami was in all but name the regime's portfolio manager, the middleman ensuring that any transaction in the country would have to go through him, at a price of his choosing, to further line the Assad clan's deep pockets.

* * *

RAMI'S PREROGATIVE

Very quickly, every Syrian, rich or poor, learned about *ramrameh*, the eponymous password that opened some doors if Rami said so. Few countries in the world would have developed the kind of vocabulary that was so unique to Assad's Syria, that was so blatantly clear in its meaning and fit for purpose. This was not a formulation denoting involvement at a state level, say like Keynesian economics, or even one depicting a particular era's policies, like Thatcherism. Rather, its essence resembled the Mafia's *pizzo* of monetary extortion in exchange for protection, which in its Assadist iteration began even before the business reached the level of needing protection—or, better said, a lack of harassment. In Assad's Syria, *ramrameh*, that made-up noun derived from Rami's name, meant an action that needed his involvement, his approval, and that he was the only person who could make it happen, for a price, from the moment someone had an idea for a new business.

Many Syrians saw first-hand how *ramrameh* worked at different levels, through a series of steps that those who needed it began to understand well. *Ramrameh* usually developed through several stages, each guarded by a smaller middleman that you had to convince to let you through, also for a price. The higher up the echelon you were, the more likely it was your appeal would reach Rami; sometimes, Rami's people would even be the first ones to reach out, if they got wind of a lucrative plan. In the Syrian state's economy that had been a tightly controlled command one for decades, a parallel financial system grew exponentially under the new godfather, with little thought given to the actual consequences that touched the entire nation.

On one of my trips from London in autumn 2003 to attend an event at the People's Palace, during the official visit of a foreign dignitary, I was catching up with an acquaintance about changes since our last respective trips to Damascus. He, a well-known Syrian-born tycoon who resided abroad, related to me some details of a one-on-one meeting he had with Assad the day earlier. As he lowered his voice in the presence of other people in his hotel suite, I thought his hushed tone was because he wanted to comment on something political, a broad field that had been our usual discussion ground. Instead, he told me he had brought up the Syrian economy and a request for the presidency to facilitate a well-planned European investment, one that would benefit the country in the tense climate following the invasion of Iraq. He was merely establishing the connection for those Europeans, this was not his project: 'I just asked Dr Bashar to cut the red tape for them, to prevent the relevant ministries from messing up this opportunity,' he told me. To his astonishment, and to mine as I listened to his recounting of the conversation, Bashar's response had been to dismiss governmental involvement with a wave of the hand: 'Speak to Rami,' he instructed, considering the issue resolved and changing the subject.

There was not even a hint of pretence, nor a self-conscious justification about the Syrian government handing over such an important financial transaction to a relative of the president who held no official title. The businessman in question was a heavyweight, expecting that the foreign investors he was introducing would deal through official channels, as they would in most other countries. 'It is possible that Syria still functions like this, in important matters at this point in time?' he rhetorically asked in a slightly bitter tone, his eyes reflecting lost hope for the promised reforms.

It did not matter how big one became in the business world; whether through direct instructions from Assad at times, or possibly after consultations with the clan's *consigliere*, nothing in Syria now worked without *ramrameh* in the Bashar era. With his firm control over large portions of Syrian economic decisions and activities for the Assad clan, and with his monopoly on financial matters that should have remained matters of state, nearly every business transaction worthy of attention was only possible in Syria with Rami's approval and his receipt of the generous corresponding commission that filled the extended Assad family coffers instead of the Syrian Treasury. Syrians had different ideas on the percentage of the economy that he controlled, some calling him 'Mr Five Percent', others raising that number much higher, but they had no doubt that he, as part and parcel of the ruling elite, had a piece of nearly every pie he wanted.

This literal ramification of the Assad process of making deals in Syria became the answer to many economic, business, or financial questions at a high—or high enough—level. Can we import this raw material for our new manufacturing, or does it need *ramrameh*, a factory owner may have wondered. Could I get the franchise rights of this brand and sell its products in Syria, or does it need *ramrameh*, a retailer may have asked. Does our company have a chance to bid for this tourist infrastructure, or does it need *ramrameh*, pondered others. Unless you were opening small companies, local manufacturing, or falafel stands, an economic endeavour that for decades had required a security clearance, the answer was that you always needed *ramrameh* for any venture worthy of the regime's attention, and the question soon became moot. Rami's *ramrameh* was the real Ministry of Economy and Finance, regardless of what the law said.

* * *

The apple had not fallen far from the tree, as Mohammad Makhlouf, Rami's father and Hafez's brother-in-law, had himself been a similarly significant player in the Hafez era. At the head of the General Organisation of Tobacco, a state-owned monopoly that liberally filled the Assad clan's bank accounts through thriving tobacco imports and sales, Makhlouf Senior was a jack of all trades in 1980s and 1990s Syria. He was also, among others, the executive director of the Real Estate Bank of Syria for two decades, a convenient position giving him *carte blanche* to systematically grab his and the Assads' cut on loans and mortgages at the only available bank in Syria.

Makhlouf was also a partner and shareholder in the Al Furat Petroleum Company, with brother-in-law Ghassan Muhanna's company providing the industrial services support. This was at a time when Syria was producing some 600,000 barrels of oil per day—peanuts for the giant producers, but significant pocket money for the Assad clan when the Syrian state's healthy oil income did not even appear on the national budget for years.

As with Hafez Assad's offspring, many of the children of this regime's henchmen would eventually outdo their fathers in whatever their fathers had done. While various regime branches and relatives were satisfied with smaller smuggling activities in the eighties and nineties, Rami and his brothers became the so-called businessmen of the late 1990s and 2000s, enjoying the free rein afforded them and them alone, taking pieces of the Syrian pie solely because of who they were. It was all in the family, a large family of entitled brats with an open playing field, for whom success was guaranteed in the complete absence of competition. For the other ninety-nine percent, the rigid laws of the regime and the archaic limitations of a nominally socialist economy applied.

Aside from the large Assad clan and its extended branches, the children of top regime officials, like General Mustafa Tlass and Vice-President Abdul Halim Khaddam, had been among the first well-known faces of that business generation in the Hafez era, with simple ventures that had high visibility. Although imports were forbidden for the vast majority of personal goods, a select group of Damascene ladies could head to boutique Al Reem (belonging to Khaddam's daughter) in the middle of Abou Roummaneh and find it packed with luxury designer clothes and accessories, flown in regularly from Paris and other European

RAMI'S PREROGATIVE

fashion capitals. For years, it was the only one of its kind in Syria. La Noisette, first open in Malki and then in Mezzeh, had been the first Western-style café-restaurant chain allowed in the country, a privilege granted to the Khaddam sons. Firas Tlass, for his part, had a variety of low-profile commercial activities from the 1980s, many in the food industry.

Then the Bashar era came, and many more of his generation, the children of the original regime hot shots—and later their own children—got hungrier and flashier and the pie had to get much bigger. The business of the Hafez era was small fry compared to what would come.

* * *

Even before Syriatel, and even before Bashar's rule, Rami Makhlouf had other lucrative business opportunities that had not been made available to anyone but him. Under Hafez's rule, in 1997, he had been granted the right to establish duty-free stores in international airports, ports, and land ports of entry in Syria. It started with his taking over the license to operate the Damascus International Airport duty-free shop, replacing the previous government-owned GOTA (General Organisation for Trade and Distribution) stores whose merchandise and presentation in all the free trade zones in which it operated, and some small showrooms in hotels where only a foreign passport allowed purchases, were more reflective of the Baathist aesthetic. For that privilege, Ramak would have to pay only one million Syrian pounds a year (the equivalent then of 20,000 dollars) to the Syrian state, for his initial contract of five years.

There had been no calls for tenders, and Rami, then aged twenty-eight and with no real qualifications apart from being the president's nephew, had simply been granted the permission by then-prime minister Mahmoud Zoubi to operate Ramak duty-free stores at every port of entry, and at the free trade zones

IT STARTED IN DAMASCUS

where GOTA operated. The prime minister's son, Mufleh, whose privileged position had given him many pieces of the pie at a time when fewer officials' children were openly competing, was Rami's partner in this venture.

In March 2000, without warning, Hafez Assad relieved Zoubi of the post of prime minister he had held since 1987 and expelled him from the Baath Party, accusing him of corruption—the usual accusation for any official the regime wanted to sideline or dismiss. It's not that he was not corrupt, of course, but this institutionalised corruption was only ever a problem or a crime when the Assads wanted it to be one.

Among other accusations, Zoubi was alleged to have pocketed a hefty commission from a French company on the purchase of several Airbus planes for Syrian Airlines. Two months later, it was announced in state media that Zoubi had committed suicide at his home in Damascus, apparently just when he learned he was about to be taken for interrogation by the authorities.

Following Zoubi's death, his son Mufleh, Rami's partner in Ramak, was just as swiftly abandoned, and the duty-free company would operate for the next decade exempt from taxes under the sole ownership of Makhlouf, enticing Syrians who wanted to discover the foreign products and brands that only Rami could sell them. For those who could afford it, short shopping trips to Lebanon became worthwhile just to go to Ramak; as they drove back through border control with a Ramak shopping bag or two in the boot, Syrians knew that the notorious searches and alleged duties they would have had to pay magically vanished. Ramak shopping bags had quickly become a guarantee of safe and swift passage.

The mobile phone concession had been his next big business, and Syriatel had at first been a joint venture with the Egyptian telecommunications firm Orascom Telecom, owned by billionaire businessman Naguib Sawiris. With its twenty-five percent stake in Syriatel, Orascom had a Build-Operate-Transfer (BOT) agreement that was a common practice in some countries, giving the Egyptian company managerial powers as the company grew for the agreed numbers of years before management and ownership were transferred to the majority stakeholder, Syriatel. Trouble quickly emerged, however, when Orascom accused its Syrian partner of trying to control the management of the company and to be sole signatory on its bank accounts, considering it an unacceptable and hostile manoeuvre.

Orascom took the issue to court expecting a prompt resolution of the problem given the clarity of the contract, and were shocked when a Syrian judge simply froze the company's accounts and assets worth about fifty million dollars. Not even a businessman of Sawiris' stature and international clout was able to successfully handle his affairs in a Syria subject to the petty thievery of Bashar and his cousin Rami. They were still at the very beginning of their greedy reign and of the *ramrameh* that would make them richer than they could have imagined possible, and nobody knew exactly where the line between the state and their family was drawn.

When the Syrian government awarded one of the first mobile phone concessions to Rami's brand-new Syriatel in 2001 (and the second to Lebanese businessman and future prime minister Najib Miqati, in whose company Investcom Makhlouf also owned shares), two members of parliament and Damascus Spring figures—Riad Seif and Mamoun Homsi—had dared to criticise the deal. Without naming Makhlouf, they argued that there were numerous irregularities in the creation of Syriatel and Investcom, and that the conditions in the contracts would result in the Syrian state losing money, unlike most other countries where mobile phone contracts had been financially profitable for the government.

A few months later, Seif and Homsi were stripped of their parliamentary immunity, arrested, accused of corruption and of attempting to change the constitution through illegal means, and sentenced to five years in prison each. The accusations were always the same, whether critics were demanding civil liberties and assorted rights, or speaking out when the government seemed to be losing an important source of income.

Mobile phone prices were prohibitive at first for nearly all Syrians, remaining an unattainable aspiration until the prices came down in the mid-2000s, especially when the regime allowed the import of cheap Chinese phones that average Syrians could afford. In 2000, after some dithering because of the excessive cost, I purchased a cell phone line for 60,000 Syrian pounds (then equivalent to 1,200 dollars); it was of course an exorbitant luxury in Assad's Syria, but I had gotten used to having a cell phone abroad and liked the small sense of freedom it gave me. That amount was just for the phone number, for the right to have a mobile line; I felt that this activation fee was really a ransom, or at the very least highway robbery.

That amount did not include various registration fees and the monthly call package, and it did not include the phone. My European cell phone was unusable in Syria: only devices imported by the government would function in Syria—basically, another commercial venture for Rami. The security checks were done for free. Besides, my salesperson already knew me well, as he did most of the people who ordered the widest range of products stashed in his tiniest of shops named after an ancient Syrian queen. He was most certainly an informant, and a well-connected one at that, but Syria worked in mysterious ways indeed: from his shop, I used to buy odds and ends of the type one finds in convenience stores like cigarettes, cheese, bread, coffee, an occasional magazine, and, of all things, my mobile phone.

Rami was not just after new business, nor was he just after a cut in other people's businesses; sometimes, he liked a business so much that he wanted to have it all for himself. Since the early

1980s, Omar Sankar's dealership had been the exclusive agent of Mercedes-Benz and in charge of every Mercedes that came into the country. After all, regime officials and their rich circle needed nice cars, and Sankar was well established with them, enduring the harshest Hafez years and his banana politics without a hitch until Bashar and Rami came along.

In 2004, Rami decided to wedge himself into that lucrative car market, and specifically into Mercedes which had worked with its same Syrian agent for decades. The Syrian government promptly obliged, following the unwritten rule of what Rami wants, Rami gets, making it compulsory for Mercedes to only sell spare parts in Syria through Makhlouf's business, thus bypassing Sankar. In the longer run, it was clear that Rami wanted to take the Mercedes dealership for himself.

It seems Mercedes did not take kindly to this power play and refused to comply with the new rule. For two years, the powerful German manufacturer refused to dissociate itself from its agent, Sankar, and equally refused to send its spare parts through anyone else. For once, Makhlouf had to give up because Mercedes did not cave. Rami consoled himself by turning his attention to another maker, taking the BMW agency and making sure the Ministry of Defence bought thousands of cars through him and sold them to retired officers.

* * *

Assad Senior's nationalisations had killed the private sector's capacity, but Junior was determined to revive it, along with his generation of nepo babies who eventually ushered in an era of foreign franchises and the imports of consumer goods that Syrians could only dream of previously. But while the financial empire reached new peaks under Bashar, with the regime's limitless appetite for money on full display as it enriched itself and its cronies, it did so at the expense of urgently needed growth of the national economy and infrastructure. There was a new air of activity and livelihood, noticed by Syrians of all social levels, but most of these new possibilities remained out of reach for the vast majority.

For the most part, less well-to-do Syrians monitored with growing anxiety the regular reductions in social welfare and in government subsidies for many basic necessities, such as bread or fuel. While these reductions were supposed to reduce budget deficits and enable public spending in other fields, they were not accompanied by schemes for the creation of employment, amongst other necessary and gradual economic steps in a serious long-term plan. It was a haphazard process at best.

That said, there were some fringe advantages to the ruling clan's ravenous appetite: in order to enjoy the products and services they wanted, they needed employees who could rise to the level, and this increased the number of service agencies and employment opportunities, including in design and in advertising, that thrived in this new atmosphere. There were fewer jobs than there were applicants, but it was still a slight improvement.

In 2007, Makhlouf set up Cham Holding with several other businessmen and investors with an initial capital of 360 million dollars. It included a large luxury real estate firm, Bena Properties, with exclusive high-end projects such as Eighth Gate and the Yafour Complex, and an aviation arm with Syrian Pearl Airlines, operating joint flights with Syrian Airlines (and causing the only other private airline, Cham Wings, to struggle to secure routes and slots). Cham Holding also included a variety of other sectors with big projects in tourism and the hospitality industry, several private banking and financial firms, media outlets and advertising agencies, private education, and a variety of transportation, healthcare, manufacturing and energy, and investment and development projects.

Although the economy had eventually opened up in the second half of the 2000s, the rise of Rami's empire and the growth of the business clique that surrounded the regime made it feel as if there were two versions of Syria facing one another: one owned and led by the crony capitalists doing Bashar's bidding, and another made up by the rest of the country watching things change rapidly, close enough and yet just out of their reach. The first group had free choice in their ventures, generous state institutions' support in every logistical aspect, and first-rate prime lands and areas to which they were given priority. The second, far larger group, was a mere spectator, observing the notion of a social balance crumble, as most of its middle class was slipping downward.

The mass consumerism that could have brought the regime cronies more money took a few years to materialise, but the regime had other creative ways to squeeze Syrians out of their money even when they lived abroad. For instance, exemption fees for military service were offered to Syrian men living abroad, so they could visit their homeland or come back to settle in Syria even if they had not done their military service. The Syrian constitution made military service compulsory and regulated by law for Syrian males for a period of thirty months, reduced to two years in 2005, except for those who were the only son in the family, or who had health issues that would impede their service. For those living abroad, there was a whole menu of regulations that changed regularly, often depending on the cash flow needs of the regime.

For years, the regime had set different fee categories for residents of the Gulf, Europe, and America (the fee for US residents tended to be higher, because the regime expected people to make a good living there). In effect, it was another ransom expats had to pay before being allowed free access to their native country, or else be dragged into the army upon returning. There was no rhyme or reason to any of the fees imposed by the regime.

In the mid-2000s, if a man had been born outside of Syria and had resided abroad continuously until the age of eighteen, the exemption fee in that category was 2,000 dollars. Those who had left Syria before they were twelve and remained abroad until eighteen had to pay 5,000 dollars. After that, it got more complicated, depending on where one lived, for how long, and what educational degree—and in which field—one had. For example, a man having left Syria after the age of twelve who now had a Master's degree or a PhD in a scientific field would have to pay an exemption fee of 10,000 dollars. But, if the man had been abroad for more than fifteen years and did not hold a graduate degree, the exemption fee would be 15,000 dollars.

Lucky Syrian men who had reached the age of fifty-two would only pay a measly 1,000 dollars, regardless of their education level. Countless Syrian men scattered all over the globe, long before the revolution, had been unable to come back home if they had not done their military service, as many could not afford these fees.

* * *

Under Bashar, Syrians still earned a ridiculous annual per capita income (a rough, unjustifiable 1,000 dollars considering the country's abundant natural and human resources). Meanwhile, they continued to watch as regime cronies obscenely flaunted their incredible wealth, having modernised an archaic *droit de seigneur* in making business a privilege, rather than a right. For years, reform schemes for the erratic economic and financial system (socialist in name, crony capitalist in reality) were not conducive to reassurance, especially when an abrupt elimination of subsidies seemed to be the only plan, one that did nothing to tackle massive unemployment and limited prospects for the hundreds of thousands of Syrians entering the workforce yearly.

Decisions made by the regime, touted as economic and administrative reform, were nothing more than a potpourri of tactical steps rather than the strategic goals needed to lift all of Syria upward. The legendary bureaucracy of the Baath Party reigned on all, while the lack of transparent and open laws and regulations further complicated matters. In such environments, the playing field was not level, and it was always more advantageous to Rami Makhlouf and the clique of businessmen who, like him, had become symbolic of the Bashar era.

As I observed them through the years, I found that this class of businessmen tied directly to the regime could be even more haughty and entitled, if possible, than the officials in government, army, or intelligence. Their businesses were certainly successful, there was no debating that, but it was not necessarily because of their superior creativity, financial acumen, or strategic minds. Indeed, crony capitalism is a wonderful—and above all an easy—thing when one holds the monopoly in an economy that is closed for most others.

That period did create a lavish lifestyle that quickly became very visible to all, including the opulent parties and the high-class weddings that were now even serving sumptuous breakfasts after long nights of celebration. But for all the fancy business ventures started by Rami and friends, in Cham Holding and through other avenues, there were still no world-class hospitals or even highly functional ambulances in Syria, if only to treat the important officials and personalities in their own capital instead of having to drive them to Beirut at times of acute need. There were no respected research centres or laboratories donated by various businessmen to advance scientific discovery or even to train promising young students. There were no serious contributions made to infrastructure, or to social projects in those years of rising business effervescence.

Rami's prerogative defined much of the first decade of Bashar Assad's rule, and his sense of entitlement was passed to his own children, just as he had inherited his from his father. They were not shy about the extravagances they still allowed themselves

IT STARTED IN DAMASCUS

when the rest of the country underwent its worst circumstances, flaunting much of it on their Instagram accounts as they posed in front of their posse of cars parked in front of mansions, even during the war years that would come the following decade. The Assad regime's toxic men had always been rich and powerful, but the younger generation, following in Bashar and Rami's footsteps, wanted to be flashy and famous as well in the age of social media.

In 2021, famous influencer Daniel Mac, followed by some fifteen million people on the major social media platforms, inadvertently showed Syrians something they had not known. His content consisted of filming himself stopping people who drove extravagant cars and always asking them the same question on camera: 'I love your car, what do you do for a living?' Many would answer that they were entrepreneurs, and sometimes name their fields or companies when they recognised Daniel.

When he saw a Ferrari 488 Spider (worth nearly $300,000) stopped at a traffic light in Los Angeles, he asked that question of the young man at the wheel who seemed hesitant to respond, but then claimed he was an intern and that he had rented that car. The young woman in the passenger seat repressed a laugh and they drove off. No sooner had Daniel Mac posted the video on his accounts than legions of Syrians commented, half shocked, half angry, that this was Ali Makhlouf, one of Rami's sons, cruising with an Israeli model at his side.

The flamboyant carelessness was nothing new to Syrians, but they still wanted to know how he had gotten a US visa when the family was under US sanctions. For everyone else, everything Ali Makhlouf and his family could do was forbidden to them by some force bigger than them. And that is how it felt for nearly everything in Syrians' lives; things were probably forbidden by the regime, and if it wasn't the regime, it was something else trying to control their lives.

7

THE PROHIBITION TROIKA

The Millennium Bug may have worried a lot of people at the turn of the century, but Syrians had no reason to share this global state of apprehension that a computing glitch would cause technological mayhem around the world. Many governments had eagerly spread internet access as widely as possible, opening the door to millions of opportunities for their people, businesses, and public services. Others were rather unenthusiastic, reluctant to allow the proletariat to experiment with a tool that was much more dangerous than satellite television.

That was a perennial dilemma of authoritarian states in those times, the challenge of looking modern using the latest knowledge and finding new ways to make money off the people, and yet still keeping them disconnected enough from the outside world. Was it even possible to control everything and censor undesirable elements that might give them ideas that they did not already have? These were not the kind of options the Assad regime left to chance: just because their neighbours had new toys did not mean Syrians could have them too. Y2K was therefore the least of the regime's problems because progress and technology also needed an entry visa to Assad's Syria.

IT STARTED IN DAMASCUS

As my trips to Damascus and extended stays had become more frequent by the late nineties, accessing my email and the various websites that I now considered essential daily reading became a priority. The arrival of the internet to Syria, often wrongly credited to Bashar, had been slowly seeping into the country under Hafez's rule, and rudimentary internet cafés began to appear in the last years of his reign. With a few computers and monitors accessible only with a formal ID, those cafés offered the novelty of ad hoc surfing sessions—followed by a guaranteed checking of your browsing history minutes after you left the café, just in case electronic Big Brother missed something.

Home internet connections were a challenge on another level, however. I had heard that it was possible to get one, but I also knew that it was difficult to get without that other type of connection we all needed, the all-mighty '*wasta*'—the link to a well-placed individual who would facilitate a given request. Even though this would be a small favour that would cost my prospective *wasta* nothing, I tried the normal way first, because I thought there was a normal way to begin with.

Advised that the Syrian Computer Society—established by Bassel Assad in 1989—was the place to go, I headed to them with one of my helpful cousins and waited for someone to assist me. A couple of men eyed us sceptically, seeming convinced that we were not supposed to be there; in retrospect, they were not wrong, we really were trespassing on their turf of privilege. I politely asked about the steps needed to obtain an internet connection at home. They did not even try to hide their sneer, doubtful of my alleged need for a connection: 'Why do you want it?' I explained that I had both professional and personal reasons to remain connected during my stays in Damascus at my family's home, and that I was told they could provide it. They proceeded with the investigation: 'Do you have an IT course certificate?' I did not, but I had been using computers and the internet for

THE PROHIBITION TROIKA

years, I reassured them. It turns out that did not matter, as they could only give it to members of the Syrian Computer Society anyway—a point they should have started with instead of demanding a justification for my use of the internet.

The Society claimed it was open to businesspeople, researchers, and academics as well, so I jumped on the opportunity: 'Excellent,' I replied, 'I would like to join the Society then.' The audacity, said their facial expressions—who did I think I was? They had never asked for my name, to gauge whether it rang a bell or was worthy of interest, nor did I offer it; I think they had figured that someone with the right connections would not have bothered to try this way, or would have led with a name that might have opened doors.

They decided among themselves that I could try to apply despite my unverifiable IT prowess, and that my request would be considered. Their snooty tone indicated otherwise, however, as they refused to even tell me how long a decision and an eventual connection would take; it was clear that I was not getting my internet from there. I had remained impassive during that exchange while these employees had been dismissive, confident of their self-perceived superiority and their power to block even though the final decision was probably not going to be theirs. Before we turned to leave, I matched their smugness by loudly commenting to my cousin: 'I know how this country works, it seems I will have to get my connection the usual other way.' And I did.

Friends had shown me zero sympathy when I shared the experience, amused that I was making life difficult for myself with pointless attempts like these. Was I trying to prove what everyone already knew, that this was a unique and unfair system? We are not in Europe, they said, everyone has to use connections if they have them, especially when dealing with little prima donnas like these. At a social event that week, a casual mention of my travails to a powerful regime insider solved the problem instantly, without my even having to formulate it as a formal request. 'Call so-and-so tomorrow and tell him I sent you.'

It sounded a bit too easy but the call was placed the next morning, as per his instructions, and the response was practically immediate; what young Syrians should have been offered as a matter of course, I got in a few hours. Later that evening, I was online with my laptop from the comfort of our living room. They could still monitor what I did, but at least there would be no sleazy informant leering over my shoulder in a tiny internet café, nor an arrogant regime employee gloating about his tiny dominance, especially when I noticed that many of the websites I was trying to reach were blocked, including my email.

In those days, every email provider was blocked in Syria, and it once took me a while to understand why an article I was trying to read on the Canadian news site *The Globe and Mail* was inaccessible, even though it was unrelated to anything that might be deemed unsuitable for our delicate Syrian eyes. I then realised that if a web address contained the word mail in any formulation, not just providers like 'hotmail' but also publications like 'theglobeandmail' or 'dailymail,' it was verboten. Even in cyberspace, we all had to learn how to circumvent the ridiculous walls the regime was trying to build. For years afterwards, those who finally accessed the internet had to use proxy servers and VPNs, even—or perhaps especially—to engage on the social media platforms that developed in the mid-2000s.

* * *

What a world of difference there was between the Syrian Computer Society gatekeepers and the multitude of charming young men in Bahsa, the area in downtown Damascus scattered with small shops selling all things relating to computing. They were always welcoming, eager to help and happy to advise without disdain, excited about the prospects of the huge advances in

THE PROHIBITION TROIKA

technology they followed as closely as they could, trying to enrich their own knowledge. Through no fault of their own, much of what they sold was bootleg and programmes were copied on CDs, and I would see some of them poring over photocopied IT books when customers were scarce, learning everything they could. What they wanted for themselves, they wanted for everyone else as well, unlike the regime's haughty employees who tried to keep average people away from what they considered to be the privilege of a few. Even after I moved to London, I would visit Bahsa often on my trips to Damascus, taking in the vibe and chatting about what was new. They always had this infectious energy, an ardent desire to learn and connect, a human need to be part of something bigger. And yet, most of what they wanted, every kind of connection they craved, was forbidden one way or another.

Steve Jobs himself, whose biological father was a Syrian from Homs, and who was often claimed by Syrians as a famous compatriot, would not have been accepted as a member of the Syrian Computer Society had he tried; as a university dropout who never studied IT, he would not have managed to get an internet connection for years without a *wasta*. How many young Syrians with a world of ambition and curiosity bursting inside of them have been disregarded, neglected over the years as well-connected people and those of certain social classes—myself included—enjoyed services that should have been universal?

The internet that these and other youngsters craved was initially reserved for the top of the pyramid and began to spread at a glacial pace over the next years, always leaving Syrians longing for more. By the end of Bashar's first decade in power, more than ten years after I got my internet in a day, just about one fifth of Syrians had regular online access. Even those who managed to access the net had difficulty securing personal computers or laptops, still the privilege of very few. It took several years for cheaper computers to become available for more people in Syria, and for internet access to open up; like everything in Syria, new things were always first the prerogative of the lucky few.

For all its potentially liberating promises and its opening of new worlds, it was thus not the internet that caused the biggest shift in young people's attitudes in the early 2000s and that triggered their thirst for more. No, what first caused them to begin asking questions about their lives was satellite television, which showed them not just the free lives they knew they could never have, but also the reasonably attainable lives of people from similar cultures.

The rusty satellite dishes that used to be banned, hidden from the view of prying eyes with blankets or plants during the day, were now openly displayed in their full naked glory on the rooftops of every city, with little difference between affluent areas and poorer ones. Turned to the sky towards a single direction, they supplicated in unison the gods of free entertainment and information for non-stop broadcasts. Pan-Arab television had become the true opium of the masses, an addiction that most governments found conveniently inoffensive and not in need of a cure. The Assad regime relented when it decided it had bigger fish to fry and could allow mere mortal citizens the freedom of television; let them watch, it was decreed, and so they did. Besides, Syrian TV also had its own satellite channel by then.

In most homes, television enjoyed a central role and even a central location as the focal point of nearly everyone's living room. The family remained a solid unit, for better or for worse, with watching television together still the main joint activity for the entire household, especially in the evening. And as they watched with their parents, teens and young adults were noticing that many other Arabs were living a different kind of life, and that other countries in the region were more open than most young Syrians had even imagined. The realisation that it would

THE PROHIBITION TROIKA

probably not change much for them began to sink in, one broadcast at a time.

Like their parents and their grandparents before them, young Syrians and others in the region were shackled by several categories of things they wanted but could not have. Most of their desires were either forbidden, sinful, or shameful, a trifecta of impositions that frustrated them and kept their expectations in check. Not only did the regime decide what was allowed or not in the political and economic sphere, but the weight of societal and familial influence was still too strong to fight, let alone reject.

The forced isolation from the world, endured by Syrians during those preceding years of solitude and isolation, had many social consequences. In addition to the fear that intensified the closeknit structure of families, society had consequently become even more insular, hanging on to traditions that were waning slightly in other countries. In Assad's Syria, the stifling weight of all these prohibitions were felt to a much greater degree than in most other countries because Syrians had fewer outlets for their frustrations. TV showed them this other world that was just out of reach; personal devices would soon revolutionise their own, and it was the arrival of the cheap mobile phones in the mid-2000s that was to start unshackling many young Syrians from the chains of all the entities trying to impose law and order: regime, religion, and tradition.

Everyone had a different set of forbidden fruits, spoken and unspoken rules of engagement that defined whether something was outright banned, or would not be permitted for the average citizen.

* * *

In Assad's Syria, there was little difference between most people with regard to the big red lines to observe. Everything relating to criticism of the Assad clan was forbidden, and dangerous, regardless of who you were. During the first year of Bashar's reign, for having forwarded an email with a caricature of the Syrian and Lebanese presidents in a compromising position, a woman from a well-known Damascene family was arrested and held in solitary confinement for six months, despite pleas for her release from several people in regime circles. Her husband and children were barred from even short visits. The punishment had been swift and harsh for such an ultimately meaningless activity, and the lesson served as a warning to others of what could happen if lines were crossed. Lèse-majesté, especially the sarcastic kind, was prohibited to all, and was enforced from the very top of the pyramid. It was nearly easier to criticise God than to belittle Assad, even though both were out of mere mortals' reach.

For anything else that did not touch the ruling family, you were either a lucky member of the velvet society who enjoyed the liberties that your social class and connections afforded you, or you were not, but there was a rather egalitarian application of prohibition on voicing opinions on the regime. The safest way to go around life was to assume something was forbidden, until it was declared otherwise. The constitution in Syria was not worth the paper it was written on, and with or without the state of emergency, laws were applicable according to your position in society—or rather, your closeness to the regime or your ability to bribe your way through any hiccup.

There were regular incidents involving—usually—the sons of regime officials who would instigate trouble by getting into fights and pulling weapons on others, or would drive recklessly and cause serious accidents. I was in Damascus when a family known personally to several of our friends went for a walk after their iftar meal one Ramadan evening—the father, the mother, and their two teens. An immature, irresponsible young man well past the speed limit lost control of his car and hit the father so hard he sent him flying and killed him instantly, in front of his wife

THE PROHIBITION TROIKA

and children. The fancy car quickly escaped. A couple of hours later, a man handed himself in at a police station, claiming to have been the driver who fled in a panic, but who realised his responsibility and came back to face justice. Like many others, he had been paid by his big boss to carry the crime and the punishment his son should have received, in exchange for financial support for his undoubtedly poor and powerless family.

Mamnou (forbidden) was a word we heard all the time in Syria, its most striking aspect being the fact that any security official, even the most junior guard at a shack in front of an official's house or office, could forbid someone from the most basic things like parking in a street or being next in line after having queued for a long time for something. In the darkest days of the eighties and nineties, they would even forbid people from walking on the sidewalk, shouting 'get down, *w'la*,' an untranslatable generic insult. They could freely insult citizens just to establish dominance, not just with their tone of voice but with insolent words that hurt people's dignity every day.

With so many officials and a wide range of security and intelligence people, in addition to the Baathist comrades with various levels of influence, you never knew from what side of the regime such orders or insults came; you could only guess how far up or down the ladder they were. Sometimes, they would helpfully shout 'Don't you know who I am?'—a question often ending with a slur such as 'you animal' (or 'you donkey', 'you lowlife', 'you dog'). For the most part, these unprompted offenses were reserved for men, but the tone of voice applied to all. The sons and relatives of officials would also intimidate powerless people by asking, braying even, variations of 'do you know who my father is?' in order to get their way, even if it was only to assert authority in a completely trivial situation, such as trying to overtake another driver—and tough luck if this happened to be another immature daddy's boy with even more unlimited privileges.

IT STARTED IN DAMASCUS

Whether such abusive behaviour was displayed by the fathers, the sons, or the employees of the higher powers, most people did not dare respond even well into the 2000s; the higher the position, or the pettier the abuser, the less likely someone would react in fear of causing an escalation. It was not uncommon for the most random of incidents to end with assault or even the imprisonment of the victim. These antisocial liberties were a blatant abuse of authority that few Syrians could escape, and the best defence was always avoidance, self-effacement, and retreat.

Most of the security forces dealing with the public had their own red lines imposed on them. They knew instinctively who they should not cross (those they knew had, or even thought they might have higher connections), and they were under instructions to never bother or even address the ladies in certain neighbourhoods. The last thing the regime wanted was to upset the upper class, the merchant class, and the conservative classes. However, in the poorer areas and in the streets where no officials lived, the situation was different, and young women were particularly vulnerable to the unwanted attentions of security men of varying power levels.

Certain prohibitions were adaptable, turning into permissions by way of hefty bribes; this often happened on roads paved with complications, for the most part unnecessary hurdles put there precisely for power to control. For example, construction of the most basic extensions in homes was strongly regulated in the city, except when a well-placed family wanted to add an entire upper floor or make other changes to a building, even one owned by several people who should have also had a say.

Unauthorised extensions in more modest homes were dealt with swiftly when well-placed or resentful neighbours would call authorities to complain that a violation of the building code had been committed. This could only end in one of three ways; either the culprit managed to find a relative or acquaintance con-

THE PROHIBITION TROIKA

nected enough to let it pass, or the culprit had to pay the official fines and the unofficial bribes, or the extension would end in a pile of rubble. I remember waking up one morning to the sound of our neighbour begging an official not to destroy what had taken him a long time to save for and to build. He had gotten workers to raise a very basic front façade and rudimentary roof over the garage space he owned, directly adjacent to his family's building. It was a vacant piece of land, and they never managed to get the permission to enclose it, if only for dirt not to pile up in it, even though it would have bothered nobody nor changed anything to the building structure. Our desolate neighbour had to watch helplessly as several municipal workers started taking down the wall with their hammers and picks.

Meanwhile, the makeshift towns developing around Syria's biggest cities were in and of themselves massive infractions, but these slums were allowed to sprawl uncontrollably because there was no social housing or regulated areas to cater for the changing demographic circumstances. The earliest informal settlement in Damascus grew out of Rifat Assad's decision to house his Defence Brigades in an uninhabited area of Mezzeh. This became known as Mezzeh 86, expanding over the 1970s and 1980s into a large neighbourhood of over a quarter million people, many intelligence and military officials having brought their families over to live with them, mostly from mountain areas around the coast. Because this was a regime-supported area, it received the necessary municipal services and public utilities (such as water, sewage, electricity, telephone lines) despite its initial unregulated status.

More slums emerged over the years, forests of naked concrete and cinder blocks as far as the eye could see, with visible pipes and tangled electric cables galore, and rudimentary drainage that made life a misery of flooding in times of heavy rain. They grew partly because of the migration from rural into urban areas seen in many countries, but also, in the particular Syrian case, because of the large contingents of security men brought in to beef up the regime since its early days. A seemingly unlimited number of employees were needed to follow orders in the various state institutions that functioned as a massive Assad empire. In the 2000s, these unregulated neighbourhoods would swell even more with the Damascenes and Aleppines who could no longer afford to live in areas within their respective city limits.

While these miserable slums sprawled, so did the posh communities that also extended beyond the city limits, which in the case of greater Damascus included gigantic villas on massive plots of land that the well-to-do built in areas like Sabboura and Yaffour. They had no problems obtaining construction permits or public utilities.

The problem was not a simple one of rich vs poor, but of blatant inequities in the most basic infrastructure that a state is responsible for providing, of opportunities it is supposed to be creating for the wellbeing of society, of prohibitions that darkened the horizons of people with no recourse.

* * *

If Syrians were not being forbidden something with the interjection *mamnou*, then they would probably be limited by the admonition that something was *haram*, sinful, although the one good thing about religious prohibitions is that they technically applied to everyone within the faith. The sin could mean different things to different people, as everywhere else, but the word *haram* was engrained in the language even when it was also used to indicate pity or empathy for someone's misfortune, and not in the sense of sin.

Religion was very much present in Syrian life, as it is in most countries in the region and the world, with varying degrees of civil liberties. Despite the secular nature of education in Syria, religion was taught to every student at all stages of school, along-

THE PROHIBITION TROIKA

side the Baathist curriculum. The major Muslim and Christian holidays had always been observed in Syria, in all their sincere depths and all their colourful consumerist kitsch, a part of Syria's identity and history of conviviality way before the Baath and the Assads arrived and pretended they protected minorities.

After the regime's massacre in Hama, hints of Muslim Brotherhood sympathies were punished and young men quickly found it was too much trouble to sport a beard, as they merely aroused suspicion among the ever-present security forces. Other organised religious groups were allowed, however, and even later encouraged to proliferate under the close eye of the regime. The Qubaysiat, founded by Mounira Al Qubaysi in the 1960s, had become a powerful women's organisation, if not an outright cult, of women teaching the Quran and the tenets of Islam. Increasingly, the group appealed to young women from upper classes who rebelled against the excesses of their social circle as the regime's liberalisation changed some societal norms. Daughters in hijab and long coats next to mothers in more revealing clothes was a sight to behold, the direct opposite of how youth was supposed to progress, many people thought.

For the daily grind, though, it was tradition that influenced what was allowed, and what was not. The past difficult decades under Assad had made Syrian society quite resistant to change, driving it to hold on to perceived codes of honour and moral dignity when the regime had imposed so many indignities in every facet of life. In conservative and, to a lesser extent, some more modern circles, these social codes of conduct applied to many areas of life where direct regime interference had no place—in family life, in neighbourly affairs, in relationships.

It is no secret that in Syria, like in most Arab countries, there was no question of romantic—and even less sexual—relations before or outside of marriage in most segments of society. Relations that had developed in a study or work environment were expected to progress to an official statement of purpose from the man to the woman's family, and usually an official engagement so that everything was done the proper way. This was so that the young woman's comings and goings with her fiancé would not be considered *ayb*, a word meaning shame in the social context, holding as much—if not more—weight as *haram*, and generally resented by every new generation that tries to fight its parents' restrictions. For the young Syrians who had started to feel a new hope in June 2000, that word was all the more frustrating when it was increasingly clear that there was no real change on the horizon.

Unfortunately, as economic circumstances deteriorated, it was difficult for most young people to consider marriage when they knew they could not afford it, or manage to live financially independently of their parents. Young adults continued to live at the parental home for longer, until they found the means to move out with their spouse, usually to ever more isolated areas well outside their city. For the rest, no marriage meant no physical relations, leading to a great deal of physical and psychological tension and frustration.

I had found the extent of harassment on Syrian streets to be shocking at first, the complete opposite of how I expected a conservative society to behave in public. As with most other things that I got to understand better over time, these unacceptable cat calls and offensive comments, gestures, invitations, stares, and even whistles had sprung from the repression that did not allow men and women to experience casual relationships. As is the case in many societies around the world, it was usually those with the bleakest outlooks on life who were the most frustrated and the most explicit in their verbal assaults (and at times the physical as well with furtive touching) on women passing their way.

For all the lewd suggestions some men made, they would have raised hell at other men doing likewise to the women in their own lives, the wives, sisters, mothers, and daughters in their family circle. Worse, they could even have blamed their female relatives for being on the receiving end of such behaviour about which women could do nothing. In very conservative families where a brother can be even more controlling than a father, such situations would make a woman's life even more difficult; often, early marriage was the only way out of an oppressive environment, with many women taking the risk of jumping out of the frying pan into the fire.

The double standards in how men and women were treated were most blatant when it came to the observance of traditional values; what was considered acceptable for young men was out of the question for young women in most Syrian households, modern or not. A man's past relationships were a private matter that concerned just him, considered a normal part of youth; a woman's were a burden to be hidden, minimised, or justified, affecting the reputation and the honour of the entire family. While religion allows or forbids behaviour equally for men and women, tradition does not, clearly absolving men of what would be, and often is, denounced as a shameful transgression of morals when women do it. A man engaging in sexual relations before marriage will rarely be chastised or disgraced; if a woman is discovered to have done the same, it can ruin her life.

The tyranny of expectations endured, as did the legal impediments to women's freedom, or at least their equality in the legal sense. In Syria, personal status laws have remained in the hands of religious courts, meaning women's rights relating to divorce, the custody of children, or inheritance would be determined by the faith into which they were born. Additionally, Syrian women married to non-Syrians have not been allowed to pass their nationality to their children, whereas men can do so regardless of their wife's citizenship, one of the most infuriating and irrational legal restrictions prevalent in the Arab world.

On the lighter side, Syrians are some of the least hung-up people about sex and intimacy in the region, as a stroll down the

IT STARTED IN DAMASCUS

Hamidiyeh Souk and shopping streets in downtown Damascus can always show; blatantly displayed in shop windows with not even the slightest sense of timidity, a huge variety of saucy and outlandish lingerie is sold by male shopkeepers who do not even bat an eyelid as they show their assortment to female customers.

Judicial principles hold the appearance of propriety to be of equal importance to the core values of independence, impartiality, and integrity. For Syrian society, as undoubtedly for many others around the world where communities still have close-knit relations and where neighbours are an integral part of one's social circle, the appearance of propriety is an issue that still matters. All Syrians will have heard their parents ask 'what will people say?' on numerous occasions, usually when berating them for being late, being dressed improperly, or being seen with someone. During youth, the response would have usually been that it is no one else's business, or that there is nothing wrong being done. And yet, as family image and reputation begin to be viewed differently with age, we often find ourselves becoming more considerate of the concept of cordiality and mutual respect in even the smallest details. For most Syrian communities, it is still important to uphold the appearance of propriety.

Many young people will consider this societal imposition to be one of the customs that need fighting and eradicating. Many others still care very much about reputation and their perceived dignity, that very dignity whose abuse on so many levels later pushed Syrians to revolt.

* * *

When legal, religious, and social restrictions like these were all put together, they built a wall of obstacles that a generation coming of age in the nineties and 2000s struggled to overcome. It was an amalgamation of frustrations, creating growing despair in younger Syrians who craved meaning and a sense of reasonable

THE PROHIBITION TROIKA

liberty, especially as they faced life with minimal financial resources and limited career prospects. When cheap mobile phones finally arrived in Syria, they cracked the wall of control and allowed young Syrians to better access the shameful, the sinful, and the forbidden in the absence of real progress. Young Syrians could temporarily escape the intrusions of family and even regime, as long as their transgressions did not cross the red lines they knew well; after all, this was a generation that had seen its parents bow silently to the authorities, who had diligently partaken in banana politics to provide for their families.

Cheap mobile phones, especially the second-hand devices that served a larger target group, became even more accessible with the option of buying prepaid units, rather than the long-term contracts that so many could not afford. These phones were a bridge to a degree of independence that would have been unimaginable before, when the phone in the family home, like the television, was in a central room and under constant surveillance. For the first time, young people could discreetly send texts to their friends and potential love interests with whom communicating suddenly became not just possible, but easy. With these unforeseen liberties came greater desires, of course—a visceral need to see something change in their lives, and that was before most of these young people even had a chance to lose themselves in the world that the internet would show them.

This restless generation was weighed down by a bleak outlook in a country with exploding population growth; satellite television and mobile phones had opened their eyes to a world of possibilities, highlighting the chasm between their static lives and the oblivious regime and velvet society.

Meanwhile, around the Arab world, other people were tuning in to Syrian lives with as much fascination as Syrians themselves had looked elsewhere for the escapes they could only enjoy in their imaginations.

8

ENTERTAINING DISSENT

In a country where mundane absurdities are unavoidable in daily life, those who can afford it usually have their go-to people, the little helpers who deal with the low-level hassles that are a grade or two below the *wasta* level in the Syrian pyramid. The consulting office I had joined relied on Abou Fares; much more than a driver, he was the unofficial manager, the fixer, the know-it-all who got things done. I quickly learned to ask for his opinion before doing anything out of the ordinary.

He walked up to my desk one morning looking annoyed: 'Madame Rime, did you order something from abroad?' I had not, of course, I knew better, but Abou Fares did not seem convinced. 'Well, we got notified they are holding something in your name, but they wouldn't give it to me and want you to come to the post office in person,' he said gravely. This sounded uncharacteristically serious for a postal matter, so I asked him who exactly 'they' were: 'Security, of course, who else is constantly sitting over our heads?'

We headed to the post office where, for the first time in my life, I saw employees and letters and the hustle and bustle that amounted to a semblance of a delivery structure, which surprisingly implied we all had recognised and usable formal addresses. Even in Damascus, many of the newer streets did not have a name that we knew of (especially as unregulated areas began to spread around the city). Meanwhile, some of the older streets had two of them—something the inhabitants would find out by chance after having referred to their own street for years under a given name, only to be told while doing some of the infamous Syrian paperwork that it was called something else altogether. My mother had thus been informed the name we had always thought our street went by had been changed; on a whim, she sent herself a postcard given to her by a fashion brand, addressed with the new official street name. The testing of this name change has been inconclusive at best: over twenty years later, that postcard had still not arrived.

No wonder people would have to provide specific instructions when giving directions: 'behind the Italian hospital', 'next door to the grocer', 'second left after the hair salon', or 'at the corner opposite the school', for instance, were perfectly valid directions. Even better, when applicable, it was common to direct people to 'the third building after Ali Douba's house' or 'across the guard shack of the Tlass house' because everyone knew where the high officials lived, and even where security branches were. I never told taxi drivers to take me to Hassan Street in Abou Roummaneh when I headed to my grandmother's house, for example; I would tell them to drive to the Air Force Command, and once there I would tell them to continue and take the first right. While relatives had certainly received the odd airmail letter now and then from their children abroad, a postman doing his delivery round was not a common sight in our streets, and discovering we had an operational post office was just as unexpected.

I followed Abou Fares to a room in the back as employees eyed me quizzically; inside were metal shelves along the walls filled with random stacks of dusty files, the usual scheme in any space belonging to Syrian officialdom. In pride of place was a metal desk with a dingy light, a stern security operative sitting behind it, salivating at the prospect of grilling me as I sat down facing him. 'Can you tell me what this is?' he asked, tapping on a large envelope in front of him that was apparently addressed to me. 'I don't know, what is it?' I responded, not at all alarmed by his dated antics, especially as I really had not ordered anything. He opened it and took out the evidence, showing me the suspicious item as if he were holding conclusive proof of my illegal activities: 'This!'

I wanted to laugh, but Abou Fares had not appreciated my attitude the last time security had come to the office to check on me, unannounced, probably told by the local informant that an unknown woman had been entering and leaving this known building every day around the same time—a building where the son of a senior regime official had an office. I had demanded to see the man's credentials and a written order confirming that he had the right to question me on what exactly I did and how much I was being paid. It was my dramatic reenactment of the confident 'do you have a search warrant?' response we see in American movies, which is funny if you know Syria.

What had been even funnier was his obvious mental struggle as he tried to establish whether I was well connected or just plain stupid, the only two options in his mind. He had glanced towards Abou Fares as if asking 'does she even know anything about the country?' She did, and she did not approve of this ridiculous interrogation. Abou Fares had answered in my place, describing vague chores I allegedly did for the salary of an average employee, wisely deciding to just get this useless confrontation over and done with. This time around, sitting in this strange room at the post office as I stared at the offending item, I did not dare to put Abou Fares through such a needless back-and-forth again, which

IT STARTED IN DAMASCUS

I enjoyed more than he did. I also sensed that this security guy was a bit higher up the echelon than the poor operative who had tried and failed to write up a good report for his superior.

Weeks earlier, doing my usual catch-up of world news online, a pop-up on the website of *The Economist* had asked if I would answer some questions about reading habits and be entered in a raffle to win one of their books. With time on my hands and not much thought put into the matter, I had completed the survey and given the office address in the improbable occurrence I won. They must have been chuffed to find a reader engaging from Damascus, because they decided I was a winner, and my prize, for which a notification must have gotten lost somewhere in cyberspace, was now being brandished accusingly by the security guy: it was a copy of their latest *Pocket World in Figures* book.

The good news was that the postal service worked, and our addresses mattered after all. The bad news was that mail from abroad was always going to be examined, and that the import of items without prior authorisation, such as foreign-language books, was always going to be questioned and viewed with mistrust at best.

I thought it best to answer matter-of-factly: 'It's a book about the countries of the world, a small encyclopaedia that gives facts about their size, their population, things like that,' I explained. More and more suspicious, he clearly thought. 'Why did you order it, and what are you going to do with it?' My honest response only made him more mistrustful and convinced him that this was not a believable story.

He started leafing through the slim book, pausing on various pages and looking at me intently to see if I seemed nervous. My impassiveness in the face of this interrogation, this epitome of absurdity, seemed to trigger him, but even Abou Fares was getting irked by this nonsense, now that he had been reassured that I had not crossed any big red lines.

ENTERTAINING DISSENT

Security guy asked me a couple of times to read and explain some of the titles, passages, and graphs. I obliged calmly, wondering how he would be able to tell if I was being truthful when he clearly knew no English. He posed a few more flash questions and I gave him straight answers in an increasingly exaggerated articulation; he knew that my composed demeanour projected even more disdain of his ludicrous probe than any sarcastic retort could. Try as he might, he could not find fault with *The Economist*'s basic facts, nor could he catch me doing anything illegal. Besides, had he wanted to, he could have just confiscated the evil imperialist item.

Abou Fares eventually broke the stalemate, saying a few nice words to the effect of 'You see, it's all information that is public, and she didn't know such books have to pass by the censor first.' I did know, of course, that nothing gets past them, especially when it is blatantly mailed from London. The man responsible for protecting national security from my imprudent readings relented, handing over the book with a look that said: 'I have a feeling you're hiding something, but I'm letting it go this time.' Had this been a sitcom, as it was in my head, a laugh track would have accompanied a close-up of his face as he shook his head, watching Abou Fares and me walk out with the book.

The Assad regime, like all authoritarian states of its ilk, had a thing about books it could not inspect and censor. After my father's sudden passing abroad, a few years before, we had shipped all my parents' belongings back to our home in Damascus, where my mother had decided to settle. The huge consignment was held up as security focused on two specific things: my parents' complex phone and fax machine that was taken in for inspection, and the massive personal library they had accumulated over decades abroad. My grieving mother had been asked if any of the books were forbidden in Syria; she had flatly said, 'Yes, they probably all are.' Despite the exclusive treatment we received in every other aspect given my father's status, and despite her distress in the midst of her mourning period, my mother had still been asked to list the thousands of books in the library—from memory. She wrote down a dozen or so titles such as memoirs of public figures (some surely made up) and vague titles of history books, and the full shipment was allowed in with a little help from well-placed friends.

As we headed back to the car, Abou Fares asked me to inform him in advance the next time I wanted books, to avoid the hassle. I had already brought in books on every trip, nothing controversial or sensitive, even though I knew I would never be searched because I still had a diplomatic passport—a courtesy extended to my mother and me for years after my father's passing as a mark of respect for him. While I did not appreciate being spoken to as if I had committed a major transgression, I did not regret this experience and others like it that were showing me, firsthand, how deep-rooted so many archaic rules were in Syria. Would anything ever change?

* * *

A couple of years after this comical inquisition, I watched famed Syrian director Omar Amiralay's film *A Flood in Baath Country*. With each still of this masterful exposé of the rigid emptiness and meaninglessness of the Baath, and hence the regime, I remembered that day at the post office and thought about the farcical marriage between bureaucracy, censorship, and tentative dissent that had become Syrians' daily fare in so many aspects of life.

The truth is that art had always imitated life for Syrians, these quintessentially bon vivant, foodie, and amiable people for whom the absurdities of existence had become so extreme that they often made parody moot. Yet, even under the severe eye of a regime that had repeatedly proven its intolerance of direct or even alleged criticism, the Syrian drama industry had been innovative and avant-gardist with socially and politically laden plays and series. It was certainly easier to escape the censors with symbolism and vague allusions, but nobody was really fooled—least of all the regime.

In fact, the authorities seemed to take a perverse pleasure in allowing these artistic expressions, showing false benevolence while knowing full well they depicted them in one way or another. By pretending to turn a blind eye to the otherwise blatant metaphors, similes, and allegories that filled Syrian screens as of the later nineties, they were merely choosing when to act, or even whether to take action if they deemed a reddish line had been crossed. The elasticity of the red lines often depended on the current domestic mood and regional circumstances: the worse things got, the more annoyed and less lenient the regime became. This leeway was a calculated pseudo-largesse: allowing some criticism merely stressed the message that it was the regime, and the regime only, who could decide when, how, and against whom people could let off steam.

The one inelastic constant was that the ruler was off limits. Not even in televised drama or in comedy could Syrians imagine they could criticise or make fun of a president, even an imaginary president who was not named. As in real life, the portrait of the actual president—and sometimes of two presidents, the eternal one and his successor—hung in every office in television series set during their rule, and he would never be mentioned. There was even a notable episode in the popular *Spotlight* comedy and social commentary series that related how Syrians should not even dream of becoming president, let alone claim it openly. It showed students handing in their homework, an essay on what they wanted to be when they grew up. We are never told what one child wrote, but the teacher panics when reading it and brings it to the attention of the director, who panics as well and calls the parents, who panic even more and beg the school not to escalate the issue. They then proceed to reprogram their son, through threats and therapy, so that he understands that he can never, ever become what he wrote. For the censors, the message was that you can laugh, but you cannot dream.

The hugely popular Syrian drama series that invaded the Arab world in the 2000s, overtaking the reigning Egyptian series and popularising the Syrian accent, used fiction or even history to slip in its artistic resistance. Even noted older Syrian plays known all over the Arab world such as *October Village* (1973) or *Cheers, Homeland* (1979), both authored by renowned writer and poet Muhammad Al Maghout, seem to have stood the test of time and continued to be of utmost relevance to the Syrian context. Both these plays depict rulers who promise the world and deliver nothing but hardship and brutality, remaining evocative of Syrian reality even decades later as they tackled the usual themes of power and corruption, and the passage of villages through feudalism, socialism, totalitarianism, and authoritarianism. *Cheers, Homeland* casts an even wider net with its commentary on the sad state of Arab affairs, and the complete disconnect between regimes and their people.

The trend of shorter political and social satire began in the 1990s with the television series *Mirrors*; it mostly showed sketches on aspects of life in Syria, from the comic to the tragic, passing heavy commentary on people's justified fear of the authorities who were depicted as generally corrupt, ignorant, and incompetent. In one episode, a young author publishes the biography of a king who lived centuries before, abusing his subjects and stealing the country's wealth. Several officials jump to the conclusion it must be a novel with a thinly veiled description of their own lives, given the strong similarities in abuse of power and corruption. Rather than confirm their guilt by banning it, they each send their assistants to buy every copy they can find to get it off the market, never realising that this bad king had really existed and that, for once, this was not about them.

ENTERTAINING DISSENT

The even stronger series *Spotlight* took off in the Bashar era starting in 2001, with similar skits on social, political, and cultural life that covered the same subject range through a more modern approach, and in a simultaneously bolder and more subtle way. With a new cast of rising talent who looked, dressed, and talked more like the younger generation, *Spotlight* strongly appealed to Syria's (and the Arab world's) youth majority. Pre-revolution, it managed to get away with heavy sarcasm, despite the extremely vigilant censorship that did not seem to always know what to cut or how to decide what was more dangerous.

It is very easy to criticise or make fun of presidents, officials, situations, and public personalities in democratic countries; we have choice overload with talk shows, standup comedy, newspaper columns, cartoons, and even politicians making fun of other politicians. In countries like Syria, this was impossible, and writers went to great lengths to create compelling scenarios within the limits of a conditional leniency that could be revoked for any transgression.

There were always critics who considered clear references to the regime unnecessary, wondering why the daring directors and actors would go through all this trouble and bring punishment upon themselves. The same was said of the intellectuals, the dissidents, the writers who were always getting summoned, regularly imprisoned, and worse. Why? Because of the human need for expression and sharing, because people have opinions and want the right to have these opinions stated and respected, and because people want to hear others' opinions, thoughts, and ideas as well. The proof was in the pudding; the more Syrian series like these were produced and broadcast, the bigger their audiences across the Arab world.

* * *

Syrian comedy and satire were not alone in their growing audacity in the 2000s: drama series were getting equally bolder with their tales of a hypocritical society and the violent excesses of officials who ruled them. It was, again, always about the sons, the brothers, the traitors, the corrupt officials, the overzealous security forces, the greedy businessmen and their respective cliques—they were the ones making life difficult for normal people in these exciting and well-produced drama series, never the president or his close circle.

Big Syrian drama series made by regime loyalists also reflected regional moods. During the honeymoon period with Turkey in the years preceding the revolution, historical series did not broach the Ottoman era, focusing on Syrian life during the French Mandate and the impact of Western colonialism and imperialism. Before that, when relations with the Turks were sour under the rule of Hafez Assad, drama series would address the sins of the Ottoman Empire and its collaborators.

The regime understood the power of the Syrian drama industry and the impact of its unparalleled popularity in the region. It was another reason why greater liberties were given to writers and directors, and why regime cronies themselves began to invest heavily in the business, allowing for ever sleeker and modern production means.

The mid-2000s also saw an explosion in the popularity of Syrian period dramas, specifically ones depicting Damascene society of the late Ottoman era (until World War I) and under the French Mandate which lasted until the end of World War II. These certainly did not directly fall under dissent or creative resistance, but they appealed to the public because they showed much of what was now missing from their lives. Nobody really wanted to go a hundred or so years back in time, when rulers were as omnipotent as today's. There was, however, a collective subconscious wish for a return to a world with the qualities seen in these period dramas: they found it to be a world with values, a world with honour, a world with community belonging, strong neighbourly bonds and unbreakable family ties, a world when a word was the only guarantee needed. These were the very things they felt were now missing.

For several years in a row, the series *Salhieh Nights* and *The Neighbourhood Gate* (so well-known that most people abroad have heard of it in its original Arabic name, *Bab Al Hara*) were the most watched on their first broadcasts on numerous Arab satellite channels during Ramadan, and on many reruns throughout the years. Both these series, and others like them, were strongly criticised by serious writers for showing sexism, idealistic morals, the exaggerated depiction of Damascene traditions, and the pronounced drawl of the old-style accent. I found that these critics of the early seasons (*Bab Al Hara* has thirteen as of this writing) miss the point by being so dismissive of many societal trends that prevailed, whether or not we like them. Moreover, most international literature before the twentieth century—or depicting pre-modern eras—would have to face similar scrutiny. These series proliferated after the audience explosion for *Bab Al Hara*, leading to a succession of period pieces belonging to the same Shami (Damascene) environment.

The usual themes of women's rights—or lack thereof—were common in series spanning many eras. Many also addressed children's education, the thorny issue of corporal punishment, and the freedom of children to choose their own path in life, given the strict personal status laws, and the religious institutions' dominance in matters of marriage, divorce, births, deaths, and inheritance. When the story of a Muslim man in a relationship with a divorced Christian woman was told in *It Is Not a Mirage*, the series did an excellent job of provoking a debate on the degrees of religiosity of both Muslims and Christians, and the need to consider civil marriage and civil education to benefit Syrian society. In addition to these strong legal and intellectual themes, it spoke to the essence of free speech, not in a political sense but in a social one, often an equally controversial issue mired with sensitivities.

Syrian series tackled corruption, the abuses of people in power, life under dictatorships, absurd lose-lose regional situations, the intimidation of the security forces, and the practical enslavement of employees, soldiers, and other 'lesser' people by regime cronies. However, not every act of creative resistance was against the regime alone. Increasingly, Syrian dramas dared to address the other limitations imposed on people and on society, by people and by society, with intense narratives that posed daring questions about the struggles of the classes, youthful emancipation attempts, the growing distance between tradition and modernity, and at the same time the return to religious roots that some found more grounding. The social commentaries were deep, rich, provocative yet respectful in presenting subjects that remained points of contention for Syrians facing the prohibition troika.

* * *

While televised drama, comedy, and satire had found a way to navigate the rules and the moods of the regime, it was more difficult for other forms of communication to escape censorship. Media had been completely controlled under Assad Senior, but when Bashar came, it started going one step forward and two steps back.

Like several Arab countries, Syria had abysmal state media, and the newspapers were barely readable for many years. Then in 2001, the regime passed Decree 50 that overturned the Baath's outlawing of privately owned publications nearly forty years prior. This was revolutionary, ironically, but the small print was full of restrictions that made publishers and journalists even more susceptible than before to the control of the regime. They would now be forced to reveal their sources to substantiate claims they made, and they would face the usual punishments if they failed to do so or, even worse, if they published 'falsehoods' or 'fabricated reports.' This was, after all, a law that allowed media that was private, not free.

Political articles would only be allowed in political publications, and 'propaganda publications' of the foreign kind, with foreign funding, were banned altogether. Private media would also not be allowed to publish 'calls for changing the state constitution through unconstitutional means'—that was a privilege reserved for the regime's own parliament, after all.

There were more hidden catches. The prime minister had the prerogative of refusing any application to launch a publication that was deemed to harm the 'public interest' as defined according to the whim of the regime. While this was a very broad definition, the law specified that a ban would face any publication that might harm national security, the army's security (publishing information about the army's strength and armament was prohibited), the national economy, monetary and financial security, the unity of society, and even Syria's international relations, reputation, and dignity. In other words, the usual generic terms the regime whipped out any time it needed them.

Naturally, any publication calling for civil disobedience—as if anyone would dare publish such a call—could be shut down, and the publishers would be apprehended. Heavy financial penalties and three years of imprisonment faced anyone foolish enough to ignore these warnings.

Before Decree 50, you could only write in the state's publications. After Decree 50, you could write in other people's publications too. The limitations remained the same, however. Still, some Syrians bravely accepted the challenge and established independent newspapers. About one hundred initial applications were sent to the Ministry of Information in the first year, but only a dozen or so made it to the publication stage, mostly in the safe fields of entertainment, sports, and classified ads. The first and most well-known 'serious' publisher outside these parameters was the renowned political cartoonist Ali Ferzat, whose first edition of his weekly satirical newspaper *Ad-Domari* in February 2001 flew off the newsstands, selling over 50,000 copies (and being read by many more). *Ad-Domari*'s sales well exceeded the joint dismal figures of the three official state publications, to the extreme annoyance of the government.

Syrians were delighted to read reports and editorials with a twist about the exasperating aspects of the government's bureaucracy, wastefulness, corruption, inefficiency, and rhetoric. Of course, the regime was waiting for an opportunity to clamp down on Ferzat, using a combination of warnings, financial impediments (forcing Ferzat to use only the official state distributor, forbidding state companies from advertising in it, and 'advising' private companies not to do so), and plain harassment (apparently cutting off the paper's electricity supply). The Ministry of Information was constantly on *Ad-Domari*'s case and tried to stop publication of articles deemed overly judgmental of the government.

When Ferzat was forbidden in June 2002 from publishing a critique of the government of Prime Minister Mustafa Miro, he upped the ante and defiantly refused to replace the original two-page spread that had been censored with other content. *Ad-Domari* was published with two completely blank pages in the middle, thus giving Ferzat's strongest criticism yet of the government without saying a word. This infuriated the Minister of Information to no end, and no doubt his big boss as well, and Ferzat was prohibited from attempting the same trick again; he was forced to obtain written permission before publishing any future edition.

Like many, Ferzat had been against Saddam Hussein in 1990, and had remained so over a decade later, publishing anti-Saddam cartoons in a Kuwaiti paper. Without notice, the state's *Tishreen* newspaper attacked him, republishing his cartoons on two pages, questioning his nationalism and accusing him of being pro-American, a serious claim in the tense post-invasion atmosphere. A demonstration was hastily organised in front of his office, where a few dozen people angrily protested his stance. The country that had attacked Saddam Hussein for years was now attacking the people who attacked him, because positions that happened to counter anti-Americanism did not suit the regime.

Ferzat's experience in Syrian publishing was frustrating, short-lived, and ended in an incident worthy of the theatre of the absurd. Unable to get the required prior permission for publishing, as the minister held it back for weeks for each edition, Ferzat suspended publication in May 2003. He was then warned that if he did not publish at least eight issues every three months (which the ministry made impossible), he would no longer be allowed to publish. The regime kept its word, and *Ad-Domari*'s license was revoked in August 2003.

The only nominally private publication to have survived this initial period after Decree 50 was passed was *Al Iktissadiah*, an economic and business weekly that seemed to instinctively toe the line; the fact that its owner was Rami Makhlouf just might have had something to do with that.

* * *

The regime had controlled many aspects of people's lives and muffled numerous independent voices, but it had difficulty controlling the artistic and creative resistance online. Even though social media had at first remained off limits to Syrian youth, satellite television, mobile phones, and the internet had gradually made censorship more difficult as new generations of dissenters found new ways to express themselves. This would have a tremendous impact on the young activists, whose creativity exploded with the advent of the revolution that opened their minds further. Unlike the writers, intellectuals, and artists who had sparked the Damascus Spring in 2000, and unlike the multitude of prisoners of conscience who continued to pay a heavy price for their serious writings, the revolutionaries who came of age in Bashar's Syria were as determined as their fellow millennials worldwide to select different forms of expression and wider channels of dissemination.

The dissidents had paved the way, and the revolutionaries had followed. Even in the darkest hours, under Assad's sieges or under his bombs, Syrian humour produced a deluge of slogans, memes, jokes, and the inimitable peaceful protest banners of towns like Kafranbel that millions of Syrians eagerly awaited each week to proudly share on their social media accounts. Despite the tragedy, art prevailed as a form of resistance in anticipation of better days, especially as freedom of speech and opinion were among the first demands of the protesters.

The drama series and the comedies had been like comfort food, an escape from the harshness of Assad's Syria for many people, an artistic adaptation of what they lived and felt. They reflected much of their own lives, their social customs and their economic hardships, and their urge to shout back at the forces blocking them from the basic rights they craved. Years later, the slogans and the chants of the Syrian Revolution would unleash a new wave of creativity we could not have imagined.

But the revolution also ended up bringing a new characteristic to the creative resistance that had been flourishing for decades. As art continued to imitate life for Syrians, there was a noticeable increase in the depiction of violence in most drama series, a violence to which Syrians had become accustomed after a decade, in a metaphorical as well as a physical sense. Several series showed scenes of abuse and of belligerence, of despair and aggression that would have felt out of place before the war. The more time passed without a hope that life would improve, the more writers and directors veered towards the most violent elements that had permeated Syrian society—from the militias, to the drug dealers, to the state's violence, to the poor who turned to petty crime, to the rich whose wild ambitions made them crush anyone standing in their way, to the people who had lost touch with their moral compass as they justified the means to survive or to dominate their little worlds. In 2022, the highly successful drama *Breaking Bones* was a specimen of how Syrians, and the art that imitated them, had become nearly numb to the violence around them.

* * *

Hatem Ali was one of those artists whose every piece moves you a certain way, a multifaceted creator of poignant and beloved Syrian drama series, and one of the most prolific and brilliant directors we have ever known. For decades, he depicted our lives in all their excessive beauty and cruelty, their maddening contradictions, their comforting familiarity and simplicity. Even those who did not know him personally felt he was a friend who knew them so well, weaving their stories into the beautiful series and cinematography that became his signature. He was gifted, genuine, humble despite his immense popularity, a creative prodigy who has left a social, historical, and cultural treasure that will always be an important part of Syrians' common heritage and collective memory. When a heart attack took Hatem Ali from us in his prime at the age of 58, in December 2020, many Syrians wept.

In an episode of *The Four Seasons*, one of his much-loved early social dramas that ran in 1999 and 2002, one of the main characters watched the massive popular funeral of our national poet Nizar Qabbani in Damascus, reflecting tearfully that a nation that respects and loves its poets will be well. Indeed, Syrians love their poets, their artists, their writers, their musicians, and thousands accompanied our great director to his final resting place in the manner he deserved, for the beauty of his art, for the magnitude of his legacy, for the soothing balm he had applied to our Syrian pain and dreams.

When they brought out his coffin from the mosque after the funeral prayer, the crowd erupted into applause, calling out 'Your jasmine has opened, Damascus' in honour of his return to his native soil after years of post-revolution exile. Thousands of Syrians around the world had shared this scene of a painful goodbye that came much too soon, all shaken, as I was, by the powerful emotions his death triggered in them.

In the last scene from one of his most deeply moving series, *Big Dreams*, from 2004, eldest son Omar reflects on his life with his father, saying: 'The world is upside down. Those who do the right thing will fall on their face, break their bones, break their head. And those who do the wrong thing will land on their feet.' Omar had abandoned his dream of studying abroad to support his family when his father became ill, and the principled man he had become clashed with his brother who cut shady business deals, bent rules, and paid bribes to get rich in the Syria of the early 2000s. 'The world has become his and anyone like him,' he tells his father. 'When I look at my situation, I find myself so empty. Neither the hopes were fulfilled, nor did life go the way we used to dream of long ago, even though the dreams were very big.'

Like Omar's, Syrians' dreams were big, and like Omar's, they were shattered.

9

SIBLING RIVALRIES

I had made a deal with Damascus when we adopted each other: I would live, love, work, and play in its warm embrace, but I would also slip away to Beirut for long weekends every few weeks to breathe deeply by the sea, meet friends and family, and dive into its much wider bookshop selections of which my post office security guy might not have approved. In the midst of a rebuilding spree downtown, triggering vigorous Lebanese debates on design aesthetics and the soul of beloved pre-war Beirut, those of us who regularly came for bouts of consumerism and relative freedom found the energy to be bubbly and ambitious. When the intensity of Damascus got overwhelming, the agility and continual charm of Beirut would feel welcoming for a while.

From a purely Syrian perspective, indulging in the liberties of Lebanon was cathartic—you could read, you could shop, you could talk. Yet, until the mid-2000s, certain subjects remained taboo for many who preferred to err on the side of caution while the Syrian presence was still pervasive; there were far fewer military checkpoints by then, but just as many intelligence agents as ever. One evening, during a dinner at a family friend's apartment overlooking the Corniche, we broached the subject of domestic developments in Syria: 'It's all pretence and fake reform, but everyone is making it sound like Bashar is the new messiah,' I casually remarked. Our hostess opened her eyes wide: 'Shh, someone could hear you,' she whispered. Although we were on the balcony, I was a little taken aback: 'We're on the fourth floor, there's nobody around us. And I say things like that in Damascus too,' I reasoned. 'Well, in Damascus you can, in Beirut you can't,' she said. Surely she was being overly cautious, I thought, but the Lebanese did know the Syrian regime well enough to worry about needlessly putting themselves in thorny situations, or saying something negative about Assad.

There had been an active Syrian army and intelligence presence in Lebanon for a long time, and they seemed like a permanent fixture. From 1976 to 1990, as the Lebanese war raged, Syrian forces had propped up various allies as they tried to establish dominance over other factions and over Israel, which occupied southern Lebanon for twenty-two years. That was the difficult period for the Assad regime, and for everyone else. With the new US–Syrian understanding of October 1990, following the invasion of Kuwait, things had changed and a period of relative calm would endure for the next decade, under the sole management of the Assad regime.

At the height of Assad Senior's isolation and paranoia in the late eighties, visits to Lebanon had a different flavour and few Syrians managed to travel there. My first road trip to Beirut had been as shocking as many firsts I experienced in Syria; with one of my well-connected relatives, we had driven into Lebanon through the military lane, a distinct stretch close to the border that ran somewhat parallel to the main road, with its own border crossing and its own rules. This was yet another indulgence shared among regime-friendly figures, regardless of their connections to the army. It seemed senseless to me that people travelling for leisure should be given special treatment, but experiences like these were also helping me form a better understanding of how things worked, and for whom they worked best. It was also the first time I had witnessed the pervasive destruction in Lebanon, the Syrian military checkpoints, and the large posters of Hafez Assad and his brotherly slogans outside of Syria, where he declared that we were one people in two countries.

I could never get used to seeing Assad's invasive gaze so frequently in Lebanon. Of course, it was bad enough for the Lebanese, but I also felt sorry for the Syrians who were surely feeling hounded and pursued wherever they went; prohibited from travel to Iraq, and because of bad relations with Turkey and tepid ones with Jordan for a long time, most Syrians only had Lebanon as an option for brief escapes from their Assad-enforced routines, only to find him there too, waiting for them. In the late nineties, I had once flown straight into Beirut from Cairo, on a work trip that did not leave me time to pass by Damascus. As we deplaned and I entered the airport's arrival hall for the very first time, I was startled by the giant face of Assad greeting us with a smug smile. By the luggage carousel, Bassel Assad was there too, on a wall, giving a military salute. Was this all the dominion of Assad as well?

There were other dimensions to the Syrian presence in Lebanon. While the army and intelligence were quite visible, although less so in Beirut, there were many more Syrian workers and manual labourers who had come for jobs in the construction and agriculture sectors, for the most part, throughout the nineties. Their numbers ranged from half a million to a million, depending on the season and on the ones complaining about their presence. While there were no exact figures given the prevalence of undocumented work, Syrian workers always received much lower wages than their Lebanese counterparts did (though still higher than those they would have received in Syria); this is why they were preferred by the employers. It was common knowledge that many Syrian workers were mistreated and abused by their Lebanese employers and others, perhaps because the latter could not take out their frustrations on the regime, perhaps because they felt that Syrians were taking jobs meant for them, perhaps because foreign workers tend to be treated miserably all over the world. And like all these workers everywhere, they persevered and endured the humiliation as long as work was available and money could be sent to family back home.

Not all Syrians were handled like these poor workers, of course. The folks who descended on Beirut for rest and relaxation, for weddings and for shopping, were treated quite differently to those who came to help rebuild the country; these clienteles were welcomed, and their Syrian pounds were an accepted currency at a time when Syrians could be imprisoned in their own country for owning foreign currencies, especially the US dollar. The shopping trips also happened in reverse, with Lebanese often coming into Damascus or Homs where most goods were more affordable and stayed cheaper well into the 2000s. Before every trip back to London, I would stock up on Syrian sweets and often see Lebanese customers choosing, like me, their boxes of our famous *maamoul*, the small butter cookies filled abundantly with nuts or dates, and small and impeccably presented baclava variations, less syrupy than the Turkish or Balkan versions. I remember getting a naive sense of joy when I would see big boxes loaded into their cars, thinking there is so much that Syrians can do well when they're given a chance to do their thing, no matter how small or ordinary.

The upper classes and the established families in both countries knew each other particularly well, through their financial ventures and business deals, and the marriages that bonded so many Syrians and Lebanese throughout their common history. My maternal grandmother was from the Yafi family, split for

SIBLING RIVALRIES

generations between Lebanon and Syria like many others and forming complex family trees that disregarded modern borders. I could hardly keep track of who were first cousins, who came from our side to theirs and vice versa, but this interconnectivity was common.

Despite this history and proximity at certain levels, a chasm had grown between Syrians and Lebanese since Assad had come to power and extended his reach over his neighbour. Under Assad's restrictions, many Syrians felt that Lebanese people tended to look down on them, considering themselves superior in the advantages they had over Syrians. For instance, their schools taught foreign languages that Syrians in public schools, shackled by Baathist education, could barely speak. While my grandmother and her generation spoke French, as did my mother and most of her friends who attended the renowned École Laique when the influence of France had diminished post-Mandate, most students in Syrian public schools only reached a rudimentary level of English or French, especially after the Baath and Assad came to power. Their Arabic, however, was top notch. This would change in the age of satellite TV as English material in particular became more widespread and accessible to Syrians, but the perceived slight about the educational gap with Lebanon and everything that went with it was felt, sometimes deliberately shown, and it was resented.

Moreover, the closed economy that the Assads had imposed on all Syrians meant only the most privileged classes had access to the consumer goods that had become common fare in most of the region, or were able to follow the latest trends in everything else. Many Lebanese seemed to forget the hardships Syrians continued to endure, often not distinguishing between the regime and the people; this would become a point of contention in later years, returned in kind when Syrians began associating different segments of Lebanon with their respective leaders.

IT STARTED IN DAMASCUS

These mutual perceptions were going to prove particularly problematic when Valentine's Day 2005 would set the two countries with one people on fire, after a continuous build-up of tensions that had one common denominator: Bashar Assad.

It all began to unravel ten years after a sudden invasion in the middle of the night had changed Syria's place in the world, when the retreat of another invader in the dark of night was going to establish a new pecking order in the Levant.

* * *

The Israeli occupation of southern Lebanon ended abruptly, unannounced, discovered by the world one fine morning two and a half weeks before the death of Hafez Assad. On 24 May 2000, the Lebanese had woken up to the news that Israeli troops and their local ally, the South Lebanon Army led by Major Saad Haddad, had precipitately retreated to Israel as Hezbollah calmly retook every village and post they had vacated. Israel quickly declared it had fulfilled its responsibility under Security Council Resolution 425, passed in 1978 following its invasion of Lebanon.

This was a great victory for what most Lebanese and Syrians back then still considered to be 'The Resistance,' as Hezbollah referred to itself. Although it had been a much smaller organisation at the time, there was no doubt that it was Hezbollah which had single-handedly forced Israel's exit from the entirety of Lebanese land it had occupied for twenty-two years.

Great celebrations were underway when it occurred to many that this situation posed a new problem: if Lebanon was now free of Israeli occupation, what was there left to resist? And, importantly, if there was no occupation left to resist, did Hezbollah not have to disarm itself like all the other Lebanese groups, as per the Taif Accord that had been reached between all warring parties in 1989 and ratified by parliament? The latter called for the disbanding of all Lebanese and non-Lebanese militias, and for their weapons to be delivered to the state of Lebanon within a period of six months, leaving the fundamental task of defending the homeland to the armed forces, as in every other country in the world. For the last ten years, Hezbollah had flaunted this accord, maintaining that the continuing occupation justified their presence.

If the Assad regime could change a constitution in a few minutes, as it would do on 10 June, it could also decide that Syria's Shebaa Farms, a small area located between Lebanon and the Golan Heights and still occupied by Israel since 1967, could be passed off as Lebanese for the time being until the demarcation of the area. This automatically gave Hezbollah the needed justification to retain its arms until it liberated all 'Lebanese' land, including the twenty-two square kilometres that some thought was Syrian land, and were assured still had to be liberated by the resistance.

This had been the first big decision taken by Bashar Assad after the Lebanon portfolio was given to him by his father in 1998. Lebanese affairs had previously been the responsibility of seasoned vice-president Abdul Halim Khaddam who, with Major General Ghazi Kanaan, head of Military Intelligence in Lebanon and de facto proconsul, had overseen the smoothing of relations with various Lebanese personalities through quid pro quos or threats, but mostly through agreements that were found tolerable to both sides. From any perspective, it was quite an important responsibility to give to such an inexperienced man with such a rapidly expanding ego.

By the end of the Lebanese civil war in 1990, Kanaan had established an understanding with most Lebanese leaders within this new era of Syrian–Saudi cooperation that had emerged after the liberation of Kuwait. As many Lebanese will probably agree, despite having endured the brunt of Syrian military occupation and the assassination of key Lebanese lead-

IT STARTED IN DAMASCUS

ers under Hafez, Bashar made things worse nearly immediately after becoming president.

In late 2002, out of the blue, Assad recalled Kanaan to Damascus and appointed General Rustom Ghazaleh in his place, a man without a single diplomatic bone in his body and no experience dealing with the intricacies of political manoeuvring, who was sure to rub every Lebanese—friend and foe alike—the wrong way. Many quipped that his only relevant qualification for that specific job was that he did not outshine Bashar. From the moment Ghazaleh set up camp in the border town of Anjar, the mood began to sour in Beirut with several politicians who would have preferred to maintain their relationship with Kanaan; with Bashar's big plans, however, it probably did not matter much by that point. Instead of reducing the heat under the simmering Lebanese pot as the world dealt with the repercussions of the 11 September attacks, Assad had begun to burn bridges.

* * *

The growing resentment towards Syrians was becoming more apparent, expressed increasingly openly even in the most unexpected places and the most ridiculous situations. In August 2003, there was a frenzy of excitement as audiences in the Arab world, engrossed in the first season of the talent programme *SuperStar* (the pan-Arab version of Britain's *Pop Idol*), were about to vote on the last three contestants in the penultimate show: Melhem Zein from Lebanon, Rouwaida Attieh from Syria, and Diana Carazon from Jordan. When Melhem Zein was voted out, fans lost their minds; people in the audience started throwing chairs, and protesters in front of the Future Television Network in Beirut (where the show was recorded and produced) chanted their support for Zein in the manner of the pledge reserved for political leaders, 'with our soul, with our blood.' In the commotion, the last two female contestants fainted and were rushed out, and the live broadcast was stopped abruptly.

SIBLING RIVALRIES

The rumours circulating that week were based on a simple premise: the Syrian intelligence network had rigged the voting by discounting votes in favour of Zein, forcing his elimination so that the Syrian contestant could win the show. This seemed to make perfect sense to many otherwise rational people; Syria controlled Lebanon, and therefore controlled *SuperStar*, and the Lebanese could do nothing about it. Zein had been yet another victim of Syrian machinations, despite—or maybe because of—his superior talent.

As the last show approached, Syria and Jordan were also caught in a whirl of theories about who would win: rumour had it that the Jordanian contestant would be getting the votes of the entire Jordanian army, on the orders of its king, whereas the Syrian contestant would receive the support of the Syrian army and intelligence services. Syriatel launched an actual campaign of support for Rouwaida Attieh, with billboards all over the country asking Syrians to do their national duty and vote for her (each vote making Rami Makhlouf and his cousin a bit more money). For most Lebanese, it was clear that the Syrian would win because the regime always had the upper hand in Lebanon.

Tensions were high as the results were announced: Diana Carazon, the Jordanian candidate, had won with fifty-two percent of the votes. Far from disproving the conspiracy theory about Syria, however, this unexpected victory merely created a new angle to clarify it: Syria had decided to allow the young Jordanian woman to win, so that its interference in the voting would not be too blatant. Had the Syrian won, people said, it would have been too obvious, and therefore the Jordanian's victory actually proved Syrian meddling. Elementary, really.

The entertaining *SuperStar* agitation that year was partly escapism from the heavy mood in the region after the invasion of Iraq; it could be dismissed as an anecdotal commentary on the vapid state of popular culture, or an incident that was easy to ridicule. Smart observers would have also understood that it nevertheless exposed frustrations with Syrian hegemony and a growing willingness to be vocal about it, even in social contexts during that period. Naturally, Assad was not about to heed serious warnings, let alone popular chatter. He had more important issues to rig in Lebanon.

* * *

The term of sitting president Emile Lahoud, a staunch Assad ally, was coming to its end in November 2004; even though the Lebanese constitution prohibited second terms, Assad had already decided Lahoud would remain president. Constitutions had not stopped the regime before, so Syria began a campaign of intimidation that year to force Lebanese MPs—including Prime Minister Rafic Hariri—to vote an amendment to the constitution that would allow the extension of the presidential term for three years in exceptional circumstances.

Assad had been particularly angered by Hariri's stance against amending the constitution and extending Lahoud's term, and had summoned him to Damascus in late August to make it clear he would tolerate no dissent. According to Rafic Hariri's own account as relayed to several close associates and aides following his short meeting with Assad, the Syrian president had disrespected him, raising his voice and threatening to 'break Lebanon over your head' if he did not cooperate. It was probably the first time, and the only time, Hariri had ever been addressed in that manner.

In the build-up to the invasion of Iraq, relations between the US and France had sunk to unprecedented lows, and Assad ignored the warnings that came from them and other powers about his plans for Lebanon, assuming they would amount to nothing. But after having disagreed on Iraq, France and the US reconciled over Syria and co-sponsored Security Council Resolution 1559 calling for the removal of all foreign forces from

Lebanon; it was passed the day before the Lebanese parliament voted, the sponsors having understood in advance that Assad would not back down. For the first time, Syria was directly in breach of a Security Council resolution. Shocked by the turn of events, having miscalculated how the EU would be so willing to align itself with the US, the Syrians tried to save face by pointing to the fact that the watered-down resolution had not mentioned Syria by name. Even regime supporters were embarrassed by this ridiculous reaction.

Assad realised, too late, that Resolution 1559 had been made possible through the sway of Hariri and his position on the unconstitutional extension, demonstrating his stature in the world. Hariri was simply too big, too rich, too powerful, and too influential with much stronger countries like France, the US, Saudi Arabia and many more. Bashar should have known it would be difficult and ineffective to intimidate Hariri and make him submit to his whims.

He got his way with the parliamentary vote on 3 September 2004 (with ninety-six MPs approving and only twenty-nine daring to refuse) that allowed Lahoud to remain until 2007. The Syrians could have chosen anyone else for the job and kept their influence. If Assad had meant to project strength, he only demonstrated immaturity and a superficial reading of international relations, as he later found out.

On 14 February 2005, a large convoy carrying Rafic Hariri was blown up by 1,000 kilograms of TNT that detonated as his motorcade drove near the St. George Hotel in Beirut. Causing a massive crater, it killed Hariri instantly and twenty-one people in his entourage.

It was a moment every Lebanese and every Syrian remembers, for it suddenly changed many parameters that had remained fixed for years and that touched lives in both countries. Like several friends and peers at the time, I recall being both convinced the regime did it, and equally convinced it could not have carried out such a blatant and madly counterproductive assassination. Most of the world was pointing the finger at Syria and Hezbollah, and a sea of outraged protesters in central Beirut began to shout slogans that had never before been said out loud. At every huge demonstration that took place all over Lebanon, demanding the immediate withdrawal of Syrian troops, and with every insult that was hurled at Assad, Syrian jaws dropped across the border. Even after thirty years of Syrian occupation, nobody had ever talked about the Assads that way, that loud. It felt exhilarating, and it was disquieting as well, as we all knew that the Lebanese would inevitably pay a price for slighting Assad.

Caving to immediate pressure, as it always does when there is a credible threat, the regime withdrew its troops in April 2005, organising big welcoming crowds in Syria for the soldiers who were coming home. As Israel had done following its retreat from Lebanon in 2000 with regard to Resolution 425, Syria informed the United Nations it had complied with Resolution 1559.

* * *

The scenes in Beirut were causing much commotion in Damascus, with rumours swirling about the regime's fears of isolation from abroad, and its fears of derision at home. Indeed, Syrians seemed less afraid to mention Lebanon, its demonstrations, and the string of assassinations that continued to target critics of Syria, including well-known journalists Samir Kassir in June and Gebran Tueni in December. Lebanon was in disarray, and Syrians were wavering between dismay and exasperation, sensing the usual danger of crossing the regime when it was cornered.

The Lebanese protesters lashed out at ordinary Syrians too, thoughtlessly spreading anti-Syrian sentiment that did not seem to separate the people from the regime. The abuse was physical for those who still found themselves in Lebanon, like the Syrian taxi drivers who made the Damascus–Beirut trek several times a week and had begun to arm themselves with pictures of the late Rafic Hariri, displaying them on their car windows as soon as they had crossed the Lebanese border. Chtaura, the border town a short drive from Damascus to which I often popped with family or friends, mainly to go to our respective banks (where many Syrians had accounts in the absence of private banks back home), quickly became a ghost town, its livelihood—the heavy Syrian traffic—having stopped very suddenly. One of our friends had gone to Chtaura with his elderly mother, who waited in the car as he went into a bank; a group of youngsters started to insult the frightened lady, banging on the car and kicking it, and he had to rush out and was barely able to talk some sense into the young men. Incidents like these had become common.

What every Syrian watched on television ended up being the most damaging to Syrian–Lebanese relations. In these mass protests of Lebanese demanding the withdrawal of Syrian troops, and then demanding bringing the perpetrators of Hariri's killing to justice, signs and chants started targeting not the regime, but the Syrian people. They imitated Syrian accents, badly, exaggeratedly, crudely, and made numerous derogatory comments. Instead of endearing themselves to people who knew exactly what the regime was capable of doing, they alienated them, and Syrian sympathy for the Lebanese as a whole began to fade under the intensity of these unwarranted insults.

Shortly after these events, the Lebanese government, as opportunistic as the Syrian regime, declared that Palestinian refugees who were born in Lebanon would now be allowed to work in the country—a right they had been denied for decades. This was not the end of rampant discrimination, but the upgrading of Palestinians to the level of the Syrian labourers (of whom at least thirty had been killed during those weeks) who left Lebanon after Hariri's killing. The 400,000 Palestinian refugees could still not work as doctors, engineers, accountants, architects, scientists, or teachers, and they would still be refused the right to build permanent homes in their twelve refugee camps, but they could now do the menial jobs that Syrians used to do.

Assad had still not begun to make the Lebanese pay for demanding he leave them alone, and his revenge was drawn out and petty. After the Syrian troops had withdrawn, he blocked the border with Lebanon for weeks, effectively strangling Lebanon and leaving hundreds of Lebanese trucks stuck at the border, their goods rotting in the sun. Several Lebanese fishermen were also apprehended by Syrian authorities when they crossed slightly into Syria's waters. The Syrian regime also suddenly noticed the killed Syrian workers, demanding compensation from the Lebanese authorities. Nobody in Damascus seemed to think this was opening a huge can of worms, but thousands of Lebanese would also have been acting fully within their rights to demand equal compensation for offenses they endured, and for the killing of family members. Syrian media also demanded an official apology from the Lebanese government for insults made to Syria. And as a final touch, without warning, the regime expelled hundreds of Lebanese employees from Syria, claiming their work permits had expired.

All of this ensured that the few Lebanese who did not yet resent the Syrian regime were by then livid, while the Syrians who had initially sympathised with their neighbours felt insulted by both. But Assad was not yet done—his next act of revenge against Lebanon would be something he did in Syria, to Syria.

* * *

The Tenth Baath Party Congress had been called for June 2005, exactly five years after its ninth had anointed Bashar Assad as head of everything. In the weeks that preceded it, amidst the repercussions of the Hariri assassination, the regime spread rumours around the country of huge upcoming changes; Assad himself had stated in March, during a speech to parliament, that the congress would be a great turning point.

While some could not help but be cautiously optimistic, still desperately waiting for change five years on, what was being said quietly in Syria was that the regime was acting from a position of weakness, of humiliation, and that we should remember that making empty promises was its signature move. Suggestions that the state of emergency would be lifted and that multiple political parties would be allowed were taken with many grains of salt; Syrians by then already knew that Bashar was full of air.

The congress announced some decisions that seemed to indicate advancement in the allowance of political parties, but those who spoke Baathese and who read the small print understood that like the media law introduced a few years prior which had in fact shackled media further, the new political decisions merely clarified what was still forbidden.

But there was one change, and it was a major one even though nobody could explain its exact parameters in Syria at first: after nearly forty years of Baathism and its closed economy, the regime introduced a 'social market economy' just over a month after Syrian troops' withdrawal from Lebanon. From one day to the next, Syrian doors were flung open to imports and free trade. On the surface, this was mostly to comply with the economic reforms required by the EU Association Agreement, which the regime now suddenly wanted to have after stalling for years (the clauses on weapons of mass destruction and human rights not being agreeable to Assad). At the same time, it was thought this decision would appease Syrians as they faced ostracism from the world.

An equally important consideration for the regime, however, was the detachment from Lebanon and the punishment of the Lebanese for having dared to humiliate Syria. With an open Syrian economy, there would be less dependence on Lebanon, which was going to lose a huge Syrian clientele that did not need to cross the border any longer for most of its needs.

Over the next months, the regime's message to Syrians was clear: unless you absolutely must, do not go to Lebanon until we tell you. The exit fee that Syrians must pay every time they leave the country, by air or by road, went up by 300%, from 200 to 800 Syrian pounds (from 4 to 16 US dollars) per person; this made regular visits—especially day trips—no longer financially viable for many families.

The regime did not want the Lebanese to benefit from even the smallest purchase, so returning cars were now searched thoroughly and goods entering Syria taxed. In previous years, border guards had only given perfunctory looks into car boots when it was clear the shopping was limited, especially when they were filled with bags from Ramak, Rami Makhlouf's duty-free shop. Now, even Rami could lose a few dollars if it meant punishing Lebanon.

It was also decreed that cars could now only cross into Lebanon with a maximum of twenty litres of petrol. On a trip in early 2006, I saw for myself how every car, ours included, was checked as border officials opened the gas tank and dipped a measuring stick inside to determine the amount. The fine was hefty, in the thousands of Syrian pounds, if you had the misfortune of having filled up before your trip. With less than twenty litres in their tanks, Syrians had no choice but to fill up in Lebanon where petrol was more expensive, another deterrent to making the trip. The regime truly tried to think of everything that could make life difficult for Lebanon and people wanting to go to Lebanon.

Some shops in Beirut which catered to an exclusive Damascene clientele were feeling the cold front. The luxury chain Aïshti, well known to the velvet society and regime circles, was one of several Lebanese retailers trying to woo back customers by offering to send selections of designer clothes to the clients' houses, where they could choose at leisure. Unfortunately for them, the regime had quickly allowed the import of the highly desired foreign labels to keep its clique satisfied. A few months later, the Villa Moda Emporium opened in old Damascus, in a converted khan in the middle of Medhat Basha (the Street Called Straight) that was transformed into a dreamhouse for wealthy shopaholics. In a street where ancient tiny shops adjacent to the souks had been trading for centuries, one could now buy designer labels whose jeans cost hundreds of dollars and handbags thousands. There was one less reason to go to Lebanon, and one more way to tell the Lebanese they had become irrelevant.

The effect of these various anti-Lebanese measures was felt in varying degrees by Syrians. Many were not touched directly and soon stopped caring, but some in my extended circle went through waves of contradicting emotions. I remember arguing with a close friend, an educated, cosmopolitan, well-travelled lady who had been living in Beirut for a few years. She had always hated the regime, but as she poured her heart out about how frustrated and insulted she felt by the general anti-Syrian attitude manifested by so many Lebanese, she defended it. I confronted her, insisting that Lebanese chauvinism did not justify becoming a regime apologist, but she readily admitted feeling too hurt to retreat to a neutral position. This exact feeling was shared by many Syrians who had become fed up with what they perceived to be their neighbours' sense of superiority and self-righteousness. The huge wave of sympathy that had initially blown across the border had quickly been replaced by exasperation and indifference; unfortunately, the attitude of some Lebanese had served the Syrian regime's interests well.

* * *

Some of Syria's civil society activists paid dearly for voicing support for a relation of equality between Syria and Lebanon with

IT STARTED IN DAMASCUS

the Beirut–Damascus/Damascus–Beirut Declaration of May 2006, calling for improved ties and the mutual respect of the sovereignty of both nations. Signed by hundreds of Lebanese and Syrian intellectuals, writers, and activists following the Lebanese imbroglio, it led to the Syrian regime's arrest and imprisonment of several signatories, hammering a big nail into the coffin of any domestic opposition movement. It was a dangerous time for Syrians to express anything but full support for the Syrian nation and its maligned authorities.

The regime was under the spotlight for months after the assassination of Hariri, isolated and forced to deal with the UN-led international inquiry under German prosecutor Detlev Mehlis. His report to the Security Council in October 2005 would be published online 'by mistake' in a version that showed the names of several Syrian and Lebanese officials (including Bashar's brother Maher and his brother-in-law Assef Shawkat, and the head of Lebanon's Security Directorate Jamil Sayyed). These names were replaced in the final report with 'senior Lebanese and Syrian officials.' Two weeks before Mehlis presented his initial findings to the Security Council, it was announced that General Ghazi Kanaan, who had been Syria's man in Lebanon for two decades until Bashar replaced him with Ghazaleh, had committed suicide in his office. The Syrian grapevine ventured the deed had been done with two bullets.

When we thought every possible repercussion to the assassination of Hariri had already happened, we were treated to the first ever defection from the regime at the highest level, that of former vice-president Abdul Halim Khaddam, a friend of Hariri and the only Syrian official who had gone to his funeral. On 30 December 2005, from Paris, he went public in a long interview on Alarabiya television; he spoke at length not only about politics in Syria and in Lebanon, but also about Bashar Assad's character, temper, and inaptitude for the job. It was the first time that a senior official had spoken of such things. The next morning, all the members of the Syrian parliament were called in to recite, one after another, their allegiance to Assad and their disdain of Khaddam, enumerating his many faults and voicing outrage at his wealth. It was the most entertaining session of parliament we had ever seen, but the embarrassing antics pointed to a deepening isolation of the Assad regime.

Because of Hariri's Saudi citizenship and his closeness to the Saudi ruling family, his killing had been considered a particular affront to Saudi Arabia; Syrian–Arab relations reached their lowest point since the Iran–Iraq war—quite a feat for Bashar, who had done all of that in less than five years. In January 2006, standing in front of a huge sign that stated, in English, 'Defending Syria is national right and duty,' Assad explained that, once more, a big conspiracy to hurt him was also going to hurt the whole region: 'What is happening between Syria and Lebanon is part of a global plot against all Arabs.'

In July 2006, Hezbollah killed three Israeli soldiers and kidnapped two from the border, triggering an Israeli ground invasion and an air and naval blockade on Lebanon. Thirty-four days later, after some 1,300 Lebanese and 165 Israelis had been killed and over a million Lebanese displaced, Hezbollah and Israel both declared victory. Israel had destroyed much of Lebanon's infrastructure, expecting Lebanon would crumble and Hezbollah would be destroyed; it was not, leading Hezbollah leader Hassan Nasrallah to declare it a divine victory for the group.

Syrian media had run non-stop footage of the hundreds of thousands of Lebanese seeking temporary refuge from the ferocious Israeli bombing, welcomed with open arms at every level of the Syrian state and society. With renewed vigour and confidence, having done nothing himself or said a word for the duration of the war, Assad gave a speech the day after the ceasefire in which he fiercely attacked the 'half men' who did not stand up to the Israeli aggression. The offense was directed at Arab leaders he resented, in particular those of the powerful Gulf states whose fury at Hariri's killing had not yet abated.

He watched smugly as his ally Hezbollah, the most powerful Iran-backed militia in the Middle East, brought life in central Beirut to a complete standstill with a sit-in that began in December 2006, aiming to bring down the government of Prime Minister Fouad Siniora supported by Western powers. After over a year of paralysis, Hezbollah fighters took over Beirut on 8 May 2008, following the Lebanese government's attempt to control its communications system that included surveillance cameras over Beirut Airport. After days of fighting that killed around a hundred Lebanese, Arab states stepped in to mediate a return to calm, with Qatar taking the diplomatic lead and sponsoring negotiations that led to the Doha Agreement of 21 May. As it saved itself, Hezbollah had also saved Assad, whose re-entry into the world was introduced by Qatar's decision to involve Syria, facilitated by an unlikely change of direction from Paris.

* * *

The growing Qatari role in the region had coincided with a strategic foreign policy shift from France following President Jacques Chirac's end of term in office in May 2007. He had been an early Syrian ally and a close friend of Rafic Hariri, turning into a committed Assad opponent when things went awry in Lebanon. With his departure, the slate was mostly freed of the links between the French presidency and the Hariri family's allies. Nicolas Sarkozy's election in May 2007 had heralded a new approach which centred on personal involvement from the presidency itself at the time of the Lebanese impasse of 2008, at the expense of the Quai d'Orsay and Foreign Minister Bernard Kouchner. It was this diplomatic engagement from France that would enable Assad's rehabilitation and open doors anew for him.

10

THE DOCTOR'S TURN

'Your father, may he rest in peace, was a big patriot who served his country for many years.' I could only nod in subtle agreement looking in my interlocutor's general direction, fully catching his gist and the insinuations behind this introduction. As he praised my father's various achievements and virtues, over a decade after his passing, I was bracing myself for what was going to follow during our so-called 'chat over a cup of coffee,' the notorious non-negotiable invitation that every Syrian fears receiving, even from a run-of-the-mill local intelligence branch, let alone from much higher up. Mine had come from the mother of all branches.

The Assad regime may have been quick to lash out when it was under outside pressure, arresting those who trespassed and often following with a lot worse. It was even more dangerous in better days, when it had survived yet another challenge and had time to turn its attention to certain critics—those considered annoyances, those who had ruffled royal feathers one time too many, or those with media presence and an audience.

On one of my trips to Damascus in 2008, I was all of those in one, a nuisance if not a threat to national security, abruptly summoned to one of the regime's most powerful and feared men.

IT STARTED IN DAMASCUS

Days before my planned return to London, I had been picked up in a Range Rover with tinted windows and driven to that well-known building that we all passed on the way to the airport, that building we dreaded ever having to enter. As the gates had opened, I noticed the lush garden and the tidy lawn, hidden from sight if you were lucky enough to just drive past, and the ever-present men in black standing on the steps, watching me get out after the car dropped me in front of the main entrance. I looked straight ahead, trying to avoid every glare as I followed a man across a large hall leading to a staircase, and to the big boss upstairs. Conscious of my kitten heels tapping on the tiled floor, I was fixated on controlling my apprehension, praying that I would soon walk out in the same way I had walked in, not dragged or led forcibly to another intelligence centre. My heart tightened as I imagined, despite myself, what and who lay in the basement beneath my feet, wondering how many young men could be writhing in agony and begging for mercy as I walked over their heads.

I was determined to pretend I was not afraid, but my convocation had been unexpected and alarming. Most other alleged troublemakers did not generally merit the attention of Assad's most senior officials, and I had heard that only one other writer, with whom I was acquainted, had been personally seen by General Ali Mamlouk, the head of the General Security Directorate to whose office I was being led.

He was taller than I expected, a slim and intimidating figure. As he came towards me to shake my hand and gesture to the dark leather sofa in the sitting area, facing a gigantic portrait of Bashar Assad on the wall, I thought his calm voice contrasted with his piercing gaze. He took the armchair to my left, the closest seat to me, and ordered coffee for us even after I had declined one. Then, he began with the niceties, rarely taking his eyes off me as he sang the praises of the great diplomat and

THE DOCTOR'S TURN

national figure he said my late father had been. He neatly moved into the challenges 'we' faced in the world today, and our need to be careful in how we viewed situations and what we said about them. We had quickly reached the purpose of my convocation, and it was clearly not to liken me to my father but rather to berate me for not being as patriotic as he had been.

Mamlouk noticed I was not drinking the coffee placed on the low table in front of me, knowing I was being disrespectful in silent protest at being there. He leaned forward in his armchair and reached to grab my cup, turning fully to his right and waiting for me to take it from his outstretched hand: '*Tfaddali*,' he said, 'please take it, or do you want me to think that you are refusing my hospitality?' To this day, I wish I had been strong enough to do just that, but my mother's words resonated in my ears just then. An hour earlier, as I said goodbye, she had held my daughter who had just turned two and cautioned: 'Do you want her to grow up without her mother? Hold your tongue and don't argue with him, even if he provokes you.'

We both knew this was hyperbole, that the likelihood of my not returning (at that stage at least) was small. My family name had undoubtedly protected me until then, as had my position at Chatham House at a time when few people around the world— and even fewer Syrians—worked on, researched, and wrote about the country. These factors, and my frequent media appearances from London, would probably warrant some news coverage should the meeting not end as we hoped—not that this had ever helped Syrian detainees. Even so, we had already agreed on the well-placed person my mother would call in the unlikely case I did not return after a couple of hours. Knowing I had never hesitated to respond in person to Syrian officials' absurd comments and accusations, and that I was furious at being summoned in this manner since the call had come as if I had committed a crime, she wisely reminded me that this anger was harmful, and pointless.

IT STARTED IN DAMASCUS

I heard my mother's voice and saw my baby daughter's face at that moment. Dejected, I accepted the coffee from his hand and took a sip as he watched. Mamlouk sat back and nodded towards a large folder on his desk at the other side of the room, implying it was my file: 'You know, we follow everything you write and say,' he started. I had assumed as much, especially as this was not the first notice I had received from various sources over time.

The previous year, an official at the Syrian embassy in London had told me he had no choice but to write a report about a well-circulated briefing paper on Syria I had written for Chatham House, but that was common practice. Two years before that, a friend passed a direct message from Assad's father-in-law saying, verbatim, 'tell her she has no right to speak badly about Syria' after he watched me on the news explaining Kurdish protests in Qamishli and the regime's typically violent repression that killed and injured dozens. That one was particularly surprising as we saw each other regularly and he could have told me that face to face, or called me directly; then again, he probably did not want to hear my immediate response.

Several Syrian officials whom I met on various occasions on their London visits had also, at sensitive stages of Syria's headline news exploits (not least of which the aftermath of the Hariri assassination) told me my comments were dangerous and inappropriate. One thought he would have more success by addressing himself to my husband, so that he could tell me to go easy in my criticism of the regime.

Mamlouk said there were positions I should not have taken on various occasions, on domestic affairs and beyond; I prudently countered that those of us who love and are attached to our country feel issues should be exposed and discussed. Besides, I added, providing analysis and commentary on the region was part of my work. He smirked: 'But why are you so critical? Don't be negative, you should try to see the glass as being half full.'

THE DOCTOR'S TURN

He was particularly cross about an admittedly acerbic piece (that many readers had found quite amusing) I had written a few weeks before about the regime's dismal defence of its own declared causes, and the raison d'être of its continuing state of war with Israel. I had already gotten word that the '*O Golan, Where Art Thou?*' post on my blog, the first Syrian blog to have been created years before, had been shared around Damascene circles and had made some noise. 'What I wrote is the truth and the blame should be on all the institutions I mention, not on me,' I brazenly challenged Mamlouk, asking him to tell me what exactly was incorrect. He could not; his silent glare, however, told me I had touched a sensitive regime nerve, and that pushing further was futile.

I veered slightly, feeling I needed to insist on the larger scope of my work: what about the articles I had written and commentary I had given in mainstream media, I asked, which argued for the Syrian national position? It turned out one did not receive credit for what the regime considered its due, or so I gathered from Mamlouk's evasive nod. For everything else, the response was always 'now is not the time'—the mantra Syrians had been hearing for nearly forty years.

I was surprised to realise he really did follow what I wrote and said, judging from the many details he was mentioning that 'you do not need to say,' to which I tried to interject that I was not wrong. I was still apprehensive, sitting in the presence of this powerful man scolding me, especially when his tone and mood visibly toughened: 'I'm telling you, be careful, because like this you are helping the enemy.' In other words, treason. Even though I dared respond that the enemy had its own sources and hardly needed my writings to know what was happening in Syria, my motivation to defend my right to state facts diminished significantly and anxiety weighed on my chest. While the entire meeting had itself been a stark warning, Mamlouk's closing remarks to me were next level up in Syrian regime lingo, going from cautionary to threatening. It ended on that note, with the clear message that I was not to criticise the regime and be useful to our enemies. Some forty-five minutes after I had entered his office, he smiled again and said he hoped we would not meet in the same circumstances next time, but in better ones. I prayed I would never have to meet him again and spent the next months trying to get his voice and piercing gaze out of my head.

* * *

During that eventful week of July 2008 and General Mamlouk's unequivocal warning to me, Bashar Assad was gallivanting in Paris at the invitation of President Nicolas Sarkozy for the launch of the Union for the Mediterranean, sponsored by France. Three years after Hariri's assassination, three years after being ostracised for his actions in Lebanon and pressured over his role in fuelling chaos in Iraq, the Syrian dictator was seen beaming at the Grand Palais in the company of over forty heads of state and government. He did not even try to hide his satisfaction: 'This is for me a historic visit, an opening up to France and to Europe,' Assad told French newspaper *Le Figaro*.

The following day, the UN Secretary General, EU leaders, and their Middle Eastern and North African counterparts rubbed shoulders on a podium at the Champs-Elysées to watch the famous 14 July military parade celebrating France's National Day. Observers wondered whether they should read something in the short distance that separated Assad from Israeli prime minister Ehud Olmert, but it was just a wily photo op that denoted nothing of substance, a clickbait moment generating a lot of empty talk. The real news—some might say the travesty—was Assad's meeting with another of Syria's neighbours, the newly elected Lebanese president Michel Sleiman, who had replaced Assad's man Lahoud when his unconstitutional term expired, and the

THE DOCTOR'S TURN

announcement that diplomatic relations between the two countries would be established for the first time since their respective independence from France.

Leading the Syrian delegation's media and PR for the three-day visit to France was former Lebanese Minister of Information Michel Samaha; as Assad spoke of embassies in Syria and Lebanon, the irony was lost on many. While many Lebanese politicians of various parties had never stopped doing the regime's bidding, they were now able to do it openly once again. This was taking things to a new level, however, and Assad's reliance on a Lebanese rather than a Syrian to handle his communications during that Paris trip was a national embarrassment—or, in effect, two national embarrassments as it reflected badly on both countries. It was a slap to the Lebanese, who were trying to project strength and independence, and to the Syrians, who wondered how not a single one of them had been considered competent enough to do the job, if only for the prestige of the country.

Four years after his highly visible Parisian gig for Assad, Michel Samaha would be arrested in Beirut for organising the transport of vast amounts of TNT from Syria into Lebanon, on the orders of the same General Mamlouk who had warned me about treason and threatening national security with my writing and public speaking. Samaha was secretly filmed relaying Syrian instructions to assassinate Christian leaders, and to place bombs at various iftar meals during Ramadan; this was meant to trigger sectarian violence in Lebanon during Assad's second year of war on his own people and to claim that the anti-Assad camp (on whom these terror acts would be blamed) was a danger to all. By spreading Assad's killing machine into Lebanon, yet again, Samaha was to help push the lie that the regime—in supposed contrast to extremist killers—was secular and a guarantor of stability in the region.

* * *

IT STARTED IN DAMASCUS

After Paris, more world capitals would roll out the red carpet for Assad once again, as if nothing had ever happened. In September 2008, on the pretext of attending a mini summit with the emir of Qatar and the prime minister of Turkey, Sarkozy became the first Western leader to visit Damascus after the Hariri assassination. Having considered the decision to open embassies with Lebanon to be a positive step, he had chosen to increase engagement with Syria, although other French and European figures were less enthusiastic. He also inaugurated the new Lycée Charles de Gaulle of Damascus building during that visit.

This successful rehabilitation at the highest level allowed Assad to expand his reach over the next couple years, touring several countries in South America and popping over to Kyiv to toast Viktor Yanukovych, the new Ukrainian president who would become one of Putin's protégés as well. The hard times seemed to have passed, and the Assad regime felt strengthened as detractors' attempts to isolate it continued to fade away.

Sarkozy's pivotal opening to Assad had come just as President George W. Bush was serving the last months of his second term. His neocon administration that had considered the regime a low-hanging fruit for its meddling in Iraq, that had reconciled with France over Lebanon, that had ensured Assad would not attend the New York UN World Summit where 170 world leaders met in 2005, was on its way out. The hope that a Democrat would bring the change many Americans seemed to want, especially following the invasion of Iraq, was ardently shared by the Syrian regime; it waited for the storm to pass, like it always did.

As anticipated, many around the world welcomed Barack Obama's election. For Syria, it had come at a perfect time and put the regime in an excellent mood, especially after Obama's Cairo speech of June 2009 when he promised a new beginning between the US and the Muslim world. One year after their Paris escapade, the Assads embarked on a rather blunt charm offensive. 'The fact

THE DOCTOR'S TURN

is President Obama is young,' Asma Assad told Sky News in July 2009, 'and President Assad is also very young as well, so maybe it is time for these young leaders to make a difference in the world.' Bashar went even further, later adding an invitation to his wife's opening salvo: 'We would welcome him in Syria. Definitely. I am very clear about this.' Unfortunately for them both, Obama did not take the bait; he was just not that into them.

The US did appoint a new ambassador to Damascus in 2010, five years after the US had recalled its previous ambassador to protest the killing of Hariri. As luck would have it, with the confirmation delays and usual disagreements on Capitol Hill, he would only take his post in January 2011.

* * *

Towards the end of Bashar's erratic first decade in power, life had gotten very good at the top, and increasingly bleak at the bottom. After the extended Lebanon fiasco, few Syrian critics dared make a sound, let alone sign new statements amid worsening social conditions and the continued stifling of opinion. Many so-called dissidents remained in jail for years, for having had the temerity to question Bashar's actions in Lebanon, if not his governance of Syria. Assad had quickly killed the first Damascus Spring by 2001, and had just as ruthlessly ended the second spring of 2006 with its Beirut–Damascus/Damascus–Beirut Declaration, the fruit of Syrian–Lebanese solidarity. For Syrians, only the right to remain silent prevailed.

With a whopping 99.82% of the vote and an astonishing voter turnout of 95.82%, Assad had been re-elected in 2007, inspiring Interior Minister Bassam Abel Majid to proudly proclaim that 'this great consensus shows the political maturity of Syria and the brilliance of our democracy'—and nobody dared to argue with him. As always, it was 'not the time' for the magic word—reform—because of regional circumstances, and because Syria could not carry out political reform under outside pressure. Besides, why would Syrians complain when regional and foreign media regularly told them how much better things had gotten?

Some private schools (such as the International School of Choueifat, owned in Syria by Bashar's cousin Rami Makhlouf) and even some private universities (such as the Syrian Private University, owned by Rami Makhlouf) had opened around Syria, though still only the privilege of very few. Likewise, six private banks (including Al-Baraka Bank, Cham Bank, and Byblos Bank, whose Syrian branches were owned by Rami Makhlouf) had opened during Assad's first nominal term. These economic reforms were duly praised in state media and in the new private publications that had also been decreed permissible, such as *Al Iqtissadiya* (owned by Rami Makhlouf) and *Al Watan* (also, as luck would have it, owned by Rami Makhlouf).

Despite the hundreds of new laws, legislative decrees, and instructions that were issued in the name of Bashar's reforms, about which so many journalists wrote approvingly, *ramrameh* was still the only real game in town. But if, as General Mamlouk had berated me, I should not have been looking at the glass as half empty, why were other Syrians doing it as well?

Dissent may have looked dead on the surface, but resentment was rife as disparities grew. These were years that felt busy, in a stimulating, entrepreneurial, forward-looking way that excited many of those who were merely missing the forest for the trees. In reality, it was a chaotic period, showcasing a veneer of progress laid on weak foundations that supported neither the weight of expectations nor of needs. You could feel the hustle and bustle that seemed to lift Damascus higher and higher as signs of change continued to appear, but if you remained stuck in the vibes of your own privileged social circle, you would have been unaware of the anxiety that reigned over a growing segment of society.

There was a perceptible rumble mounting from the slums that were developing at an alarming rate, barely hiding in plain sight

THE DOCTOR'S TURN

as they attached themselves to the metropolis. Unable to afford living in the city any longer, more and more young Damascenes were forced to move to these unregulated areas or to increasingly distant new developments, giving themselves the added frustration of long and difficult commutes in crowded and irregular micro buses. More cars were clogging up the main arteries of Damascus as import duties had decreased, but there were no concurrent measures taken to regulate traffic, to adapt roads, to create parking spaces, or even to provide sufficient petrol stations that would cater to the expanded automobile needs.

The voices of discontent, at first murmured, were increasingly loud and blunt as subsidies decreased on a regular basis, justified by the regime's claims of ongoing reform and the disengagement of the state in favour of market forces. While wages in the public sector were regularly increased, they did not match the price hikes that affected basic necessities, and better-paying jobs in the private sector were limited. Poverty increased exponentially during that decade; like inflation, it was visible, and it was rampant.

Amidst the total lack of planning or the creation of employment schemes, the angst and frustrations of young students who had also struggled to graduate without paying bribes grew, facing the bleak reality of unemployment rates of at least thirty percent, according to estimates. Qualified but unable to find work, they found themselves trying to enter a frail job market, along with hundreds of thousands of Syrians escaping the drought that had since 2006 destroyed their agricultural lifeline, in the absence of the state's planning and a well-designed investment in irrigation infrastructure.

The traditional middle class was being overtaken on both sides; more people were becoming poor, and more people were becoming rich. For the latter, luxury boutiques and consumer goods and services had multiplied since the exit from Lebanon and Assad's decision to finally allow Syrians—at least some of them—a semblance of a market economy. Fancy boutiques with trendy designer labels sprouted about town, becoming the velvet society's new local shopping meccas, as more luxury cars than ever were seen sticking out among the battered vehicles most Syrians could not afford to replace. Their shopping done, they could head back to sip frappuccinos at the still sparkling new Four Seasons Hotel, or have coffee at places like Art House, rejoicing at how great life had become. These were the golden days of the velvet society, blinded by its own light and insensible to the hardship the vast majority of Syrians were facing as they watched the chasm grow.

Families, couples, and even groups of young people would be seen roaming the malls around the city, and the main shopping streets filled with people in the evenings. For the most part, they bought nothing from these shops; they watched, they wished, they waited. While such disparities and instances of crony capitalism were not exclusive to Syria, most of the other countries in the region had made sure that copious investments were made in the public sector. Under the Assads' severe mismanagement, neither roads, nor basic infrastructure, nor reliable services were ever delivered to a nation that was repeatedly told to just be patient. Even the tourism industry that should have thrived during that period of renewed engagement and a recently opened economy remained tentative, unable to rely on the necessary state services or competitive alternatives—including water, electricity, sanitation, and the roads and accompanying travel infrastructure worthy of a rich country like Syria.

The travails of Umayyad Square, Damascus's inescapable central point where seven major avenues converge, had become emblematic of the Syrian regime in the early Bashar years. Plans for renovations aiming at reducing congestion were drawn up, with the building of an underground tunnel for cars going from Mezzeh to the Old City to free valuable space above ground. For

THE DOCTOR'S TURN

two years, the square remained a massive construction site, even after the tunnel had already opened by 2005, driving Damascenes to despair as it closed and re-opened periodically with no evidence that anything had actually changed.

There could be no logical reason for this chaotic outcome of a seemingly straightforward civil engineering task. At every gathering in Damascus, in shops and in homes, people openly mocked the situation, blaming it on gross negligence, mismanagement, the usual corruption, and plain incompetence. For a long time afterwards, every frustration, every contradiction, and every failure in Syria's public, political, and economic affairs was compared to Umayyad Square. It made no sense that a city like Damascus could not handle a simple job like that and all the others like it.

* * *

While all Syrians dealt with these infuriating struggles at every level of their lives, another issue was weighing on Damascus and greater Damascus. Both Aleppo and Damascus, and to some extent the smaller major cities, were continuing to expand as people from rural areas moved to urban centres, but Damascus alone was experiencing a surge with the concentration of Iraqi refugees there. Very few refugees had come following the Anglo-American invasion of 2003; as of 2006, however, as sectarian violence flared following a bombing of Al Askari Mosque in Samarra, up to 1.5 million Iraqis sought refuge in Syria, with ninety percent of them settling in and around Damascus. Because of the way the regime dealt with refugees, their huge number affected Syrians directly, in their daily lives.

Syrian officials often prided themselves on welcoming refugees without erecting a single tent for them. Indeed, unlike neighbouring countries and others where millions of Syrians themselves would later end up, tents were nowhere to be seen when people seeking refuge arrived, the understanding being that in Syria, refugees slept in proper homes. That is only because the Syrian government provided no shelter or housing assistance. Refugees could come to Syria and would be welcomed as brothers and guests, according to official rhetoric; unfortunately, they would have to fend for themselves once they made it across the border, and it was left to organisations like UNHCR to manage the flow.

As they were granted six-month residence permits rather than asylum, Iraqis would be forced to leave Syria at the end of the allowed stay and come back again to obtain permission to remain another half year, and so on. This was difficult and expensive for families: not only they would have to spend money to travel to the Iraqi border and back, but they would also have to pay the departure tax imposed on everyone in Assad's Syria, and then pay another fee for the new visa allowing them to stay another six months. Many Iraqis ended up staying beyond their permit and tried to remain off the radar, unable to work or send their children to school for fear of being discovered flaunting the rules.

The Iraqis fleeing civil strife were renting apartments that housed several families. Many Syrians, facing their own financial limitations, had taken advantage of the situation and charged inflated prices; inevitably, this caused a significant rise in rents in those neighbourhoods, pricing out Syrians and increasing their resentment of Iraqis who they felt were to blame.

Taxi drivers eventually started to prefer picking up Iraqi customers, just as they preferred the business of Gulf visitors in the summer months, less likely to argue about the fare than Syrians. In areas like Jaramana, Sayyida Zeinab, Qudsayia, or even Yarmouk, you could practically hear more Iraqi than Syrian accents in the streets during that period, and this quickly became a bone of contention that was completely disregarded by the regime.

Refugee children had been allowed to exercise the same right to free education as Syrians had, and to attend Syrian schools, a

THE DOCTOR'S TURN

nominally wonderful initiative that cost the regime nothing. Most schools, however, were already bursting at the seams with many classrooms squeezing in thirty or forty students, to which Iraqi children were added. UNHCR helped build some schools and refurbish others in the affected areas for which the regime had no time, and even helped institute a system of shifts so that all the children could access the education they deserved at different times of the day. By the 2007–08 school year, 100,000 Iraqi students had joined Syrians in Damascus schools.

Healthcare services, also free to refugees as they were to Syrians in state-run facilities, were already struggling before the influx of refugees. As with education, the regime gave little thought to how this might affect everyone, and resentment had risen and spread.

One day, my bad habit of putting my purse on the roof of the car while I settled my daughter into her car seat nearly paid off for a passing thief in downtown Damascus. When I raised my head, I saw the purse was missing as my mother noticed a young man walking briskly away with it. I instinctively ran after him, my fear of losing cards and documents giving me wings. As he heard my steps and looked behind, seeing me getting closer, he started running as well as I screamed 'thief' at the top of my lungs. Surprisingly, this scared him into dropping the purse and darting into a side street when he saw several men heading towards us to help me.

When I told some friends what had happened, one immediately responded 'it must have been an Iraqi.' 'How do you know?' I asked. 'Did we not have thieves and crooks in Syria before they came?' She doubled down and berated me for not fully realising how bad things had gotten. This incident gave me pause to consider, to reflect even more on the tense Syrian social dynamics of the late 2000s. It was clear that the refugee issue had only exacerbated Syrians' sky-high frustrations that had accumulated year after year, finding no outlet. Taking it out on Iraqis was not only allowed but even encouraged, I felt, as it helped the regime blame problems on everyone but itself—on the invasion of Iraq, mostly, and on US imperialism.

I wrote back then of my fears that our country and our region stood precariously at the edge of an existential precipice. The huge young population was running out of options for education, employment, or any sort of economic security. Even in large urban areas, many were often denied the most basic infrastructure, lacking access to healthcare, sanitation, water, and even rudimentary transportation. Increasingly, faced with no prospects and realising there would be no miraculous change on the horizon, some were succumbing to idleness and religiosity, the most dangerous of combinations, lounging around with nothing better to do than to watch mind-numbing shows or—even worse—indoctrinating satellite television channels.

* * *

My columns for *Syria Today*, an English-language monthly that had been created in 2004, came to an abrupt end in the spring of 2009, nearly a year after my convocation to General Mamlouk. Its friendly editor told me they had been surprised by Mohsen Bilal, the-then Minister of Information, summoning the publisher to announce that they were not to accept any more of my articles, and that I was henceforth banned from writing in Syria. When asked why, the minister had replied: 'The order comes from above.' This meant the presidential palace which, despite my focus on writing about social issues for *Syria Today*, still followed what I wrote and said elsewhere, and still resented it.

In my last piece for the publication, I had advocated for Syria to allow think tanks and teach students to think for themselves, arguing that students now stood at a disadvantage: 'Following an educational regimen that generally favours memorising over

THE DOCTOR'S TURN

understanding, that rewards conformity over initiative and that penalises independent thinking and deviations from the straight path, they will never be as well-equipped to think about situations or to solve problems.' In Bashar's pretend reformist environment at the end of the first decade, these words and thoughts were blasphemy, and the sentence had been censored.

A Syrian journalist had reached out to me the following year, hearing from someone that I was back in Damascus. He had seen some of my analysis and commentary on regional affairs and asked to interview me; I told him that he would not be able to quote anything I said, or even mention my name. He insisted on the interview, and I obliged, knowing it was for nought. A few days after our talk, he called again to apologise for having wasted my time and for not having realised I was banned not just from writing myself, but from even being referenced. The era of pretend reform was well and truly over in every field.

The regime was euphoric from its successful rehabilitation and spreading its wings again, oblivious to the agitation and waves of disquiet simmering all around Syria. In July 2010, to celebrate Bashar Assad's tenth year in power, a huge Syrian flag was raised on a 107-metre pole in Tishreen Park in Damascus, where it flapped as a constant reminder of the regime's omnipotence nationally and regionally, come what may. The ceremony was attended by the usual regime officials and oligarchs. Rami Makhlouf was all smiles, full of joie de vivre as he mingled with fellow cronies; on his lapel were two shiny pins, one of the Syrian flag, the other of the head of Bashar.

* * *

In December 2010, the Assads treated themselves to another Paris round, high on their own buzz on an official two-day visit where they did not even need to share the limelight with others this time. Before the visit, Reporters Without Borders had written to President Sarkozy to remind him that repression had stepped up significantly in Syria and that the population still lived in constant fear of the security services, asking him to intercede for the release of numerous journalists and writers. Likewise, Human Rights Watch, Amnesty International, and several other NGOs wrote an open letter to Sarkozy about the repression suffered by civil society, the continued persecution of human rights defenders, and the government's stranglehold on the judiciary, blocking any prospect of developing the rule of law in Syria. Even if Sarkozy brought this up with Assad, the effect was the same: relations with France flourished, and no prisoners of conscience were liberated in those final months of that erratic decade, despite the numerous appeals of the few organisations still watching Syria. It seemed all was quiet on the eastern front, but the calm was deceptive.

Ten days after that Paris visit, when protests began in Tunisia on 17 December, Assad felt unconcerned and unstoppable. Why would he worry when he had always gotten away with doing exactly what he wanted? Besides, negative repercussions to decisions he had made thus far had always been explained as the fault of others: this included the mythical old guard, and the domestic enemies who threatened national security with demands they had learned from hypocritical democracies who did not understand local circumstances. Regional calamities were always the fault of Syria's enemies, of imperialism, and of the conspiracy against Syria that never seemed to abate despite the international engagement Assad was enjoying again.

His decade in power had amply revealed that he had not been a reluctant heir at all, relishing his power over Syrians and many of their neighbours, imagining himself to be a statesman of the highest order on the world stage. Like all narcissists, he demanded admiration and adulation, allowing no one to shine in his presence except for his wife—and then only, one could speculate, because she reflected positively on him. Over the years, it had

THE DOCTOR'S TURN

become obvious that he could not tolerate having charismatic and articulate advisors or ministers around him; those who inadvertently received praise or gained their own following were promptly sidelined. Those who remained were either old-style Baathist dinosaurs, or they were so junior in rank that they posed no competitive threat to his image.

* * *

When a spontaneous protest erupted in downtown Damascus on 17 February 2011, after a young shopkeeper in the Hariqa shopping area was insulted and beaten up by security forces, it sent shockwaves around the country—not just because it had happened in the first place, but because Syrians had dared to film it openly, holding their phones high with outstretched arms as they chanted 'the Syrian people will not be humiliated!' The young man's friends and commercial neighbours could no longer bear the gratuitous violence of these non-uniformed security forces, more powerful than the police and impossible to confront—until that moment.

This scene stupefied everyone. We watched the quickly uploaded clips online, the raw shaky footage spreading like wildfire on our social media. We recognised the streets and the awnings of the shops, and saw the famous white domes of Al Darwishiah Mosque in the background. I had expected to see a few dozen people protesting, but there were hundreds crammed in the area, chanting as people came out on their balconies and joined them. When the police arrived, they surrounded their cars and shouted 'thieves, thieves' repeatedly.

The regime was just as stunned as we were, and quickly sent in its operatives who started counter-chants of 'with our soul, with our blood, we sacrifice ourselves for you, Bashar.' None of the protesters had mentioned him, but the regime is a one-trick pony: in case of doubt, praise the leader. The minister of the interior had rushed to the scene to try to limit the damage done with a mixture of cajoling and warnings as he stood by his car, telling them not to turn this into a demonstration and promising that the culprits would be punished for their violence on the young civilian.

That incident is an important one to recall as we recount the history of the Syrian people's search for dignity and freedom, and how they began their descent into hell. The Arab Spring did not 'reach Syria' as has been endlessly repeated in retrospectives of the region. It may very well be that protesters in Tunis, Cairo, and Tripoli had opened the way, and that they had indirectly influenced Syrians to stand up for their rights as well. And it is undeniable that the brave protesters in these countries encouraged those in other countries to also make their demands.

The Syrians' Arab Spring, however, had already started years before in Damascus with young people's hopes, with the initiatives of those who signed letters to push for reform, with the pleas from writers and artists and economists and architects and doctors who presented ideas and offered solutions that would help the country they loved. Bashar Assad's intransigence, greed, and megalomania had ensured none of that, and none of them, would matter.

We did not know it then, and we still thought a full-fledged revolution was unlikely given our forty-year history with this regime, but all hell was about to break loose. Weeks before the children of Daraa's graffiti had proclaimed 'Your turn has come, Doctor,' as these young men in Damascus had finally refused to accept the continued affront to their dignity, as they stood tall and proud documenting their rejection of this abuse and their discontent to the world, it was clear that something had finally snapped.

That's the thing: as the communications adage goes, nothing kills a bad product faster than good advertising, and people now knew full well that Bashar's promised winds of change had been nothing but dust in the wind.

PART THREE

THE REVOLUTION FOR DIGNITY

11

ANATOMY OF EXTERMINATION

A few months before Hafez's death, one of our accomplished relatives had been surprised to be appointed minister in a new government, the first openly Bashar-dictated cabinet about which he—still without an official position—gave statements to Syrian media. My father's cousin was a man who believed he should give back to his country, even though his studies and PhD in the UK and Switzerland had been privately financed by his family. A competent, erudite, open-minded man, he was a rare case in Syrian government of being the right man for the job in his field of expertise. Having people like him entrusted with important portfolios and, above all, allowed to do their job and improve the situation in matters of high national interest, was a good thing. He had been given no choice in the matter of his appointment, much as my own father had been appointed a decade earlier, without being first asked, to lead Syria's negotiations with Israel, but he gave his best upon his appointment in March 2000.

On 13 December 2001, Bashar Assad named another government, in the same manner as he had the one before it, but for the first time in his official capacity as president. Our relative walked out of his office shortly after the announcement, at the end of the day, and waited for his car and driver at the entrance. They never came, and it was a guard who informed him that his car was not available any longer as he was no longer the minister in the new government. This respectable man found himself walking out of his own ministry to stand on a busy Damascus street trying to find a taxi to get himself home, shocked at the disrespect he had just been needlessly shown. As he told the family later, the manner of his dismissal had been as abrupt as his appointment: in both cases, nobody spoke with him, nobody asked him if he would consider becoming a minister, and nobody had told him that his duties were coming to an end until the decree came out.

His case was far from unique; the regime dealt with most people in this manner. One of my acquaintances was an economist who had been told by a highly placed regime official that he was to be named minister in the upcoming government. It was a done deal, even though nobody discussed it with him. Fully assured that he would have to take up that position in a matter of days, he told the staff at his small consultancy the office would remain open, and that they would keep their jobs even though he would not be with them. The next day, the new cabinet was announced on the news, and Assad had changed his mind again, naming another person who had not expected it. Stories like these were a dime a dozen.

Losing a job like that mattered, but what mattered just as much was the manner in which such positions were given, whether considered a reward or an imposition, and then taken away just as arbitrarily. It would have cost the prime minister nothing to give his minister and the rest of the cabinet a courtesy call to inform them of such consequential decisions; then again, he probably did not know himself until the last minute.

ANATOMY OF EXTERMINATION

As with royal appointments throughout history, when people were moved around and things were done at His Majesty's pleasure, so were they in Assad's twenty-first-century Syria. But with everything being subject to the whims of this ill-equipped and temperamental ruler, the slightest deviations from complete submission were considered an affront to him, and to his kingdom—even if it was a partial disagreement, or a counsel or professional opinion that he disliked, because he knew best. As in all such realms, lèse-majesté was an offense punishable by any means the monarch deemed suitable. Syrians (and many Lebanese) spent the next ten years discovering the high cost of displeasing him as they learned that there was only ever one dignity that mattered.

* * *

When protests had erupted in other Arab countries at the end of 2010, Bouthaina Shaban had gotten very excited. In her column of 31 January 2011 for the Saudi newspaper *Asharq Alawsat*, Bashar Assad's senior advisor had gleefully wondered: 'Has the moment come when Arab masses take to the streets to force their will on their governments, the governments which for decades have imposed their will, slogans, failures and disagreements over millions of them and without achieving their hopes and aspirations?' Her question seemed to be rhetorical, because she exuded confidence that the answer would be a resounding yes from practically every Arab country, except her own. In the warped mind of hardcore Assadists, the Assads were cut from another cloth, of course, but her confidence must have also stemmed from the knowledge that forty years of repression had frozen Syrians' incentives to achieve their aspirations. Who in the regime would even ask such a question if they believed there was the slightest chance a Syrian would dare respond yes to that about their own turf?

IT STARTED IN DAMASCUS

That same day, an interview with Bashar Assad was published by the *Wall Street Journal*, in which he posited that unlike other rulers in the region, he was immune to the anger of his struggling population: 'We have growth although we do not have many of the basic needs for the people; despite all that, the people do not go into an uprising,' he boasted. Such assuredness must have not completely persuaded the Syrians for whom he was speaking, judging from the spontaneous outburst of anger in Hariqa a couple of weeks later, and from the March uprising Assad was sure would not happen.

Assad's conceit was more than matched by his wife's own borderless vanity. For the March edition of *Vogue*, Asma Assad orchestrated the publication of an astonishingly vacuous puff piece titled 'A Rose in the Desert,' a piece for which it later emerged she had demanded full editorial control. Not only did it glorify her physical image and style, a given for an iconic fashion magazine, but it also waxed poetic about her and her husband's 'wildly democratic principles'—applied at home with their children, allegedly, if not with the struggling population. Ironically, the piece claimed her central mission was to change the mindset of six million Syrians under eighteen, encouraging them to engage in what she called 'active citizenship'—something they and others could hardly wait to do when the protests began.

As they lectured from their thrones, it would have looked to the untrained eye like the Assads had neither gauged the temperature in the country after ten years of empty promises, nor even noticed the extent of the population's growing resentment. They had suddenly granted Syrians the right to access major social media platforms that had been blocked until 8 February, including Facebook, Twitter, YouTube, and Blogger, all vital elements of communication that would unite Syrians in their revolution. The simmering pot that was noticeable to everyone else, the rumbling emanating from the population that Assad himself had already conceded lacked many basic needs, did not worry the aloof Assads much, however. Comfortably perched atop their gilded tower, they were certain that nobody would protest in the way others in the region had done, not because they had nothing to complain about, but because they would not dare. The regime had spent the past four decades training Syrians to be docile, to accept their fate, to fear dissent and avoid trouble; they knew the consequences they would have to bear if they poked at its supremacy and forgot the lessons of Hama.

That is why when the first signs of protest began to appear, it was not news to the Assad regime members and all the accompanying cliques that the population had had enough of their restrictive lives as they watched the velvet society live it up at their expense. What was new, and what shocked them, was the fact that the Syrian people now seemed determined to do something about it, to challenge the regime directly. That, in itself, was a revolution.

* * *

Like everyone else in the region, Syrians had been watching on the edge of their seats the live coverage of protests as they spread in Tunisia, Egypt, and Libya. The resounding calls of massive crowds demanding the fall of Arab regimes were electrifying, resonating in the homes of millions around the Arab world who had never imagined such events could be possible. Like their regime, most Syrians were quite certain that this would not happen in their own country, well aware of what the regime would do if they dared to make a move. Full of youthful energy and driven by their rebellious teen spirit, however, some children in Daraa were not as reticent in voicing their own demands: adopting the Arab Spring slogan 'The people want the downfall of the regime,' they sprayed it on a school wall and added the ominous 'Your turn has come, Doctor.'

IT STARTED IN DAMASCUS

On 6 March, security officers arrested nineteen schoolboys they determined were responsible for this graffiti and held them in one of the state's security branches. For days, their concerned parents searched for them as word spread about their disappearance; forming a group of leaders from other well-known families and elders, they went to Atef Najib, head of Political Security and cousin of Bashar Assad, to demand the release of their children. He derisively told these apprehensive fathers to forget they ever had these children and to go home and make new ones with their wives, adding: 'If you don't manage, bring us your wives and we will do it for you.'

This was not an impetuous reaction, but a calculated affront to the dignity of these proud Syrian men of the conservative region of Hauran. Like so many of the regime's deliberate humiliations, it was like a punch in the gut of people the regime thought were still shackled by fear, unable to respond. That March of 2011, in Daraa, it was this insult that broke the first link in the chain that had held the people back all these years.

15 March had already been declared a Day of Rage on the Facebook page of the Syrian Revolution and shared on the newly accessible social media, but it only led to small protests filmed in Damascus and Aleppo, without creating much traction yet, especially as the regime stood ready to apprehend protesters. On 18 March, however, numerous demonstrations sprouted all around Syria after Friday prayers, and the regime began shooting into the crowds, killing several in Daraa as news of these events was spreading to other Syrian cities. Two days later, furious protesters set fire to the Baath Party office in Daraa, an incident which finally seems to have triggered Assad to intervene by sending a negotiator, but not a diplomat. Of all the people he could have sent to Daraa, he chose General Rustom Ghazaleh, the man who had helped him bring chaos to Lebanon. Ghazaleh finally agreed to release the children two weeks after their arrest, in a

belated attempt to pacify people. He thought that would be the end of it and that the parents would not dare to take it further.

When the children arrived home, their families were shocked to discover their physical state and the extent of the mistreatment and torture to which they had been subjected; they had marks of beatings all over their bodies, broken limbs, and fractured skulls, wounds whose images were shared online as outrage spread. With all Syrian eyes now on Daraa, the protesters quickly grew from hundreds to thousands; the more protests, the more the regime fired into the crowds and killed more people on a daily basis. This turned each funeral into an occasion for more people to come out and chant against the regime, and for the regime to shoot and kill even more, only for their funerals to be even bigger the following day, and for the killings to increase as well.

On the night of 23 March, Syrian special forces violently stormed Al Omari Mosque where protesters had gathered for safety, killing five and wounding many. A significant historic site dating back to the seventh century, the mosque was built in the era of Caliph Omar Ibn El Khattab, a revered Muslim figure who was a companion of the Prophet. By then, the regime had killed thirty-seven unarmed civilians since the protests had begun less than a week before, and the video footage of the assault on the mosque shocked and enraged even more people around Syria.

Facing this massive outrage, Assad replaced the Governor the next day, and removed his cousin Atef Najib from his post, but he never apologised or reached out to the people of Daraa, or even just to the parents whose children had been abused by his forces. Assad's actions thus far were typical of his haughty character, revealing once more that his self-perceived majestic position meant he did not have to admit failure or show empathy, let alone regret. People would soon start to lose steam, he must have assumed.

Thinking this would calm matters quicker, he had his advisor Bouthaina Shaban announce a new decree reducing taxes and raising the salaries of government employees by 1,500 Syrian pounds (about thirty US Dollars). In response, in a pointed reminder that this was about their dignity, protesters at the funerals for the people killed in Al Omari Mosque began chanting 'Ya Bouthaina Ya Shaban, the Syrian people are not hungry' and 'the Syrian people will not be humiliated.' The regime shot into the crowds again, killing another fifteen unarmed Syrians who were burying their fellow civilian compatriots. By Friday 25 March, the Assad regime had killed nearly sixty Syrians, and protesters all over Syria were coming out of Friday prayers to chant 'with our soul, with our blood, we sacrifice ourselves for you, Daraa.'

On 30 March, Bashar Assad decided to pour a huge canister of fuel into the fire, with an address to parliament watched live by millions of Syrians who had been waiting for an apology, a promise, condolences, a pledge to right the wrongs of the last weeks, and to rectify the mistakes of the last years. Instead, Assad spat out a crazy, rambling diatribe accusing protesters of sedition, of being foreign agents and conspirators against the nation, of attempting to cause sectarian strife, of being armed, and of killing people at random. He accused foreign news channels of incitement, causing unrest, and spreading lies. He even compared the Daraa events to 'what happened in 2005' (referring to his hasty exit from Lebanon) and the virtual war on Syria then. He also listed all the reasons that prevented him from committing to his promised reforms, starting with the attacks of 11 September 2001. The only promise he made to the people was that the conspiracy would fail, to enthusiastic applause from the parliamentarians.

Assad might as well have declared the official launch of the Syrian Revolution at the end of his preposterous speech. In the days that followed, he fought the conspiracy by inserting the message 'Bashar Assad, we love you' in packs of bread sold in government bakeries, and by suddenly deciding to grant Syrian citizenship to tens of thousands of Kurds, lest they decide to join the conspiracy as well. Two weeks after the first speech, he spoke again to announce the end of the state of emergency that had been the law since 1963, a puzzling measure at best when Syria was allegedly being attacked by such a massive conspiracy, as he had explained. Mostly though, Assad continued killing his way through peaceful demonstrations and funerals on repeat.

* * *

During the first weeks of the revolution, several journalists had asked me and other Syrians about our optimism on Syria's prospects now that the Arab Spring had reached it, as they put it. They wanted to know when I thought Damascus would experience a Tahrir Square moment, referring to the tens of thousands of Egyptians who had gathered there for eighteen days until President Hosni Mubarak resigned. They even asked what the chances were of Assad fleeing the country, like the Tunisian dictator Zein Al Abidine Ben Ali had after a month of protests.

I had been working on and writing about Syria for over a decade by then, and already knew just how much the nature and the modus operandi of this regime remained a mystery to most media, even to Middle East regulars. The Assads would never leave voluntarily, I explained repeatedly, and there would never be a Tahrir moment—not because there were not enough Syrians who dreamt of seeing the end of the regime, but because potential protesters would be arrested, or shot and killed before even getting to the main squares of Damascus. Public spaces were off limits to large numbers of people; the only way Syrians could gather was for Friday prayers at mosques, and that is why demonstrations started happening every Friday as men finished midday prayers, often joined by others as the demonstration proceeded.

IT STARTED IN DAMASCUS

Despite our certitude that Syrians would never be able to have their liberation in that manner, there was one point about which I was particularly, foolishly confident: the regime would not be able to massacre Syrians as it had in Hama, I rationalised, because this time the world was watching and would not allow it. I was proved wrong very quickly. We knew the Syrian regime only responded to credible threats to its survival; that is why it had expelled Abdullah Ocalan and his PKK at the eleventh hour when the Turkish army was positioned close to the border, why it had stopped grandstanding on Iraq's invasion, and why it had withdrawn from Lebanon in 2005. What we did not know, having believed that declared red lines and promises of 'never again' mattered, was that the powers who could issue similar credible warnings to stop Assad just never did.

Many Syrians could not help but feel energised, even slightly hopeful at the beginning. The first protests took our breath away when we saw all these hurt, indignant people suddenly dare to face regime forces and demand a life of dignity. At first scattered in small groups, they became better organised as their protest sizes grew with the mounting number of casualties. We watched regime snipers openly shoot on unarmed civilians in broad daylight, and, the next day, shoot on the funeral processions of those it had killed. As of March 2011, in Daraa and beyond, not a day passed in Syria without casualties; as the killing methods multiplied, so did the daily number of victims, from a few, to dozens, to hundreds all over Syria.

There was a blatant logic to the Assad regime's systematic responses to the peaceful protests; they all aimed at breaking Syrians' spirits, eradicating the mere notion of change, driving them to despair, and then back to resignation. The regime was going to beat to a pulp every attempt at personal initiative for civic and political participation, crushing the very basic freedoms the protesters—and all those who for decades had tried to be heard—were demanding. It was an extermination of any inkling of hope, done step by step, little by little. For having lost their fear of the regime, Syrians had to be terrorised into submission again. Besides, regime supporters quickly adopted and spread the menacing slogan 'Assad or we burn the country'—a dichotomy they took literally.

To try to contain and punish Daraa, birthplace of the Syrian Revolution, Assad imposed a full siege in April 2011, a measure that would be replicated all around Syria as more people joined the uprising. Syrians were shocked to see electricity, water, and phone networks cut off from the city that was encircled by the army, when its inhabitants' only crime had been to manifest their anger after the arrest and torture of school children. In a show of solidarity, a petition was signed by over a thousand public figures around Syria, including many well-known writers, directors, and actors, demanding that the state allow access to food and milk for the sake of the children of Daraa, who could not be accused of being conspirators. It became known in Syria as the Milk Statement, and it enraged the regime. Not only did the siege continue, but many of the Statement's signatories were pressured and harassed into retracting their positions, and then paraded on Syrian television to describe the uprising as lies, conspiracies, and treason.

Two weeks after Human Rights Watch had documented in a new report that the torture of protesters was rampant in Syria, 13-year-old Hamza Khatib joined his father and several members of his family in a peaceful demonstration in Daraa on 29 April calling for the end of the regime's siege. When security forces began shooting at the crowd in Jiza, on the outskirts of Daraa, the boy ran amidst the chaos and was separated from his father, who soon found out he had been arrested. Just over three weeks later, Hamza's horribly disfigured body was delivered to his parents. Even though they had been ordered to immediately bury him, friends of the grieving family photographed and filmed Hamza, and the horrific images quickly spread online and on some television channels. Young Hamza had been heavily beaten, lacerated, burned with cigarettes, and tortured so badly his body had turned purple and was bloated nearly beyond recognition. His jaw and kneecaps were shattered, and, in an act of utmost savagery, the boy's genitals had been mutilated.

The regime's primary goal in returning the body was terrorism in its simplest sense, intimidation to scare others from daring to protest and show them what would happen to their loved ones, and even their children, if they persisted. Instead, the images of this new level of cruelty incensed Syrians everywhere and sent them in droves into the streets, chanting 'We are all Hamza Khatib'—much like 'We are all Khaled Said' had become the rallying cry of protesters in Egypt months earlier, after the 28-year-old man had died in police custody in Alexandria. The popular indignation at Hamza's torture and death became so widespread that the regime had to broadcast a response on Addounia television, in which a doctor who claimed he had supervised his autopsy said the boy had been killed by armed gangs but not tortured, and that his body had merely decomposed as authorities tried to find his parents.

* * *

The killing of peaceful demonstrators, young and old, had just been the start. Soon, the regime turned its attention to the thought leaders, the pacifists, the creatives, the idealists, the writers, the dreamers, all considered much greater threats to the regime than armed factions. With every one of these killings, Assad amplified the status of these icons of the revolution, even as he tried to push the peaceful uprising into an armed one that would justify a ferocious response and give people a false dichotomy between the state and 'terrorists.' These were the events that continued to fuel Syrian anger and sorrow, the acts of brutality that drove more people to the streets to say enough, the unhinged escalation of unilateral violence that many of the regime's apologists would later ignore as they decried an alleged civil war.

In September 2011, the bold, beautiful, and brilliant youth of Daraya, a town on the outskirts of Damascus known for its cultivation of grapes, became the epitome of dignified non-violent activism, brandishing flowers and distributing cold water bottles to the security forces tasked with repressing them. Among them were Yahya and Maan Cherbaji, and Ghiath Matar, all arrested for daring to defy Assad.

Twenty-six-year-old Ghiath was a tailor and a leader in Daraya's youth movement. Arrested during one of these peaceful protests, he was tortured for four days until he succumbed at the hands of the regime's abusers. His sadistically tortured body was thrown in front of his pregnant wife's front door a few days later, as a warning to others in the peaceful activism circle of the fate that awaited them should they proceed with their calls for dignity and freedom with flowers and refreshing water. The senseless torture and death of Little Gandhi, as he was known because of his commitment to nonviolent activism, made of him one of the lasting icons of the revolution. It took seven agonising years of waiting for the Cherbaji family to receive news of their beloved disappeared sons; in 2018, they were informed that Yahya had been executed in January 2013, and that Maan finally succumbed to his tormentors in December 2013.

In October 2011, the regime assassinated the popular Kurdish opposition leader Michal Tammo, a strong proponent of a pluralistic democratic Syria with equal rights for all. His murder ensured that potential for a united Arab-Kurdish opposition would fade quickly without seasoned, well-liked people like Tammo to play a leading part in it. Having denied Kurds most of their civic rights for decades, the regime spent the next years in a strategic ménage à trois with the Kurdish armed factions led by the PKK (whose activities in Syria had flourished again under Bashar after Hafez Assad had kicked them out) and its Syrian branch the PYD, even as they worked under the US umbrella in the oil-rich eastern region.

Bassel Shehadeh was a young filmmaker who had joined the early peaceful demonstrations. He had gotten arrested in Midan, Damascus but was released just in time to start his Master's Degree in Film Production at Syracuse University in the US, through the Fulbright scholarship he had been granted before the revolution had begun. Feeling he could not stay away while his compatriots struggled, he abandoned his scholarship and returned to Syria, dedicating himself to training as many citizen journalists and revolutionaries as he could in filming and documenting events. He was killed in May 2012 by regime gunfire in Homs, with several others, and buried there. When many of his devastated Damascene friends tried to conduct prayers for him at his local church in Damascus, they were blocked by security forces.

In November 2012, regime forces barged into the home of respected Damascene intellectual and economist Omar Aziz, confiscating his and his wife's phones and computers while arresting him for having helped distribute aid in besieged areas of Damascus, and for guiding revolutionaries' organisational capacities. They had learned that Aziz had helped found the first local council in Barzeh, Damascus, leading to the creation of the Local Coordination Committees that would spread all over Syria, connecting with one another, learning the concepts of self-governance, of keeping records of all events and casualties, and of providing the civil society structure that Syrians needed. In his discussion paper on local councils in Syria, he wrote: 'A revolution is an exceptional event that will alter the history of societies, while changing humanity itself. It is a rupture in time and space, where humans live between two periods: the period of power and the period of revolution. A revolution's victory, however, is ultimately achieving the independence of its time in order to move into a new era.' His poor health deteriorating quickly from ill treatment and torture, Aziz died in prison in February 2013.

Bassel Khartabil (known online as Safadi) was a young Palestinian-Syrian open-source software developer. An advocate of free speech and peaceful resistance, he ran Aiki Lab from Damascus, a collaborative technology and art space that offered tools for Syrians to communicate and share their work online, and that became a Creative Commons affiliate. In 2012, he was ranked by the magazine *Foreign Policy* as the nineteenth most influential thinker for 'insisting, against all odds, on a peaceful Syrian revolution.' Khartabil was arrested by the regime in March 2012, and charged in December with spying for an enemy state even while a strong international solidarity campaign was pushing for his release, with the participation of technology giants including Mozilla and Wikipedia. Allowed to marry his sweetheart while still in jail, he then disappeared as his wife and family desperately sought news. In August 2017, they found out he had been executed two years prior in Adra Prison.

Rami Hennawi, a pacifist from Suwayda, joined his city's peaceful demonstrations against the abuses of the regime. He would be arrested in 2012 and tortured for years, a manifestation of the regime's knowledge and fear of the strong underground opposition to Assad in this predominantly Druze area. It was only in April 2018 that his distraught family was informed he had died in prison, although his body was never returned to them so they could bury him.

None of these Syrians had ever carried arms, nor had thousands of others like them who were killed by the Assad regime for wanting freedom and for helping others seek it peacefully. They were all eliminated one by one until there were no more flowers left, not even to throw on their graves. Assad killed the peaceful, killed the thoughtful, and along the way also killed the world's conscience, and got away with it.

* * *

Syrians' online skills gradually improved as the revolution expanded. Very quickly, the Facebook page of the Syrian Revolution grew to nearly two million followers on a platform that had only just been unblocked to Syrians, and there was a proliferation of new YouTube accounts that uploaded videos of the protests, the repression, and the horrors to which Syrians were subjected, but also the meaningful and the beautiful moments of the revolution, and the characters that played a role in unifying Syrians in search of dignity. Assad's crimes, and those of his enablers, were amply documented as they happened; we discovered that the regime's men often filmed their own acts of violence on protesters, prisoners, and other people, and their clips were either shared directly on regime-friendly pages, or found on the phones of captured or killed regime soldiers and officials when the revolution turned into an armed conflict.

Just like the Assad clique had never been shy about any of its excesses, these were not men who were trying to hide their crimes. More notably, they had not committed them reluctantly, displaying nothing but glee at the despair of their victims. The regime's pyramid of violence and corruption, built over decades, had increased the sadistic leanings of many who revelled in showing normal Syrians that they were superior to them, and that protesters would pay dearly for their audacity in rising up and in demanding freedom.

During that initial period of peaceful protests, security and armed forces would scornfully shout 'Is this the freedom you want?' at Syrians in their custody, seen on countless clips shared by the perpetrators themselves as they slapped, beat, kicked, abused, and then sometimes shot the poor souls who had dared go to demonstrations, or who had dared to smuggle food to besieged areas, or who had dared to treat those wounded by Assad's thugs. Many other clips showed them abusing prisoners as they repeated 'Who is your god?' until battered men, sometimes boys, were forced to respond 'Bashar Assad.'

At the same time, however, defections in the ranks of regime forces had also begun to spread, with memorable scenes of armed soldiers being carried on the shoulders of grateful compatriots they had vowed to protect. Many Syrians were brought to tears as they watched videos of army officers showing their ID cards, giving their name and rank, declaring they would not turn their guns on their compatriots. The first to defect in that manner was Lieutenant Colonel Hussein Harmoush, bringing his ID card up close to the camera so viewers could read it as he announced the creation of a Brigade of Free Officers. Videos soon appeared of other officers, and even of entire squads defecting, announced by their leader on camera. One of these defections warmed many hearts when the leader of the defected group of soldiers signed off with a heartfelt 'Long Live Assad's Syria' out of habit, as the entire group behind him burst out laughing and he signed off again with 'Long Live Free Syria.'

Colonel Riad Asaad, who had defected from the Syrian Air Force in July 2011 to join the Free Officers, was the founding leader of the Free Syrian Army (FSA) and was its Commander-in-Chief in the early phases. Slowly, the FSA began to take shape, giving many people hope that more would join in refusing to kill other Syrians, sparing the country from the ravages of the Assad regime's vengeance. As the FSA grew, but more specifically as the regime's violence increased exponentially, more of the revolution's initial protesters joined the armed resistance to the regime. Without substantive supplies, and without the air support that protected the regime and its many Syrian and non-Syrian militias, the FSA was heavily outnumbered. Still, some of its figures, whether they were soldiers or civilians, reached legendary status amongst many Syrians praying for liberation from the regime.

We had all watched a man in the early days of the revolution, teary-eyed, his voice hoarse and cracking as he recounted the humiliating and painful abuse he and others had received, as soldiers had shoved them, stepping on their necks with their boots. 'I am a human being, not an animal, and all these millions of people are like me,' he had cried, his words like daggers to our hearts as the clip became another defining moment of the revolution, as violence escalated and refugees fled in greater numbers. A year and a half later, he reappeared on a new clip, armed and in military uniform, declaring he, Mohammad Ahmad Abdelwahab, was now at the head of a squad with the FSA in Khirbet Al Jouz in northern Syria. The dignity he could not receive as a civilian had driven him to pick up arms.

Colonel Youssef Al Jader, known as Abu Furat, had defected in June 2012 and joined the revolution after refusing to follow orders to attack the Al Haffa region north of Latakia. Back in his town of Jarablus, east of Aleppo, he led *Liwa Al Tawhid* (The Oneness of God Brigade) as part of the FSA and helped take parts of Aleppo from the regime. Upon liberating the Infantry Academy, he lamented the situation in a widely shared clip: 'I am sad because these tanks are our tanks, the ammunition is ours, these soldiers are our brothers, and I swear every time I see one of us or one of them killed I am upset.' Many Syrians mourned him when he was killed by regime forces in December 2012, at the same Infantry Academy where he had touched the hearts of so many.

In that same *Liwa Al Tawhid* was the prominent and charismatic figure of Abdul Qader Al Saleh, known affectionately as Hajji Marea, a civilian who had evolved from organising peaceful demonstrations to joining the FSA as a leader in the brigade that grew to some 8,000 fighters. Wounded several times, Hajji Marea

ANATOMY OF EXTERMINATION

had gained a following when people discovered his bravery at the frontlines, always at the side of his men raising their spirits. He was so well-known that the regime had a bounty on his head. When a regime airstrike killed him by the Infantry Academy in November 2013, he was buried in a grave he and his men had already dug themselves in anticipation of victims from the intense bombing. Countless young, liberal, secular Syrians changed their profile pictures on social media to display his smiling face, in mourning for a fighter they viewed as a simple, pious, honest man who had fought for their collective right to freedom and dignity.

* * *

From the beginning of the revolution, one small town in southern Idlib Province had become a media sensation with its depiction of all these opponents of Syrian revolutionaries. I instantly equated Kafranbel with the fictional indomitable Gaul village in the French comic series *Asterix*, often attacked by Romans but inevitably victorious because of its inhabitants' tenacity and the magic potion that made them invincible. Kafranbel's magic potion was its banners that Syrians, and eventually the world at large, waited to discover every Friday. With humour and irony, with precision, with immense creativity in Arabic and in English, these legendary banners gave a running commentary on events and created a history of the Syrian Revolution, of its suppression in the most violent manner, and of its desertion by the world. Their creator, founder of Radio Fresh and the Kafranbel Media Centre, was revolutionary icon Raed Fares, a Syrian opposed to both regime and Islamist groups like so many of his compatriots. Having survived assassination attempts and numerous airstrikes, he was shot and killed in November 2018 by unknown assailants, along with his colleague Hamood Jneed, killings that locals blamed on Islamist groups.

IT STARTED IN DAMASCUS

In December 2013, prominent human rights defenders and observers Razan Zaitouneh, Samira Khalil, Wael Hamada and Nazim Hammadi were abducted from their joint office at the Violations Documentation Center in Douma, greater Damascus, a centre founded when the protests began in early 2011. They were most instrumental in investigating and exposing war crimes committed by the regime, including as eyewitnesses to the 2013 chemical massacre in Ghouta, on which they provided vivid testimony to international sources and media. As of this writing, their fate remains unknown, but it is widely believed that an Islamist militia, possibly in cahoots with the regime, is responsible for the disappearance of the group.

Like the Douma Four, as these revolutionaries became affectionately known by revolutionaries, the fate of Father Paolo Dall'Oglio remains unknown. Father Paolo was an Italian Jesuit priest whose attachment to Syria and involvement with Syrians' quest for freedom was profound. When he took part in the funeral of Bassel Shehadeh, leading prayers for his fellow Christian, Father Paolo was issued an expulsion order by the Syrian regime. He left Syria in June 2012 but could not bear to stay away; he came back in July 2013, only to be kidnapped by ISIS (Islamic State of Iraq and Syria) as he walked in the city of Raqqa. His fate remains unknown, but his name and the memory of his acts of kindness, his morality, and his wisdom are ever present in Syrian minds.

These were some of the highly recognisable and beloved figures of the Syrian Revolution, and there are many others whose bravery and devotion to the cause of Syrian freedom and dignity have been widely documented. Hundreds of pages would not suffice to give justice to their collective actions and words that Syrians treasure and honour to this day. There is one figure, however, who seems to have taken up a slightly bigger space in Syrian hearts and memory, one whose name and voice began to resonate with us all in the early days. Daraa had been the birthplace of the revolution, but protests increased in size and frequency elsewhere, as did the repression. After a sit-in by thousands of peaceful demonstrators had gone on for days at the Clock Tower Square in central Homs, regime forces surrounded the demonstration and launched an assault on thousands of unarmed civilians in the middle of the night of 18 to 19 April 2011. The exact number of victims remains unknown, as regime forces quickly removed the dozens of bodies before the day had broken. By then, Homs had become the capital of the revolution.

Abdel Basset Sarout was the goalkeeper for Al Karama Football Club. Aged nineteen when the revolution started, he joined the peaceful protests in Homs and began to lead them through chants and songs with his husky voice and simple melodic style. *'Janna wallah ya watanna'* (our nation is paradise), he would sing as hundreds swayed, chanted, and jumped together as they had in the football matches they used to attend. Sarout would be joined on occasion by Syrian actress Fadwa Suleiman and the two would lead chants of 'One one one, the Syrian people are one,' cherishing the unity that the regime wanted to break and showing their refusal to 'sectarianise.' These remain some of the most meaningful memories of the revolution for many Syrians—a popular Sunni football player, and a beautiful Alawi actress, together in song and in hope for their country, seeing themselves and each other only as free Syrians.

In the months following that first massacre in Homs, the Free Syrian Army took control of several areas in the city. The regime's devastating assault on the Baba Amr area began in February 2012, as armed forces incessantly shelled and killed hundreds of trapped civilians. Like many others by this point, Sarout had decided to take up arms and join the Free Syrian Army. We still saw him singing sadder songs, huddled at night in small rooms with other fighters, holding his weapon in between battles. As the regime's pounding increased, Sarout formed the Bayada Martyrs Battalion, whose fighters were nearly all killed. When Homs had been decimated and many of its inhabitants forcibly displaced by the regime in 2014, Sarout headed north and became distinctly Islamist-leaning, now viewing jihadist groups as the only ones capable of fighting the regime. The days when he sang 'the Syrian people are one' with Fadwa seemed so far away; she had fled to France, and he to religious struggle.

Sarout's trajectory was captured in Syrian director Talal Derki's film *Return to Homs*, and it seemed that Sarout had returned to his non-Islamist roots after a period of disillusionment and hiding from various groups. He resurfaced in 2018 fighting with the Jaish Al Izza faction, affiliated with the Free Syrian Army, only to be killed in June 2019 by regime artillery in northern Hama, at the age of twenty-seven, the last of five Sarout brothers to die under regime fire. His death triggered a rush of emotions in revolutionary and opposition circles, who saw how regime brutality and world apathy had affected him. This charismatic, earnest goalkeeper had gone from peaceful chants to armed resistance, then to extremist groups, and then finally back full circle to continue fighting for a Syria that was free of the Assad regime. The Syria he sang about with Fadwa when their dreams felt achievable, when the regime appeared to be faltering under the magnitude of the uprising, seemed distant; his Fadwa had passed away in exile, and both their voices were now silenced forever.

The revolution's goalkeeper, as Sarout continued to be known, was one of many who became and remained beloved icons of people who demanded freedom. There were many heroes in the military who did everything they could to avoid killing Syrian civilians, and many civilians who took up arms when they felt abandoned in the face of the regime's incessant assault. The more violent the regime became, as it quickly did, the more they

ANATOMY OF EXTERMINATION

armed themselves and fought back, which was exactly what Assad wanted to justify moving to the next level of repression.

Amidst so much more loss and pain, Syrians were holding on to their hope that diplomacy and serious political pressure would eventually bear fruit and restrain the regime.

12

DEATH OF AN ILLUSION

Syrians' descent into hell and the deluge of turmoil it triggered happened gradually at first, but rather predictably. And yet, even with the certainty that the regime would go to every length possible to maintain power and bring the population to its knees, it was one thing to imagine how much worse things could get, and quite another to live through the exponential increase of the regime's violence. Those who did not know it yet quickly discovered that hell hath no fury like an Assad scorned.

It took until the summer of 2011 for significant diplomatic action to emerge in response to the regime's actions. Qatar had been one of Syria's steady allies since facilitating the rehabilitation of Assad in 2008, ending years of Syrian isolation after Hariri's assassination. During the first weeks of protests, Qatar's Al Jazeera channel had been strangely subdued, not giving the Syrian demonstrations the same focused reporting it had given similar events in other Arab countries. Protests had at first been mentioned as news items, but without much elaboration and with none of the live coverage the channel was known for. Then suddenly, in the middle of April, something changed: Al Jazeera began showing demonstrations filmed by activists in Syria on a loop, city after city, sometimes without commenting, allowing the strong voice of the people to be heard loud and clear.

Since Qatar had held some sway over Assad, Al Jazeera's abrupt change could only mean that attempts by the Emir of Qatar to cajole Assad into taking a different approach with protesters would have been rejected by the Syrian dictator. In July, regime supporters stormed and damaged the Qatari embassy in Damascus because of that coverage; a few days later, Qatar withdrew its ambassador and closed its embassy for good on 18 July, four months after the start of the revolution.

Having tried behind the scenes since March to moderate Assad's response to the protests, Saudi Arabia also recalled its ambassador on 8 August and condemned Assad's killing machine, as did other Gulf countries. Ten days later, in a coordinated move, the US, Britain, France, and Germany called on Bashar Assad to resign, five months after the start of the revolution, and the following week, numerous members and factions of the opposition formed the Syrian National Council.

The Turkish position changed after weeks of diplomacy, and several trips and consultations by senior Turkish diplomats to convince Assad to choose a different path. Like Qatar, Turkey had invested much time and effort in its relations with Assad, which had led to a free trade agreement between the two countries and warm relations between Assad and then Prime Minister Recep Tayyip Erdoğan. In October 2009, the two countries had signed cooperation protocols in several fields, and Turkish and Syrian ministers lifted a bar at the border to symbolise the removal of visa restrictions between them. On that day, Turkish Foreign Minister Ahmet Davutoğlu had declared: 'From now on, Turkey will continue walking on the same road as Syria, sharing a common fate, history and future. We are going to walk hand in hand and work all together to revive our region as a centre of civilisation.'

DEATH OF AN ILLUSION

A year and a half later, these goals and the Turkish policy of 'zero problems' with the neighbours collapsed in one fell swoop when Bashar Assad refused to listen to any of his allies, triggering for Turkey a nightmare scenario of chaos on its southern border and the prospect of huge numbers of refugees. On 9 August 2011, Davutoğlu visited Damascus to try to end the crackdown after an estimated 2,000 people had already been killed by the regime. He was reported by the Turkish *Hürriyet* newspaper as saying: 'Stop crush on people or face Gadhafi's fate.' Covering the same meeting that day, Syrian news agency SANA wrote: 'He stressed that Syria under the leadership of President Assad will become a model in the Arab world after accomplishing the reforms announced by the Syrian leadership.' It was the last trip by a Turkish official to Damascus, and Turkey finally cut ties with Syria on 21 September, more than six months after the start of the revolution. So much for the conspiracy.

After all these states had given up on coaxing Assad into dealing with the protests differently, the League of Arab States made an eleventh-hour attempt, as an institution, to stop the killings. The attempt was short-lived. On 2 November 2011, the Arab League announced that Assad had accepted its proposal to immediately cease violence, free prisoners, and hold talks with the opposition. Ten days and some 300 more Syrians killed later, the Arab League suspended Syria's membership eight months after the start of the revolution, and imposed sanctions until Assad adhered to the plan he'd already accepted. On 27 November, the Arab League went a step further, imposing a travel ban on Syrian officials, suspending flights to Syria, and banning transactions with the Central Bank of Syria. This did not even slow Assad down.

Still, the Arab League tried again with a new proposal that would include dispatching monitors from different Arab countries, and Assad accepted again. Sixty-five monitors arrived in Syria on 26 December; one month later, they had all left after

IT STARTED IN DAMASCUS

having seen the killings, noticing army tanks that were barely hidden from sight before rolling out again the minute the monitors left the area, and being attacked in their official cars by a crowd of pro-Assad demonstrators as they drove off, more than ten months after the start of the revolution. They were never to return. Anwar Malek, a monitor from Algeria, resigned from his post even before the Arab League withdrew the entire team, telling Al Jazeera: 'What I saw was a humanitarian disaster. The regime is not just committing one war crime, but a series of crimes against its people. The snipers are everywhere, shooting at civilians. People are being kidnapped, prisoners are being tortured, and none were released.'

It had taken many months for Assad's closest allies, regional states, and the leading international powers to give up on him. They all tried to offer support for reforms and for redressing the situation nearly a year into the killings; he pretended to agree to transition plans, then carried on killing, and continued to get away with it. What Bashar Assad had called a conspiracy two weeks into the protests had never been anything but a true popular uprising. The countries he claimed were plotting against him had all been allies who tried to mitigate the fallout and find him a way out, repeatedly, for months on end. His vow to fight the conspiracy had never been anything but a violent crackdown on people who had dared demand dignity after waiting ten years for his vapid promises that never materialised. Even the member states of the Arab League could no longer put lipstick on that proverbial pig.

* * *

For the most part, even those old enough to remember the days of the 1982 Hama massacre had not seen actual sieges and mass killings with their own eyes; its thirtieth anniversary came while the same regime was holding part of another city under siege—

DEATH OF AN ILLUSION

Baba Amr, in Homs—and launching a new assault on Hama. And while Syrian activists were documenting every incident they could, some foreign journalists had managed to witness the regime in action as well, and paid the ultimate price for it.

On 11 January 2012, while Arab League monitors were still on their observer and reporting mission, France 2 reporter Gilles Jacquier had entered Syria on a government visa and been taken to Homs with Mother Agnes Mariam de la Croix, a nun who was one of the Assad regime's most ardent supporters and apologists, as his fixer. At her urging, the team left the local shops and the merchants they were interviewing and headed to another area where a pro-regime demonstration was taking place, probably for his and other reporters' benefit. While under the protection of the Syrian regime, just as he got there, a mortar shell landed on the group, killing him and seven others. The regime immediately claimed that the 'terrorists' who do not want the world's media to see the truth were responsible, but Caroline Poiron, Jacquier's wife and fellow journalist who was with him in Syria, co-authored an entire book named *Express Attack* (*Attentat Express: Qui a tué Gilles Jacquier?*) demonstrating how the Syrian regime deliberately targeted him.

On the night of 21 February 2012, prominent *Sunday Times* correspondent Marie Colvin spoke to several news channels live from Homs, to which she and other journalists had been smuggled so they could report freely on what they saw in Baba Amr, the district the regime had been pounding daily for three weeks. As she spoke with CNN's Anderson Cooper, her team's heart-wrenching footage showed the scenes of despair the world was only just beginning to discover. A bloodied baby with shrapnel in his chest lay struggling as a doctor tried to save him, but there was nothing they could do and the baby died: 'We just watched this little boy, his little tummy heaving and heaving as he tried to breathe. It was horrific, my heart broke,' she told Cooper.

IT STARTED IN DAMASCUS

She described more of the horrors she was seeing: 'There are more young men being killed, we see a lot of teenaged young men, but they are going out to just try to get the wounded to some kind of medical treatment. So it's a complete and utter lie that they're only going after terrorists. There are rockets, shells, tank shells, anti-aircraft being fired in parallel lines into the city. The Syrian Army is simply shelling a city of cold, starving civilians.'

Barely a few hours after her distressing live reporting from the heart of Baba Amr, *The Times* had splashed the headline 'Syria Slays Its Children' on its 22 February front page, under the image of a woman comforted as she mourned two of her sons killed the day before by the regime's mortar shells. By the time UK newsstands opened in the morning, Marie Colvin had been killed by the regime under a barrage of targeted shells, as had Rémi Ochlik, the French photographer accompanying her. Journalists Paul Conroy and Edith Bouvier, of *Le Figaro*, were wounded and escaped some time later.

Gilles Jacquier and Marie Colvin had been experienced and renowned war correspondents who had travelled the world; they survived every conflict they covered, until the Assad regime targeted them, killed them, and got away with it.

* * *

Assad's killing machine had gained traction. Not only was the frequency getting higher, but everything was audible and visible first hand as it became the norm to hear gunshots in many towns and neighbourhoods, and to watch the videos of rampant regime violence shown on major television networks available to all. Soon, army tanks were rolling into more cities as brave Syrians sometimes shouted 'We are unarmed, you are our brothers,' hoping this would prevent the soldiers from shooting. It rarely did.

Gunfire had successively given way to small artillery, to heavy artillery, to gunfire from low-flying helicopters, to barrel bombs

DEATH OF AN ILLUSION

dropped from those same helicopters, to airstrikes from Assad's air force. Then, massacres of a different kind began: mass slaughters were committed with guns and with knives, with a repeated use of chemical weapons, with a widespread imposition of starve-or-surrender sieges, and with the ongoing torture until death of thousands upon thousands of Syrians, as the documentation would prove later. The army was also killing defectors, or even suspected defectors, at every opportunity. In December 2011, around one hundred soldiers were killed in Jabal Al Zawiya, gunned down as they tried to escape orders to kill more Syrians.

The regime did not deny the massacres of civilians; it just blamed them all on the opposition, who were killing their own side just to blame the Syrian army and government, went the refrain. Thus, when Assad's thuggish militias known as shabiha killed forty-five people by slitting their throats and stabbing them in Karm El Zeytoun on 11 March 2012, regime media blamed terrorist gangs who were trying to discredit Syrian forces with these gruesome murders, especially as most of the victims were women and children. Yet, the regime never mourned or organised the funerals and burials of the thousands of Syrians killed by 'terrorists' over the years.

The presence of some three hundred United Nations unarmed observers, who had followed the Arab League's monitors, did absolutely nothing to deter the Assad regime, which suffered zero consequences no matter the level of brutality it unleashed on Syrians. On 25 May 2012, over one hundred civilians, of which half were young children, were killed in Houla, executed at close range by Assad's shabiha after the army had shelled them the day before. Horrific photos were increasingly shared on social media and covered on news networks the world over; people now knew how the Syrian people were being repressed, displaced, killed.

A week after Houla, in June, eighty-seven Syrians were killed by Assad's shabiha in Qubeir, in the province of Hama; some were found burned, others slashed with knives. The murders were so gruesome, yet again, that they pushed UN Secretary General Ban Ki-moon to declare that Assad had lost all legitimacy, saying: 'Any regime or leader that tolerates such killing of innocents has lost its fundamental humanity.' UN monitors trying to enter Qubeir to report on the massacre were even shot at, and prevented by the Syrian army from entering the area. And yet, Assad got away with it, as he would with many other, similarly ghastly massacres with dozens of victims each.

Then came Daraya, home of the Little Gandhis who had tried to preach non-violence with flowers and refreshing water, who had been killed for it, and whose fellow pacifists had been driven to join the Free Syrian Army to defend their people. Between 20 and 25 August 2012, the regime upped the ante once more, leading to more empty condemnations and a desperate global search for new superlatives expressing shock. It started on the second day of Eid Al Fitr, the holiday following the fasting month of Ramadan, when Syrian troops fired mortar shells, bombed Daraya from helicopters, and cut off power and communications in the town. Syrian soldiers then entered Daraya and went on a rampage, spraying people with bullets throughout the town, going on an orgy of mass slaughter. After the army withdrew a few days later, some seven hundred bodies—including those of sixty-three children—were found and buried in mass graves. Everyone condemned the horrific massacre again, and Assad got away with it.

Between 2 and 4 May 2013, security forces and shabiha targeted the coastal area of Tartous, heading first to Al Bayda, and then to the town of Baniyas. People were shot, houses were set on fire, and some two hundred Syrians were killed. Footage showed tangled bodies of men, women, and children, some mutilated, others burned and charred. By then, it was difficult to ignore the clearly sectarian pattern the regime was using, unleashing the shabiha, mostly Alawi, on civilian villages, mostly non-Alawi and primarily Sunni.

DEATH OF AN ILLUSION

Such massacres continued all throughout Syria, unabated, in addition to the other types of killings that now had become part of the daily Syrian routine. Since their creation in the early days of the revolution, the various Local Coordination Committees (LCCs) were trying to document the daily toll of victims in every Syrian locality, with as many details as possible. Like many others, they were cognisant of the need to commit their tragedy to memory, to ensure they were recording history. When Assad unleashed his war on Syrians soon after the revolution started, I had regularly posted the daily number of verified victims on my main social media accounts, often adding the caveat 'that we know of' and sometimes including an image of one or more of the victims. The numbers, posted daily on the LCCs' Facebook page (followed by hundreds of thousands of Syrians), had reached triple digits very early, and this did not account for what we assume were tens of thousands who remained under mounds of rubble, and tens of thousands who disappeared in Assad's jails and remain unfound at the time of writing.

It would take many pages to list the LCCs' depressing data, but a random overview from my notes over the years showed just how normalised the violent death of so many Syrians had become, how numbers became statistics everyone got accustomed to seeing, if even noticed, and then forgotten. In 2012, 217 Syrians were killed on 20 July, 200 on 21 August (falling under Eid), 118 on 26 August (not counting the victims of the Daraya massacre mentioned above), 248 on 30 September, 234 on 5 November, 161 on 20 November, 76 on 23 November, 168 on 26 November, 202 on 2 December, 239 on 4 December, 129 on 9 December, 142 on 10 December, 131 on 15 December, 161 on 19 December.

In 2013, the regime killed 228 Syrians on 30 January, 140 on 4 February, 157 on 7 February, 213 on 22 February, 149 on 5 March, 154 on 10 April, 157 on 17 April (Syria's national

IT STARTED IN DAMASCUS

holiday celebrating independence from France), and 566 on 22 April—of which around eighty were in a makeshift hospital in the Damascus area of Jdeydet Al Fadel. In 2014, the Assad regime killed 165 Syrians on 2 February and 134 the next day, 164—of which 36 were children—on 13 February and 141 the next day. By that time, of course, something even worse had happened, at least from the perspective of the international community, but these were the kinds of events happening in Syria on a daily basis, the crimes committed against people who still tried to hold on to their miserable lives and their homes, who still believed someone would eventually help.

Despite the horror, compared to what would follow, we still had seen nothing yet.

* * *

There was no doubt that the regime had begun to test the waters with its usage of chemical weapons, in small doses at first. That is why on 20 August 2012, US president Barack Obama felt he had to draw the red line that many people thought would be immutable. His statement may not have been the most eloquent, but it was easy to understand: 'We have been very clear to the Assad regime, but also to other players on the ground, that a red line for us is we start seeing a whole bunch of chemical weapons moving around or being utilised. That would change my calculus. That would change my equation.' In plainer language, the message to Assad was simple: do not use chemical weapons or I will have to intervene in Syria, and neither of us wants that. It was the 'don't make me come to your room' kind of warning that parents throw at kids when they cannot be bothered to deal with the hassle, but think is effective enough to keep them docile.

Exactly one year later, in the early hours of 21 August, Obama's calculus should have therefore changed when the regime he had warned did utilise 'a whole bunch' of chemical weapons that the

DEATH OF AN ILLUSION

US president could not pretend he did not see. That day, the world woke up to the most horrific images from Ghouta, on the outskirts of Damascus. There were hundreds of dead civilians, including many children, lying in their dozens side by side, some slightly on top of others, some with foam still coming out of their small mouths, with no blood in sight. The victims were so numerous that first responders and families had stuck pieces of paper on their foreheads or chests, with a hastily written number to keep count and later identify the hundreds of victims.

In several areas of Ghouta, in the locations of the attacks, frantic people were seen trying to hose down survivors with water in an attempt to wash off remnants of the deadly chemical, with no other real tools or medicine available. Ghouta had been under siege since April 2013; the regime had taken nearly everything from them, and now it had even taken the air that they breathed.

Taking in all the sounds of people crying, sobbing, wailing in agony as they found the bodies of their loved ones, through the flows of tears that had hardly stopped for two years since Assad's war on Syrians had started, we watched from around the world, grieving from afar and crying with them, holding them in our thoughts, ashamed of our impotence. I will never forget the desolate father carrying the limp corpse of his daughter, maybe four or five years old, describing as he wept loudly, uncontrollably, what his little girl had told him just before going to bed, in what would be her last ever bedtime: 'I gave her a little food, and she told me, *baba*, today is not my turn to eat, it should be my siblings' turn.' He then laid her down next to her dead sister. She died hungry, gasping for air. All these children died the same way.

Assad's sarin had suffocated more than 1,400 Syrians to death in a few minutes. Over 10,000 people had to be treated over the next days for varying degrees of chemical inhalation, difficulty breathing, tight chests, blurred vision, convulsions, and sheer panic.

IT STARTED IN DAMASCUS

No serious, respectable, recognised expert or official agency or international organisation in the world disputes the fact that the regime was not only the one responsible, but that it was the only one which had the military and technical capacity to carry out this attack with sarin. In the years following this abhorrent war crime not seen for decades, numerous studies and reports have been published showing with great precision the trajectory of the weapon that targeted Ghouta, and detailing the entire process.

* * *

As Syrians reeled from this atrocity, as the front pages of practically every publication in the world showed images that normally would have been blurred or pixellated, the political machinations of several parties had begun. Because of President Obama's own warning a year before, there seemed to be no escaping strikes on Syria to punish and neutralise Assad's weapons of mass destruction; leading the international community's response would be the US, the UK, and France—or so we thought.

The issue had never been about getting dragged into a war with the Syrian regime. There was never a chance that punishment for the chemical massacre would entail more than a grounding of Assad's air force at most, and the demolition of his weapons of mass destruction facilities as a minimum. What was clearly understood by nearly everyone was that the response to the chemical massacre, after the US had drawn the red line, would determine the future behaviour of the Assad regime and of its allies.

British prime minister David Cameron reconvened parliament from its summer break and made his case on 29 August that the UK should take action to punish and constrain the Assad regime; the leader of the opposition, Ed Miliband, argued the UK should not. On 30 August, Labour-led lobbying against a limited intervention to disable Assad's chemical weapons facilities resulted in

DEATH OF AN ILLUSION

a vote at the House of Commons that took Britain out of the game. Cameron lost by 285 to 272, making him the first prime minister to lose such a vote on military action since 1782. As devastated Syrians followed these developments, they understood this was the first reassurance Assad had gotten since the massacre, but not that Miliband had also opened an unexpected window of opportunity for Obama.

Assad had another miraculous favour coming his way immediately following the British government's parliamentary defeat in London, with the US president's own request on 31 August for an authorisation from Congress. As US media and analysts reported in great detail, Obama had changed his mind about getting Congressional approval only after the vote at the House of Commons.

By removing the burden of responsibility from himself, well aware that Congress would be reluctant to acquiesce when it returned to work on 9 September, Obama could confidently talk the talk when he anticipated not having to walk the walk: 'Young boys and girls gassed to death by their own government. This attack is an assault on human dignity. It also presents a serious danger to our national security.' He added: 'What message will we send if a dictator can gas hundreds of children to death in plain sight and pay no price?'

History has shown that the message was heard loud and clear by Assad, and by his supporters. By then, Russian president Vladimir Putin was also realising that the mighty Anglo-American leadership of years past was waning in the region, and that a chance to exploit the gap in Syria, as a first step, was his for the taking. He swooped in, took Assad tightly under his wing, and offered Obama a way out for the long term.

Meanwhile, Assad's spokespeople were giving differing versions of 'the truth' that ranged from 'the massacre did not happen', to 'it happened but we didn't do it'; they were throwing everything they could, hoping something would stick as they waited for a deal. On 4 September, Bouthaina Shaban told Sky News in a live interview that the victims had actually been kidnapped from villages near Latakia (implying that they were Alawis) by Al Qaeda, which then drove all these children from the coastal area to Ghouta and then gassed them to death. Nobody challenged her mad lies, nor asked why her government was not helping to bring back the bodies to their home towns, nor where the grieving families in these villages were.

Obama could hardly wait to distance himself from his famous 2012 statement as he waited for negotiations with Russia to yield results. Asked about Syria at a press conference with the Swedish prime minister on 4 September, he defensively told journalists: 'First of all, I didn't set a red line; the world set a red line.' In the big picture, it hardly mattered any longer what Obama said; the die had been cast. Ten days later, the US and Russia agreed on a Framework for the Elimination of Syrian Chemical Weapons that would lead to an inspection of sites by the Organisation for the Prohibition of Chemical Weapons (OPCW), and to the destruction of equipment producing chemical weapons and filling munitions with poison gas—the gas Assad claimed he did not have, let alone use—by November. All chemical weapons material and equipment were to be eliminated in the first half of 2014.

And France, the only other Western power that had pledged to respond to Assad's crime against humanity, also had to step back. President François Hollande had been the most vocal in response to the massacre, leading with moral clarity on the issue: 'Our responsibility today is to look for the most appropriate response to the exactions of the regime,' he had said, 'because the chemical massacre in Damascus cannot be left without a response.'

That summer of 2013, Bashar Assad and Vladimir Putin learned a valuable lesson from the West: as long as you do not kill with chemicals again, or at least not with sarin, or at least not in such big numbers, you do not bother us nor will we be bothering you. As documented repeatedly over the next years, Assad would use chemicals over and over again—not necessarily sarin, but other deadly chemicals such as chlorine that killed children with their small lungs even more easily than adults.

* * *

By 2014, Syrians had already endured three years of unchecked savagery. The No-Fly Zone that many had begged for when Assad's serious air campaign had begun in 2012 was a nonstarter, a rejected and unfeasible option from the beginning from various Western powers, but the opposition had still tried to argue that a few man-portable air-defence systems (MANPADS) would help the Free Syrian Army shoot down the helicopters dropping barrel bombs. This would convince Assad to refrain from using this brutal method, thus saving thousands of lives and helping Syrians stay in their homes. As the opposition headed to Washington, D.C., in May 2014, this was the rationale that would be brought in person to the media, the State Department, Capitol Hill, and the White House.

The Syrian opposition had continued to formalise and organise itself, with the creation in November 2012 of the National Coalition of Syrian Revolution and Opposition Forces; I was hopeful that US lawmakers and media were going to see the Syrian opposition in all its variety, complexity, and authenticity. Like in every other political grouping in the world, there were good people and bad, democratic people and would-be unopposed leaders, intellectuals and fools. These Syrians were the product of over forty years of Assad's suffocating rule, having never learned how to turn disagreements and differing aspirations into fruitful discussions, collaborations, and strategic decisions, but they were trying.

IT STARTED IN DAMASCUS

Many Syrians, myself included in a communications and public affairs advisory capacity, supported the Coalition in ways we thought would help free our compatriots from Assad's killing machine. I had joined groups of consultants and advisors on several occasions, in Geneva, in Brussels, in London, and in the capital of the most powerful state in the world, the only one we thought could find a way to change the course of events, if it wanted to.

During ten days of meetings in Washington, I saw genuine interest from many, but not from the White House. We all knew that President Obama was fixated on one foreign policy goal that could not be achieved if Syrian lives were prioritised: he wanted a nuclear deal with Iran to be his legacy. A politician of Obama's calibre should have also considered the consequences of his deliberate inaction, whose repercussions continue until today. The Syria file had been happily handed over to Russia in the post-chemical massacre deal, and now the success of negotiations with Iran promised to hand its Islamic regime even more power over the entire region, and amounts of cash that would replenish its imperialist entrenchment in Syria that had expanded exponentially since the beginning of the revolution. The Iranian regime, whose good relations with Syria had started with Hafez Assad, was wholly committed to maintaining Assad in power, using Syria as its throughway to Lebanon to have a direct line from Tehran to Beirut.

There were several substantial meetings with individual politicians, and with various groups and committees, and many detailed questions about the situation on the ground from the opposition's perspective. While these politicians were already familiar with Syrian activists, thanks to the well-organised research and outreach done by Syrian Americans whose tireless efforts would culminate with major anti-Assad legislation, it was the first time the Coalition, recognised as a legitimate representative of Syrians opposed to Assad, was meeting in a formal capacity.

DEATH OF AN ILLUSION

Some politicians had turned down requests to meet with the opposition delegation, telling the Coalition's office that they would be too busy. After the delegation's first few days created some positive traction, however, last-minute requests were received from both junior and senior politicians for meetings and discussions, despite the administration's disengagement from the Syrian issue. Speaker Nancy Pelosi invited us after an initial refusal; our small group accompanying the Coalition's then-president, Ahmad Jarba, was offered tea and small cakes, and a courteous expression of sadness at the plight of Syrians.

Between meetings at Capitol Hill, a colleague and I had slipped into a subway car heading to our next call at the Senate. We were joined by a pleasant and chatty politician who asked what we were doing here; we gave him an impromptu pitch, and, as we got off, he wished us luck and success. My Washington-based colleague was surprised I had not immediately recognised Senator Marco Rubio, whose office contacted our team and requested a meeting which went splendidly, with a real discussion instead of platitudes. Like Senator John McCain, who also met the delegation and had consistently supported the Syrian revolutionaries and opposition, Senator Rubio was one of few American politicians who unfailingly spoke of the need to stop Assad's war machine and protect Syrian lives. This support from two leading Republicans was often used by regime apologists to promote the claim that the Syrian Revolution was an imperialist scheme.

The mood at the White House was less welcoming. A couple of days before my arrival in D.C., I had attended a dinner in London at which a number of Syria-focused British and American officials were present. One of them had not appreciated my comments on the Obama administration's backtracking on its own red lines, and its failure to respond in any meaningful way to the ongoing massacre and displacement of the Syrian people as it sought the nuclear deal with Iran. When I got to D.C., before we had even left the parking lot at the airport, my D.C.-based colleague picking me up said: 'I heard you caused some commotion at that dinner in London.' Did I really? It was a rather factual and regular Syrian talking point, I thought, but White House officials did not want to hear Syrians saying it in Washington. The Coalition's office was thus asked not to voice these criticisms during their entire stay in Washington, to the media or otherwise—that is, if they really wanted President Obama to meet with them.

Syrians were used to watching their words in a region where free speech was forbidden. They expected, as did I, to be able to exercise that freedom in the leading democratic capitals of the world. With the demand that we not mention the red line, the chemical massacre agreement with Russia, the Iran deal, or any position Obama had ever taken that subjected Syrians to more suffering, the opposition had been set up for failure before it even had a chance to speak. Syrians were yet again shackled as they waited to be thrown political crumbs.

The meeting at the White House was scheduled for the last day of the visit, on 13 May 2014. We met with National Security Advisor Susan Rice and a large team of officials in the Roosevelt Room; half an hour into the meeting, a door swung open and President Obama walked in and went around the table, shaking hands with every member of our delegation before settling down with a cup of tea opposite the Syrian Coalition's president, on whose left I sat. He stayed over half an hour, which in normal circumstances I would have interpreted as a positive sign. As our side spoke of the need to stop the barrel bombs that were causing the most destruction and great displacement at that stage of the war, President Obama listened and watched us intently, responding with eloquent platitudes and little substance. And while there had been no reason to expect any other result, human nature is such that one clings to hope, even the smallest of hopes, when so many lives are at stake.

Exactly two years later, in May 2016, I remembered that precise moment sitting opposite the President at the White House, when I realised it was really hopeless. I was watching Obama addressing the people of Flint, Michigan, at the height of the problem of lead in the water that the city was desperate to resolve. Mid-speech, Obama requested a glass of water, saying this was not a stunt as he really needed it; when it came, he lifted the glass as if to drink, but barely wet his lips without taking a proper sip of water and set it back down. The media had a field day with this; for me, Obama's performance in Flint was poignantly reminiscent of his performative foreign policy, and not just with regard to Syrians whom no filter could protect from Assad.

Not even the testimony of an escaped Syrian regime photographer giving evidence of the Assad regime's barbaric torture dungeons moved the Obama administration, or the rest of the world, to think of a way to help the victims of the mass murderer. Identifying as Caesar and hiding his identity from the public to protect family in Syria as he appeared before Congress in July 2014, a few weeks after the Syrian opposition had tried to make its case in Washington, he had smuggled out 55,000 images of the heavily tortured and emaciated bodies of nearly 11,000 Syrians who had been killed in regime prisons in the Damascus area. Had these photos been in black and white, they would have appeared to date back to the horrors of Nazi death camps during World War II. The Obama administration remained impassive, dismissive even, and it took another five years for Congress to pass the Caesar Syria Civilian Protection Act, signed into law by President Trump in December 2019, sanctioning the Assad regime for war crimes.

In May 2020, Antony Blinken, who had been Obama's Deputy Secretary of State, told CBS of his regrets about Syria: 'We failed to prevent a horrific loss of life. We failed to prevent massive displacement of people internally in Syria and, of course, externally as refugees. And it's something that I will take with me for the rest of my days. It's something that I feel very strongly.'

* * *

There is a crystal-clear, direct correlation between international inaction following the August 2013 chemical massacre and the increased savagery of the regime, specifically in its usage of the infamous barrel bomb that devastated most of Syria, even before Russian jets came to finish the job.

There had been only a handful of barrel bombs used in 2012. As of August 2013, after Bashar Assad was given a gentle slap on the wrist and told his chemical weapons would be confiscated, he turned to the most reliable, archaic, crude weapon he could use to destroy half of the country. As has been widely documented, these indiscriminate and imprecise barrel bombs containing explosives and shrapnel would be dropped from helicopters, with some videos showing smiling Syrian soldiers filming themselves lighting the fuse before pushing out the barrel bombs. The devastating impact was widespread, flattening buildings and ripping people apart. By 2021, the Syrian regime had dropped well over 82,000 barrel bombs all over Syria, according to the Syrian Network for Human Rights.

The significant rise in barrel bombs resulted in a corresponding significant rise in victims, and in refugees. The sieges, and the militias driving people out of their homes, had helped the Assad regime reclaim Homs in 2014, Aleppo in 2016, and Ghouta in 2018, each in horrifically violent assaults that caused human suffering and casualties on an unprecedented scale. With no meaningful reactions from abroad, the regime had consistently upped the ante with ever bolder actions as it gradually realised it had a green light. Large-scale forced population dis-

DEATH OF AN ILLUSION

placement and demographic engineering were calmly carried out, also with the full military and financial aid of Iran and its proxies, and Russia. The steady increase in regime violence, and the blatant participation of Iran-backed militias in Syria, created a space for Islamist armed groups of various levels of extremism, some of which associated with Al Qaeda. While they mostly fought the regime and each other, they also targeted civilians in regime areas, and in regions they came to control. Then came ISIS, the only killer the world thought merited intervention.

What held the regime together was not the touted unity and strength that Assad supporters and assorted non-interventionists claimed; aided by unlimited resources from two powerful military states and their myriad militias, it was its viciousness and willingness to go to any length to ensure its own survival, and to make defection and insubordination hugely costly for those who considered it.

As I reflected on how the promise of 'never again' had been broken once more, I realised that Syria was not an 'again' but an absolute first. It was a macabre *Truman Show*, an uninterrupted live reality TV programme watched globally on social and mainstream media for years on end. 'Never again' could not apply to us, for what was done to Syrians had never been done before. Indeed, our tragic fate was to be the modern age's 'never before'—not in that time span, not in that intensity, not in that degree of visibility, not in that magnitude.

Never before had the world been able to observe, in real time, unfiltered and uncensored, blow by blow, the destruction of a nation and the extermination of a people who had dared to demand dignity and freedom. Never before had a civilian population been filmed under attack with Scud missiles, barrel bombs, and chemical weapons by its own illegitimate authorities, with foreign help. Never before had starvation sieges, old-fashioned barbaric massacres and executions, and mass torture been so well documented as they happened, by their victims and by their perpetrators. And never before had the world's indifferent silence been so loud, save for perfunctory condemnations and erasable red lines, as the mightiest superpowers the world had ever known shamelessly pretended to be impotent, rejecting Syrians' desperate pleas for protection.

We already knew that this gluttonous, incompetent, brutal regime was unreformable, proving repeatedly it would use all means at its disposal to maintain its violent hold on power. And it did. The illusion that the world's great powers would ever help Assad's victims died after the chemical massacre, and I felt it was buried at the White House that day of May 2014. Syrians had already realised Assad would stop at nothing to kill their hope, but it took them a bit longer to understand that they would be left to face their demon alone.

In July 2014, Bashar Assad unabashedly swore himself in for a third seven-year term. One year later, Obama finally got his coveted nuclear treaty.

13

THE GREAT EXPOSURE

If the revolution was a worldwide conspiracy against Syria, as explained repeatedly by Bashar Assad and his media, it should not have surprised anyone that support for the Syrian rebels would come from the most unexpected places, in the oddest manner. Not even a year into the revolution, yet another cunning plot to outsmart the regime was exposed by Addounia Television, one of Rami Makhlouf's media channels. This involved not only the Qatar Foundation, which provided the much-needed kits for this plot, but also the reigning UEFA champions Barcelona, meaning the Champions League was foot-deep in the global anti-Assad conspiracy.

In a January 2012 Copa Del Rey football match against Real Madrid, Barcelona midfielder Andrés Iniesta had passed the ball to Lionel Messi who, surrounded by Real Madrid defenders, had to dribble and pass a through ball to forward Pedro, who scored a goal. At first glance, it would appear to most normal spectators that nothing on that field could have been even remotely related to Syria, but Addounia cleverly uncovered the connection and demonstrated there was more than met the eye.

IT STARTED IN DAMASCUS

When stills of these passes were superimposed on a map of Lebanon and Syria, it was blatantly obvious, Addounia explained, that they were staged specifically to show arms smugglers the route to take from Lebanon (where Iniesta had the ball), to Homs (with the ball now in Messi's control), and finally to Abu Kamal in eastern Syria (where Pedro took over and scored), to deliver the shipment of weapons to Syrian agents. They were all in on this, together, to the surprise of many football fans who discovered the great depth of Syrian media when the clip went viral.

This profound analysis was from the same Addounia which had started to explain that all the alleged protest clips seen on other channels were in fact filmed on location in Qatar, where entire film studios had been built to resemble Syrian sites, just to make the world believe that there was such a thing as an uprising against the nice Syrian government. Besides, these convenient studios facilitated Al Jazeera's incitement mission; its reporters just had to drive across town to film a few pretend demonstrations that they later broadcast and falsely labelled as anti-regime demonstrations taking place in the actual Syria. And if the protests were fake, so were the killings, of course, except when the government was bravely killing terrorists who were the only targets of the valiant army.

At the same time, Syrian television recognised that some protests did indeed take place inside the country, but they were certainly not of people who went to truly demonstrate against Assad, perish the thought, as reformed protesters told us in candid interviews. Addounia spoke to various people who, regretting their actions, admitted that they had been coerced or enticed into participating in these fake protests. Most people would go to the protests, they explained, because free sandwiches and drinks were distributed to everyone, as long as they pretended to be against Assad. More importantly, they would find a 500 Syrian pound (around ten dollars at the time) note inside each sandwich to compensate for the fake protester's time and trouble, and to entice more people to come. Furthermore, a pill had been ground into the filling of each sandwich, a kind of amphetamine that would give the protesters the energy they needed to protest a long time. Such revelations would be on replay on official Syrian channels and widely spread online; parodies soon followed, showing revolutionaries eagerly rolling money into loaves of Arabic bread and coaxing random people to demonstrate.

Syrian media was nothing if not inventive, especially when occasional events that were too visible required a different approach. In late April 2011, when a large demonstration had unexpectedly broken out in Midan, a traditional and popular neighbourhood in Damascus famous for its myriad food vendors, word had quickly gotten around as footage had been shared faster than Syrian media could manage. Would they divulge that Qatar had also built an exact replica of Midan on the outskirts of Doha? No, it turns out, this time was different: while these Damascenes had admittedly come out in droves, it was not to protest against the government, as the shameless Al Jazeera and other channels had claimed, but rather to thank God for the abundant rain 'as they always did' in a well-known Midani custom we were just discovering. Just because no person from Midan, or any other Syrian for that matter, had ever seen or heard of the tradition of blessing the rains down in Syria did not mean we should make up stories about protests.

There were numerous other ways to show Syrians, and the world, that Bashar Assad was still the most popular person alive. Where actual revolutionaries could not go, Assad supporters were invited, urged, ordered to come, or even bussed to massive pro-regime demonstrations in the big squares.

In October 2011, tens of thousands swarmed the streets and squares of Damascus to show the world their support of the regime again in what was called the million-strong march, an indirect reference to a huge anti-regime demonstration in Hama that summer that also exaggeratingly claimed a million Syrians had attended. Whereas revolutionaries chanted for freedom and peaceful unity, protesters in pro-regime events chanted 'God, Syria, and Bashar only.' In March 2012, to mark the one-year anniversary of the non-revolution and the fake protests, the regime organised another giant gathering named the Global March for Syria to which all government employees, teachers included, had to come, while others were encouraged the usual Assadist way. They did not even have to provide free sandwiches wrapped around money of any denomination; people just came.

This aggrandising of Assad was spreading beyond regional regime-friendly media. Whether or not they meant to do it, mainstream journalists contributed to a distinctive treatment of the Syrian story that other reporting did not receive, or at least not to that extent. There were exceptions, of course, with seasoned reporters who dug deeper in their analysis, who spoke to more people and spotted nuances, who relayed to their audience a more faithful representation of the many facets of Syrian opinions since the revolution. Many others, unfortunately, relied on convenient key words and expressions that, for having been repeated so often, ended up forming a simplistic and somewhat misleading narrative for years.

Countless descriptions of Assad in Western media repeatedly pointed to traits that seemed to imply he was, perhaps, not as bad as some Syrians said. There was often a hint of fawning between the lines. While his army and intelligence were busy killing Syrians in double and triple digits every day, as reported by the very media organisations in which these articles appeared, many journalists peculiarly continued to describe Assad as softspoken, as if to subliminally shed doubt on his brutality. Would a louder, stronger voice have been interpretable as evidence of a potential for violence?

THE GREAT EXPOSURE

Often, we were told Bashar wore a suit, and that was clearly a good thing, as if other leaders or even his own male population did not wear trousers. I do not recall Hafez Assad ever being described as a suit-wearing leader. To what end did the audience need reminding of this most basic sartorial detail, and in contrast to whom? The attention to his attire also begged the question: if he had not sported a suit, would it then have been more believable that he was committing all these crimes?

We were meant to be impressed that he drove his own car—sometimes without a security detail, we were told—and that he even carried his own briefcase as he arrived at his office from his humble home. Should these attributes not be, the writers might have thought, a counterweight to accusations of war crimes? Did the journalists writing such trivialities not consider, even for a moment, that this was precisely why they were put in a position to witness it? I found this usually signified one of two things: either the journalist did not know anything about Syria and found these details meaningful, which would be problematic on a professional level, or the journalist did know things about Syria and still wanted to push into the audience's subconscious an image of Assad as someone who should be admired, which would be even more problematic on an ethical level.

Besides, we were constantly reminded that the soft-spoken, suit-wearing Syrian president was Western educated, even though the time he spent abroad had been short. How could he possibly be as bad as it was claimed then, if his formation had not been entirely local? The astoundingly chauvinistic premise of this equation did not seem to have occurred to these journalists—unless it did, which would then explain the rather impertinent assessments we were given. I was asked on numerous occasions whether I did not think that Assad's Western education would have affected his demeanour and actions; in plainer words, how could someone who had trained in London all of eighteen months do bad things?

IT STARTED IN DAMASCUS

I sighed a lot during conversations like these, and would respond by asking whether no other Western-educated, or Western-born and -bred leader, had ever committed crimes. Touché, some told me, only to then go on to be equally baffled that Assad's British-born wife could support the increasingly evident war crimes. She must be a prisoner who could not leave if she wished to, they reasoned, as her background surely precluded her from supporting her husband's evil actions. After all, wasn't the rose (his wife) in the desert (all the other Syrians) different (they did not dare say better)?

Another problematic leader who really was Western educated (and not just trained), for at least five or six years longer than Bashar Assad, was never described as such by these journalists. Apparently, Kim Jong-un's formative years in a Swiss school did not matter as much as Assad's eighteen-month ophthalmology training in a London hospital. To be fair, maybe they did not get the chance to describe him as truly Western educated, because the North Korean leader did not give interviews to media, foreign or otherwise. In contrast, Assad always seemed to be talking to someone, and yet interviews with him were unfailingly described as something special, a rare occurrence, their exclusivity splashed in headlines as if we were about to discover spectacular perspectives or the scoop of the decade, as if we had not heard them many times before.

Since the beginning of the revolution, as Assad carried out the well-documented repression of practically an entire population, numerous Western and Western-educated journalists travelled to Damascus for 'exclusive' interviews with him, even at the height of the most savage bombings, documented torture, and proven chemical massacres. The channels' own headlines and subtitles boasted about their significance, with titles such as 'In an exclusive interview—Bashar al-Assad, president of Syria, tells Andrew Gilligan he will not go the way of Gaddafi' (*Telegraph*, 2011), or

THE GREAT EXPOSURE

'In an exclusive with AFP, Syria's Assad says there's a "significant" chance he'll seek a new term' (AFP, 2014), or 'BBC exclusive interview with President Bashar al-Assad' (BBC, 2015), or 'Syria's President Speaks: An Exclusive Interview' (*Foreign Affairs*, 2015), or 'Watch Full Exclusive Interview With Syria's President' (NBC, 2016), or 'Exclusive interview with Syria's Assad on Thursday' (*Kathimerini*, 2018). So just how exclusive were they?

These allegedly rare interviews included ones with: Barbara Walters, ABC, 2011; Andrew Gilligan, *The Telegraph*, 2011; Hala Jaber, *The Sunday Times*, 2011; Utkur Cakirozer, *Cumhuriyet*, 2012; Jürgen Todenhöfer, ARD, 2012; Hala Jaber, *The Sunday Times*, 2013 (for the second time); Rainer Hermann, *Frankfurter Allgemeine Zeitung*, 2013; Greg Palkot (with Dennis Kucinich), Fox News, 2013; Dieter Bednarz and Klaus Brinkbäumer, *Spiegel*, 2013; Charlie Rose, PBS, 2013; Marcelo Cantelmi, *Clarín*, 2013; Régis Le Sommier, *Paris Match*, 2014; Rana Moussaoui and Sammy Ketz, AFP, 2014; Jeremy Bowen, BBC, 2015; Hala Jaber, *The Sunday Times*, 2015 (for the third time); David Pujadas, France 2, 2015; Paulo Dentinho, RTP, 2015; Jonathan Tepperman, *Foreign Affairs*, 2015; Charlie Rose, CBS, 2015; Bill Neely, NBC, 2016; Zeina Karam, AP, 2016; Thomas Aders, ARD, 2016; Sammy Ketz and Christian Chaise, AFP, 2016; Sandro Brotz, SRF, 2016; Luke Waters, SBS, 2016; Sammy Ketz, AFP, 2017; Fabien Namias, Europe 1 and Michel Scott, TF1, 2017; TBS, 2017; Mike Isikoff, Yahoo News, 2017; Tomás Alcoverro, *La Vanguardia*, 2017; Hassan Haidar Diab, *Vecernji List*, 2017; Hala Jaber, *The Mail on Sunday*, 2018 (for the fourth time); and Alexis Papachelas, *Kathimerini*, 2018.

This partial list names about three dozen occasions between 2011 and 2018 when journalists for leading media conducted 'exclusive' interviews with a leader accused by numerous organisations, governments, and his own people of war crimes. It does not include interviews with Arab, Russian, and Iranian media, often mentioned as well in the global coverage of Syria. *Time* magazine did not interview him, but it did present an exclusive of its own in 2013 by short-listing Bashar Assad for its Person of the Year, right after the chemical massacre. Bobby Ghosh, editor of *Time International*, had rationalised the decision to include him by saying he remained influential even though he killed his people, while columnist Joe Klein compared him to *The Godfather*'s Michael Corleone, as if Assad's extermination of Syrians, and his getting away with it, was something cool. The magazine's choice of Person of the Year that year was Pope Francis, with Assad a runner-up in this bizarre and tactless exercise. How could Assad and the Pope be on the same list for anything? Would any other lethal tyrant in recent history have been treated in such a cavalier way by a leading publication, when there had already been at least 130,000 Syrians killed, over one and a half million refugees, and many more internally displaced at the end of 2013?

* * *

Some journalists had no qualms about accompanying Assad's soldiers on their outings to hunt rebels, embedding with the army accused of so many crimes. Some even interviewed what the regime said were terrorists they had imprisoned. It seemed that different journalistic standards were being applied in Syria, as one cannot imagine that other detainees in the jails of violent authoritarian regimes could be treated that way, with every prisoner 'confirming' the regime's claims that they were, in short, indeed terrorists. Why did certain international journalists for leading media not apply the basic ethical norms with Syrians?

This urge to put a spotlight on Assad did not extend to any member of the opposition. While journalists' articles did include the occasional quote from various Syrians in opposition, most of them did not seek nor conduct full interviews with active Syrian

THE GREAT EXPOSURE

politicians, thinkers, writers, and activists who had been working on Syria for years if not decades. Such interviews are the ones that would have been the rare ones, offering the audience a useful counter perspective. Instead, mentions of Syria's opposition would inevitably fall back on tired descriptive clichés such as divided, bickering, fragmented, chaotic, or splintered. These adjectives hinted that people in opposition could only be regarded as serious or viable if they were of a single opinion and in full agreement on everything regarding the struggle against the regime. Such beliefs ignored the circumstances in which Syrians had finally been able to speak out in the first place, and ignored the disagreements at the heart of most well-established political parties around the world. It seemed to imply that Syrians could not be trusted until they adhered to a standard not expected of others, even as the regime's vicious war targeted them all.

Journalists and politicians also used the terms opposition and rebels interchangeably, even though there was a difference between the political side and the armed component. They were often just called anti-Assad, a technically correct term but an incomplete one that dismisses the aspirations of Syrians and forgets their own definition of the revolution as being for dignity and freedom. By way of comparison, to name but one example, Hong Kong's opposition supporters were nearly always referred to as the pro-democracy activists; for the most part, Syria's opposition ones were not.

This loaded media approach with Assad, and the indifferent one with the opposition and revolutionaries, inevitably led to a flawed depiction of events in Syria. While Syrians at the receiving end of Assad's savagery were always frustrated to notice the poor understanding of their struggle, they especially resented the facile media usage of terms like 'civil war' and 'sectarian conflict', even before the regime itself had stoked the sectarian card. They disliked the simplistic divisions imposed on them when media described them as Sunnis, Alawis, or Christians when they did not categorise themselves that way. They resented implications that the struggle against the regime was one of Sunnis against Alawis, especially as so many Sunnis were part and parcel of the regime, and as so many Alawis themselves detested the regime and felt used by it. They resented repeated media references to the regime as secular, when it had been the most blatant exploiter of sectarianism, constantly instilling in the Alawi and the Christian community fears that they would not be safe without the regime to protect them—as if Syrians had been killing each other before the arrival of the Assads. And they resented the message that the conflict was complicated, when they felt it was quite simple to explain and to understand, if only the media and observers dropped the misleading clichés they never stopped using.

The media also awarded varying weights of credibility to statements emanating from different sides. When the regime claimed that bombings had taken place in areas it controlled, for example, they were often reported matter-of-factly as 'state media reported.' When rebels or opposition claimed they were bombed or shelled or hit by an airstrike, the word 'alleged' (or its derivatives) was added most of the time. More importantly, many clips and videos shown by the opposition were shared by mainstream media with the disclaimer that they 'could not be independently verified'—even though sometimes the live footage had been shown on some channels. In contrast, the burden of verification did not often apply to regime-provided footage; this meant that regime claims of violence by the rebels were often taken at face value, no matter how ludicrous, while opposition claims were treated with some caution until independently verified.

Every now and then, however, some journalists noticed Syrians' reports showing that regime media was not just ridiculous, but careless. In 2012, Syrian activists had documented the appearance of a man on eighteen occasions at regime-led events,

THE GREAT EXPOSURE

or at what appeared to be rebel attacks in regime areas. They produced a compilation of these eighteen clips, including interviews he gave to state media presenting himself as a normal citizen who supported the Syrian government in its fight against terrorists. He tried to change his appearance regularly, and somehow always happened to be where rebels were allegedly placing car bombs. I labelled him the Casual Bystander and posted about him on social media. In February 2013, activists noticed he had suddenly resurfaced, again as an innocent citizen who was by chance where things seemed to be happening. *The New York Times*' The Lede picked up my tweet and covered the story again.

As luck would have it, the following month, Casual Bystander was also at the Iman Mosque where Sheikh Muhammad Al Bouti, a figure known to every Syrian in his capacity as the imam of the Umayyad Mosque, was giving a religion lesson and being filmed when a blast occurred. According to the regime, a suicide bombing had killed Bouti and fifty people in the process. However, someone's camera had been filming Sheikh Bouti's lesson, and its footage from inside the mosque showed minimal damage, no other victims, and a suspicious sequence showing Bouti had survived and sat up by himself after a small bang that did not even ruffle the papers in front of him. The camera view of Bouti was then blocked shortly by a man walking towards him; seconds later, as the man made his way out and exited the camera's field, the sheikh was seen bleeding and struggling to move before he died. There was no doubt Bouti had just been assassinated, but there no was doubt either that the regime's claims that he and fifty others were killed by a suicide bomber were lies.

This time, the stature of Bouti meant that the news merited coverage, but stories like that of Casual Bystander were rarely noticed or reported by most foreign media, despite the deluge of information available through vibrant Syrian platforms, local media, and numerous citizen journalists who were documenting events on the ground and all the regime's crimes and shenanigans. When these media shortcomings were added to the unexplained obsession with Assad and the unequal treatment given to those fighting for their freedom, it is no wonder that the vast majority of people seemed confused about Syria, despite all the evidence available. I would even venture that because of this accumulation of factors, they were predisposed to mistrust the revolutionaries, the activists, and the opposition who soon became referred to as US-backed or Western-backed, even as they pleaded for help and even as Assad's bombs had reduced half of Syria to rubble.

* * *

The divine dimension is present in every component of Syrian society, unapologetically inserting itself in family life, in traditions that even the most secular and unobservant Syrians follow. It was one of the first things that people could notice on the videos documenting how the revolution developed, and how it was being repressed.

Activists uploaded dozens of videos daily in the first weeks and months of the revolution, becoming more skilled as the years passed and the massacres spread all over the country. They were so obviously amateur at first that I found them endearing, their eagerness to show their new reality quite moving. Watching their clips, one could imagine fear and a rush of adrenaline pushing them as they ran breathlessly or whispered from a hidden corner to document the humiliations and horrors inflicted by shabiha, snipers, or warplanes. It took time for Syrians' filming skills to improve; from day one, however, they always stated the place and the date of the event they were filming—the songs and dances of the revolutionaries, the crowds dispersing as gunfire filled the

THE GREAT EXPOSURE

area, the aftermath of bombings, the arrests, the first responders rescuing victims, and even the devastating sights of wounded people being brought to miserable field hospitals as a few doctors frantically tried to save lives. As they described the scenes we were discovering, as they reacted to them, they spoke naturally, without a script.

Arabic is strewn with references to God, and Syrians' vernacular, regardless of their faith and regardless of their degree of religiosity, includes many religious terms that are used abundantly in everyday life. You hear these expressions dozens of times a day, on big and small occasions, in important matters and in routine activities, not necessarily in religious contexts. Even the omnipresent 'Yalla' now used in the wide sense of 'let's go' originated from 'Ya Allah' (oh God), still uttered when asking for divine guidance or deliverance from suffering, often with palms facing upwards.

People say 'Bismillah' (in the name of God) as they start their cars, begin a meal, embark on an activity, when they are startled by someone, or when they are in true prayer mode for something to go well. They say 'Inshallah' (God willing) when manifesting a specific outcome, and, conveniently, also to give an evasive answer without committing to something. They say 'Mashallah' (what God willed) when seeing abundance, a beautiful baby, to express admiration at something so wonderful that God's hand must have guided it. They say 'Subhanallah' (glory to God) when they are amazed by something. They say 'Alhamdulillah' (thank God) to show gratitude, of course, but also to show acceptance of God's will even when they are in a state of despair. They say 'Allahu akbar' (God is great) in times of joy and when good things happen, even for a goal by a favourite football team, and also in times of fear, to call to a greater force and remind themselves that God is still more powerful than those hurting or frightening them.

IT STARTED IN DAMASCUS

When Syrians started filming the repression of the Assad regime, they were scared, shocked, outraged, and some of these expressions came naturally to them. In various stages of distress, they would repeat 'Allahu akbar' over and over, an instinctive reaction whose closest contextual version in other languages would be 'Oh my God.' And as they said it, filming the aftermath of barrel bombs dropped on homes or of Russian airstrikes decimating hospitals, their repetition of these words may have caused some unease in people who had heard it before only from extremists committing violent acts themselves. While they pitied the victims, of course, some may have also felt distant from these desperate people crying out 'Allahu akbar' under the bombs, having been conditioned to take a step back from most traditions and expressions of the Islamic faith that they usually saw in circumstances of an intent to commit violence, rarely in circumstances showing respect, love, or fear.

For some, those documenting their plight were, subconsciously perhaps, categorised as the opposite of the Western-educated, suit-wearing, soft-spoken, secular president whose rare words should be followed in the exclusive interviews he gracefully granted, telling them about the terrorists attacking Syria with the help of imperialist powers. Not only did Syrians have to struggle to survive the regime and its allies' genocidal war on them, but many felt they also had to struggle to be heard, to be seen around the world. Compared to the sympathy offered to other people's plights in activist circles, they felt that compassion for Syrians and understanding of their circumstances was at a much lower level.

* * *

The expectation that Assad would be restrained after the chemical massacre had come and gone as soon as Obama had backed out of the strikes, but the US had told the Coalition it would

THE GREAT EXPOSURE

push for negotiations based on the 2012 UN-proposed transition plan known as the Geneva Communiqué, with Russia as co-sponsor. The visit to Washington in May 2014 had come on the back of the Coalition's goodwill in January that year, when it accepted going to Switzerland for the launch of these talks despite the limitations of the plan. However, the Coalition had also flexed some muscle, to the approval of many Syrians, when it indicated it would refuse to participate if the UN's invitation to Iran—at the time the main foreign power physically active in Syria who rejected the proposed transition of power—was not rescinded. For once, the Syrians prevailed, and UN Secretary General Ban Ki-moon was forced to withdraw his offer to Iran.

Pressured by Russia to attend, the regime came kicking and screaming, its officials making a spectacle of themselves with repeated outbursts while the opposition remained calm, composed, displaying maturity. For the first time in its existence, the regime was facing Syrians it could not immediately silence as the world watched with interest.

One of my acquaintances, a Syrian benefactor of the opposition who wanted to help professionalise their communications, had asked me if I would agree to help. I had declined once before to get personally involved; now, I felt there was no option left but to play the hand we were dealt, even if it meant getting dragged into a negotiating farce, a consolation prize after the chemical massacre. Many already felt we were being set up for a vicious cycle of pretend talks that led nowhere; instead of the peace and the transition we should have been getting from Geneva, we got a bland, drawn-out process.

In the meeting rooms of the Intercontinental Hotel in Geneva, the air bristled with the energy of more Syrians than I could count. Media cameras were everywhere, covering the big story and seeking news and quotes. The communication advisors, myself included, were trying to put together a workable and logical communication plan from the busy media hub.

IT STARTED IN DAMASCUS

My communications style differed greatly from that of Coalition members, and of the consultants who had been working with them. Beyond the basics, I took issue with some of their talking points, and how they presented themselves or allowed others to present them. Several non-Syrian consultants who worked for the heavyweights in the Friends of Syria Group (the countries that had recognised the Coalition and organised aid for Syrians) did not want to diverge from the textbook, classic method of reiterating basics over and over again. They were not used to having Syrian comms professionals moving on their media and public affairs turf, but with my substantial communications and marketing background, I considered their messaging to be weak, incapable of conveying the essence of the Syrian tragedy in the fourth year of war. I also objected to the inclusion of what I considered unacceptable talking points they had drilled into the Coalition's speech.

I got straight to the point: 'You have to stop saying you are the moderate opposition,' I pressed the spokespeople who were routinely repeating this to the media. It was an absurd and damaging position to take and seemed to be, simply put, a talking point devised to protect Western backers of the political opposition, in response to claims that all the rebels and all the opposition were Islamist. Spokespeople in London, Brussels, and Washington could then respond, 'No, they're not, these are the moderate opposition.' I found they were helping to dig their own hole when they accepted point blank to be defined by an imposed measuring stick, with religious extremism on one end and religious moderation on the other. The opposition was just the opposition—an opposition that was varied and represented the many facets of Syrian society, all of which have a role to play in the future.

In addition to communicating in English and some Western languages, I believed we should have been reaching out to the

THE GREAT EXPOSURE

public in Iran and Russia, through social media, statements, interviews, and opinion pieces in Farsi and Russian. Even in dictatorships, public opinion mattered when so much of their money was being spent on propping up Assad; from my perspective, the Syrian opposition would gain by connecting with their people and sharing experiences, challenges, and the many commonalities of people seeking freedoms. Given the competing priorities, this advice was barely heeded, and I still regret the lost opportunities to gain allies in the two countries most responsible for the regime's military supremacy and its political survival.

As the talks in Geneva were taking place, the regime was blocking the entry of a dozen trucks full of aid waiting to be delivered to people under siege in Homs, which had been brought to its knees. One day, as we discussed the current talking points, I saw the prepared list was of the usual political flavour, pointing to the importance of helping people in need and pushing the regime to allow food and medicine in. These were not wrong per se, but they would not grab headlines anymore so I advocated stronger talking points: 'You need to touch a nerve and give them a reference they will understand. It's like Sophie's Choice, except here the parents are deciding which of their children will eat tonight and which will not. Tell them the children are taking turns eating; this is something every parent in the world will relate to.' I argued for moving towards soundbites that would stick, to touching and salient facts about Syrian distress; that particular point had been true for the children of Ghouta killed by sarin while they were hungry, and it was true for the children of Homs now, under siege for two years.

The ten or so people in the room were rather quiet, until one of the non-Syrian consultants shot an angry retort, accusing me of belittling the efforts of the spokespeople who had done an excellent job so far. I was surprised by this non sequitur as I had certainly not dismissed anyone's efforts, but the outburst was enlightening. I gathered that attempts to deviate from the repetitive but safe blandness would be resisted, and that support, limited as it was, was contingent on the opposition remaining rather demure even as their children starved and their people perished under barrel bombs. This was what had been imposed when we headed to the US a few months later as well, asked to refrain from criticising Obama. Syrians could not complain about inaction too loudly, nor change the way things were done. Were overly vivid and relatable comms capable of moving public opinion more, and hence of adding some pressure on selected governments to take some kind of action? We will never know, and I felt we were being relegated to the confines of a 'two sides' equation, a 'sad civil war' and, from the other side supporting the regime, the ultimate anti-imperialist accusation of 'a proxy war on the last standing Arab country.'

* * *

At first, I believe a majority of Syrians in opposition had been hopeful about the Coalition's prospects. When it was given the seat of Syria at the Arab League Summit of March 2013, many felt proud seeing its then-president, Mouaz Al Khatib, address Arab leaders eloquently and strongly. He and the team sitting behind him represented much of what many Syrians yearned for: the opposition was politically diverse, culturally and regionally representative, and unanimously patriotic. We could have had it all, it seemed.

As the years passed and Syrians' fortunes kept getting worse, criticism of the Coalition increased and they were blamed for not having adequately helped Syrians in need. We watched them manoeuvre to keep their seats and positions, moves that reminded many of the Assad regime; they even traded positions at the top when it was time to elect the president and fill senior posts, in a Putin-Medvedev-style agreement that infuriated

THE GREAT EXPOSURE

Syrian public opinion. As the political will diminished and Assad regained control over most of Syria, and as the only activity permitted for Syrians became the futile Geneva meetings of the Constitutional Committee, the Coalition was relegated to insignificance from its office in Istanbul, and most Syrians in opposition became openly hostile to it.

Despite the numerous faults of the Coalition, however, there was nearly nothing the political opposition could have done to alter the course of events in Syria. Without support in real terms—political, financial, military, and humanitarian—emerging from the Assadist nightmare was impossible. The Syrian opposition could not be blamed for having sought the support of governments with blatant double standards and less than clean agendas; struggling to be free from the devil incarnate, they did not have the luxury of selectivity while seeking helping hands.

At the same time, the opposition failed in its duty to connect with the world and convey the nature of the revolution and the consequences of Assad's repression. Global engagement with public opinion was necessary, but there was no central coherent or effective communication machine outside the official talks. Despite the mountains of evidence of the regime's crimes against humanity, provided by people in Syria who risked their lives to document, film, and send them to the world, the opposition failed to counter the offensive misrepresentations of the revolution in some mainstream media, the ruthless propaganda of the regime, and the misleading narratives and sensationalist conspiracies that often came from far-right or far-left circles who had different reasons for preferring Assad despite everything.

I have always lamented the fact that we lacked a charismatic, persuasive politician, a woman or man who could carry our colossal Syrian saga to the entire world with the gravitas and eloquence it merited, and with the likeability factor needed to connect with varied audiences. Occasionally, I would think of the

IT STARTED IN DAMASCUS

memorable foreign minister who became the face and the voice of besieged Sarajevo in the 1990s, speaking expertly and confidently to international audiences about the causes of the war in Bosnia and Herzegovina and the lives impacted by it, and drawing in so many people to work on ending it. Alas, we Syrians never had our Haris Silajdžić.

* * *

In 2014, we thought world apathy had already reached its peak when, suddenly and without warning or justification, the United Nations took the shocking decision to stop counting Syrian victims. The pretext was that it could not have an accurate estimation beyond what it said were 100,000 fatalities as of that date, a number that itself was lower than the over 130,000 victims that Syrian LCCs and NGOs had already documented. Two years later, in April 2016, UN Envoy to Syria Staffan de Mistura stated to media that 400,000 had died, specifying that this was his personal estimate—and that was before the devastating Russian air campaigns on Aleppo at the end of 2016 and on Ghouta in 2018, and the continuing war on Syrians everywhere else.

Syrians began to wonder what United Nations officials and staff were then doing in Damascus all these years, settled in the luxury of the Four Seasons Hotel from which they could hear Assad's barrel bombs dropping mere kilometres away and see the huge columns of smoke in their aftermath. Had the reason truly been their safety, they would have moved out after all opposition had been wiped out from greater Damascus. The UN's own procurement data shows that between 2014 and 2022, it had spent nearly $82 million at the Four Seasons alone, a hotel in which one of Assad's sanctioned business associates and warlords owned a majority stake. UN postings in Damascus appealed to many; not only was the accommodation top notch and the hardship allowance the highest, but they were restaurant hopping and befriending regime officials whose relatives had also been given UN jobs. The UN also awarded contracts worth tens of millions of dollars to people closely associated with the Assad regime, as divulged by British media. Meanwhile, the vast majority of Syrians lived under the poverty threshold, and half of the international aid coming into the country through the UN was being siphoned off by the regime.

Not only did Syrians feel they had to continuously prove themselves to a world whose response remained tepid, but they also had to contend with a large anti-imperialist and leftist movement around the world—although it was anti-Western imperialism only, such as that of the US and NATO, not anti-Eastern imperialism, such as that of Iran and Russia. Despite all evidence to the contrary, this large fluid group magnified the general message that Assad was a victim of a multinational regime change conspiracy. Some went so far as to say that his opponents were the ones responsible for the war, the killings, and even the chemical attacks. Some personalities who supported other revolutions and civil rights movements, and who were against occupation, injustice, or the dictators of the Arab world—who they claimed were all the same—had taken a different position with the Syrian Revolution. While some simply kept silent about Syria, others actively opposed any action that Syrians themselves would welcome, ignoring their predicament at best, and slandering them at worst.

The Stop the War Coalition (StWC) had been very active in trying to prevent Western interventions of any kind in Syria, regardless of the trigger. For years, Syrians tried to engage with the group without success. In November 2015, at a StWC meeting chaired by Labour MP Diane Abbott to discuss Syria with a panel featuring no Syrians, several activists had raised their hands to speak, including several Syrian ones. Abbott did not give them the floor, and as the activists raised their voices to be heard, police were called to escort them out.

IT STARTED IN DAMASCUS

Roger Waters, the British musician and Pink Floyd bassist who has a large following because of his pro-Palestine activism, made several statements about Syria. At a concert in Barcelona in April 2018, he was filmed saying that the White Helmets, those Syrian first responders who spent years digging Syrians out of the rubble with their bare hands following Russian airstrikes and Assad barrel bombs, 'are a fake organisation that exists only to create propaganda for the jihadists and terrorists.' In a post on his Facebook page in May 2019, referring to Assad's chemical attack of 2018 which had finally merited a brief military response from the US, UK, and France, Waters wrote: 'The White Helmets probably murdered 34 women and children to dress the scene that sorry day in Douma.'

When the US had responded to another chemical attack in Khan Shaykhun in April 2017 with cruise missiles to a regime airbase, following Assad's killing of some hundred Syrians, the Black Lives Matter Twitter account posted: 'The people of #Syria are carrying the weight of American fascism. 206,500 pounds of missiles launched by #DFT today, to be exact.' The children and adults gassed to death by Assad were never mentioned, nor were the hundreds of thousands of Syrian victims of the regime since the start of the revolution.

This had particularly pained many Syrian activists who had thought their revolution would be respected by civil rights movements around the world. After the killing of George Floyd in 2020, Syrian artist Aziz Asmar painted a portrait of Floyd on the rubble of a bombed building in Idlib, a poignant illustration of Syrians' solidarity in times of pain. The images of that mural were shared widely on social media, with many posters attributing it to a Palestinian artist from a site bombed by Israel, not even acknowledging Syrians.

Some longtime respected journalists and academics also took questionable positions on Syria. Seymour Hersh, who uncovered

THE GREAT EXPOSURE

the My Lai massacre in 1968 and the abuse in Abu Ghraib prison in 2004, began sharing conspiracy theories very early in the Syrian Revolution, laying doubt on the chemical massacres despite OPCW's solid conclusions assigning responsibility to the regime. This has also been the case with Noam Chomsky and other writers of his stature who had always stood with the oppressed.

This phenomenon of anti-Syrian but 'pro-Syria' (the touted Assad's Syria allegedly being attacked from all sides) would expand on the social media platforms with little oversight on truth and facts. In 2022, an investigation by the Institute for Strategic Dialogue identified a network of Syria conspiracy theorists, backed by a Russian campaign, that sent thousands of disinformation tweets aimed at preventing international intervention and creating confusion about Syria. There have been many other such organised attempts over the years, but also many organisations whose credibility is beyond doubt as they refute attempts to mislead the public, such as Bellingcat which is trusted internationally.

The list of accusations seems to have been dictated by Assad's media: the opposition were paid stooges of the West, helping a conspiracy against their own country that remained the last bastion of Arab resistance, as it faced the machinations of NATO, the Zionists, the Ottomans, the Gulf oil sheikhs, and dark Islamic forces, all of which were united in fighting the regime—and yet, despite their collective might, did not manage to bring Assad down.

The notion of resistance played a big role in the animosity towards Syrians. As long as a greater cause (in critics' eyes) remained active, many anti-imperialist activists have blamed Syrians for rocking the boat and allowing their case to overtake the Palestinian cause, even though the cause is embraced by Syrians too. Yet, there was little acknowledgement of the suffering of Palestinians in Syria when it was Assad and Hezbollah laying siege to the Yarmouk refugee camp in Damascus; there is little doubt that this abuse of Palestinians would have triggered much bigger reactions had it been perpetrated not by Assad, but by Israel.

In January 2014, UNRWA visited the Palestinian camp of Yarmouk in Damascus, besieged by Assad's forces and Hezbollah. An image taken by the agency's official photographer shook the world; thousands of people stood in a huge crowd, waiting for food and aid in the apocalyptic scenery of bombed out buildings that bore Assad's signature. It barely made a ripple in the circles that usually report and highlight crimes against Palestinians, and who mostly could not bring themselves to accuse Assad and Hezbollah. And yet, according to Palestinian Syrian figures, the regime had killed some 6,500 Palestinians by 2023, including more than 600 in prisons, and had disappeared 1,800 since the start of the revolution.

This indifference towards Syrian victims can be better understood if the question is posed about victims of the Syrian regime relative to others. From many Syrians' perspective, as they discovered over years under attack by Assad and his allies, being killed by Israel, the West, or ISIS creates action, and condemnation. Being killed by Assad does not have the same effect. And while victims of ISIS were mourned, those of Assad's war machine were barely mentioned.

In September 2014, David Haines, a British aid worker who was helping Syrians in IDP camps near the Turkish border, was kidnapped by ISIS and murdered a year later in the most gruesome manner. Prime Minister David Cameron called his murder an act of pure evil. In November 2012, another British citizen had also gone to the Turkish border to help Syrians in need: Dr Abbas Khan, an orthopaedic surgeon from London, crossed into Syria to help medical staff at an Aleppo hospital, and was arrested at a regime checkpoint. For an entire year, his family

THE GREAT EXPOSURE

tried to get him out, having finally found him in a Damascus prison. His mother headed to Damascus in July 2013, knocking on every door to try liberating him and even managing to see her son, who she was told in December would be freed in two days. The day before his scheduled release, the regime told her he had killed himself in jail by hanging.

Cameron read a statement in Downing Street about David Haines, but not about Dr Abbas Khan. Being killed by ISIS receives the revulsion and condemnation it deserves; being killed by the Assad regime and its allies does not. In many countries, the media was much more likely to give space to the killing of people by ISIS than to the killing of people by Assad. And yet, with regards to killing civilians who oppose them, ISIS and Assad were two sides of a coin—except that Assad had killed hundreds of thousands more.

It seemed that if you belonged to a 'minority' in Syria and were persecuted by Islamists, many would want to rush to your aid, and people would engage and post 'Save them' appeals on social media. If you were part of the 'majority,' however, as were the overwhelming number of Syrians targeted by the regime or even by ISIS, you were less visible, no matter how much documentation you provided.

By paying lip service to the ouster of Assad without facilitating significant support to his opponents, Western democracies had also inadvertently contributed to this disdain of the Syrian Revolution by some parties. With every hint of action, usually in response to yet another Assadist atrocity against Syrians, the 'Don't Bomb Syria' signs would come out. In over a decade, however, there never was a much more needed 'Don't Bomb Syrians' sign.

Syrians felt they were damned, no matter what they did. When all they did was protest peacefully at the beginning, they were told their numbers were insignificant and most people still supported Assad. When they took up arms in self-defence, they were accused of escalating the violence. When they organised opposition conferences, they were described as fragmented. When the opposition united, they were compared to the Iraqi groups who had lobbied for an invasion. When they created brigades with religious names, they were called terrorists and jihadists. When they pleaded for international protection, they were called traitors who were part of a big conspiracy. When they refused to dialogue with the regime while it killed with impunity, they were accused of prolonging the war. When they entered dialogue with the regime, they were accused of carrying foreign agendas.

Nobody marched for Syrians. No world capitals were brought to a standstill under the roar of chants for their freedom. No demonstrators demanded the protection of Syrian civilians under relentless bombing for years. No one tried to convince others that boycott, divestment, or sanctions on the Syrian, Iranian, and Russian state perpetrators of war crimes and crimes against humanity would help achieve justice. No social media campaigns were organised to help raise awareness or money for Syrian victims. No celebrities adopted the cause of Syrian detainees and prisoners of opinion.

Infantilised and disrespected in their struggle for dignity, mocked and belittled as if they had no agency and were mere puppets in a bigger game, ignored and dismissed even when their genocide reached unimaginable levels, Syrians had been let down by everyone they thought would have supported them as the Assad regime wiped them and their homes off the face of the earth. The Syrian Revolution exposed everyone, everywhere.

14

NEW DOMINIONS IN GREATER SYRIA

In July 2015, we watched jubilant Iranian diplomats greeting the international press from the balcony of Palais Coburg in Vienna. They had reason to rejoice: with the persistence of the Obama administration and the determination of the Islamic regime in Tehran, a deal had just been reached on the Joint Comprehensive Plan of Action (JCPOA), supported by the P5+1 (the five countries on the Security Council in addition to Germany) and the European Union. The JCPOA would remove long-standing sanctions on Iran in exchange for the dismantlement of most of its nuclear programme and the regular, extensive international inspections of its facilities.

Iranian foreign minister Javad Zarif proclaimed 'the world has changed' in one of the most ominously truthful statements to ever come from the Islamic regime. While his perspective was a positive one referring to all countries respecting a new global order, Syrians knew their plight was about to get even worse; the sanctions relief would liberate billions of dollars in assets that had been frozen while Iran worked on its nuclear programme. It would inject the massive cash flow Iran needed to pursue its strategic goals and strengthen its position in a world that it had already helped change, not for better, much before the JCPOA. If Iran had managed to spread its wings so widely while strapped for funds, imagine what it would do now, thought both friends and foes in the region.

As many observers had anticipated long before he achieved his goal, Barack Obama wanted this nuclear deal to define his foreign affairs legacy, complementing his primary domestic legacy of the Affordable Care Act, also known as Obamacare. This global bequest would come at the expense of many geopolitical and humanitarian considerations that should have given the US pause. With its immediate empowerment of Iran and with no limitations on the latter's steady regional expansion, the effect would not only be felt in the neighbourhood, but well beyond. As is the norm with many regimes, Iran's officials never hid their aspirations when speaking to a domestic audience but had an entirely different approach abroad; that's why for Syrians, ignoring the actions of Iran in Syria was tantamount to appeasing the regime.

While the Bush administration's 2003 invasion of Iraq had unintentionally been a gift to Iran, removing its greatest foe and destroying the institutions that could have held the Iraqi state together, the Obama administration was effectively delivering Syria to the Islamic regime on a silver platter. For all their folly, Bush's neocons of the early 2000s seemed convinced that removing Saddam Hussein would eventually result in a nascent democracy for Iraqis, which would contribute to the stability they wanted in the region. In contrast, Obama's Democrats the following decade acted as if the region was not fit for the bills of rights and the civil liberties others had, preferring to deal with the strongmen that supposedly ensured that stability. As Iran revelled in its growing clout, Obama's 2009 speech heralding 'a new beginning' and preaching mutual respect as he addressed the Arab world from Cairo had never sounded hollower.

NEW DOMINIONS IN GREATER SYRIA

Iranian officials were not even shy about their regional aspirations and boasted about their influence in several Arab countries. In February 2012, Mehdi Taeb, the head of the think tank Ammar Headquarters affiliated with the close circle of Supreme Leader Ayatollah Khamenei, observed to a gathering of Basij (Iran's notorious paramilitary force) that Syria was more important than some of Iran's actual provinces. 'Syria is the 35th province and a strategic province for us,' he said. 'If the enemy attacks us and seeks to take over Syria or Khuzestan, the priority lies in maintaining Syria because if we maintain Syria, we can take back Khuzestan. However, if we lose Syria, we won't be able to hold Tehran.' In 2014, a member of parliament, Ali Reza Zakani had asserted that 'Three Arab capitals have today ended in the hands of Iran and belonged to the Islamic Iranian Revolution' and that Sanaa was becoming the fourth, after Baghdad, Beirut, and Damascus.

Control was not just political; it was becoming a physical reality. The infamous starve-or-surrender sieges Assad imposed all over Syria, assisted by Hezbollah and other Iran-backed militias, were holding numerous areas hostage. Surrenders would be immediately followed by the so-called evacuations of civilians; in fact, they were forced deportations of tens of thousands of Syrians to the north of the country, allowing the demographic engineering that Iran had been planning for years before the revolution. They would be led to waiting buses that would drive them hundreds of kilometres north to the province of Idlib and abandoned there. This pushed refugees and defeated opposition fighters into a single enclosure closer to the Turkish border, swelling the population of the province that the regime and its backers planned to retake last.

One by one, numerous Syrian districts, neighbourhoods, and villages were emptied of their inhabitants and replaced by people brought in by Iran, with Bashar Assad's full support and orchestration, in what was being called the open 'Shiification' of Syria. It was a calculated move to change the social fabric and the cultural essence of a mostly Sunni Syria, an analysis that numerous observers and experts shared. Iran's hegemonic drive was facilitated by a Western laissez-faire attitude, by the oversight of Russia which was not concerned with either changing or protecting the Syrian identity map, and by the Obama administration's focus on a nuclear deal legacy to which Syrian lives were irrelevant.

In effect, the nuclear deal was drawing new lines in the sand, a century after diplomats Mark Sykes and François Georges-Picot had divided the region between Britain and France as the Ottoman Empire was nearing its end. While official borders remained unchanged this time around, different zones of influence had now amalgamated to form an uninterrupted stretch of friendly territory for Iran, with the compliments of its sponsors. This served as a conduit for the flow of arms and the militias that kept the self-designated 'Axis of Resistance' in control. One could even remark, and not necessarily in jest, that Greater Syria had gone from Sykes-Picot to Kerry-Zarif in one hundred years, given Secretary of State John Kerry's tireless efforts to secure the deal for Obama. Unlike Sykes-Picot, however, this deal only had one major beneficiary.

The domino effect of Iran's expansion was chilling but entirely predictable, having started much before its repression of the Syrian Revolution. Under Hafez Assad, relations with Iran had cost Syria the goodwill of nearly every other Arab country, especially during his support of Iran during the war with Iraq. After Bashar came to power, Iran not only benefitted from the removal of its major enemy in Iraq in 2003, but also from the creation of that wide passage to Syria (and from there to Lebanon), where it began fortifying a presence that would not have been achievable during the Saddam and Hafez years.

NEW DOMINIONS IN GREATER SYRIA

Bashar's first decade allowed Iran to gain unprecedented military, political, and economic influence in Syria, and by extension in Lebanon. His second decade allowed Iran free rein in the violent subjugation of revolutionary Syrians, and introduced a new level of geopolitical engineering with an even more powerful patron.

* * *

Since the collapse of the red line after the 2013 chemical massacre, barrel bombs had been brought to the forefront of Assad's killing arsenal, becoming his most lethal weapon without causing a single international crisis, no matter how high the number of victims. With the signing of the nuclear deal, an even more potent weapon to kill Syrians in their thousands was added to the mix: the Russian air force. President Vladimir Putin's decision to fully join Assad's war on his people has often been explained as resulting from an Iranian appeal to intervene, at a time when even Iran and its many militias were not managing to keep Assad securely in power. Supporting that theory was the claim that Qassem Soleimani, commander of the Quds Force of the Islamic Revolutionary Guard Corps (IRGC), had flown to Moscow shortly after the nuclear deal to convince Putin to start an air campaign and bolster Assad's position.

Taking the credit for getting Russia all in is typical of Iran loyalists' tendency to exaggerate their influence and to flaunt their sway in the region. The regime was powerful, but Putin did not need a strategy lesson from Iran, nor was he waiting for them to issue a formal invitation. He had been looking for some time to expand Russia's role in the region, and was ready to swoop in when Obama needed to pass the ball after the chemical massacre. While Iran was now the biggest regional player in the Levant, Putin had invested enough political capital in Syria to not allow Iran full control: he neither wanted the increasingly tiresome Assad to fall, nor the expansionist Iran to be the leading power broker. With many cumulative reasons behind Putin's decision, there is no doubt that Russia's big Syrian military debut in September 2015 was also a consequence of the nuclear deal, and of Obama's laissez-faire.

Syrians were already three years into their Revolution for Dignity when another one started some 3,000 kilometres away. In Ukraine, the February 2014 Maidan anti-government demonstrations (that participants also called a Revolution for Dignity) protested the government's refusal to sign an association agreement bringing it closer to the EU. In a few days, dozens of Ukrainians were killed by security forces, inflaming public opinion and forcing President Viktor Yanukovych to agree to an interim government, and then to immediately flee Kyiv. When parliament voted him out on 22 February, Yanukovych decried this as a coup and, like clockwork, pro-Russian protests erupted in southern and eastern Ukraine. Putin's invasion and subsequent annexation of Crimea, a turning point in the history of Ukraine and Russia, would have long-lasting repercussions most people could not foresee at the time.

Putin waited for the backlash and, sure enough, condemnations and an assortment of synonyms expressing disapproval dominated headlines, quoting concerned leaders around the world, just as they had following Assad's chemical massacre, and just as they had in 2008 after Russia's incursion into Georgia. They also urged Ukrainians, the victims, not to escalate.

Putin had killed the second Revolution for Dignity against one of his protégés; he was still a few years from believing he had managed to kill the first. But as of September 2015, his air force was instrumental in changing not only the destiny of Syrians, but also the political trajectory of many countries far beyond their borders.

The months following the nuclear deal brought new dimensions to the Syrian tragedy and to regional dynamics: the aban-

NEW DOMINIONS IN GREATER SYRIA

donment of Syrians had been implied in the 2013 OPCW agreement led by Russia, but it was formalised with the Iran nuclear deal and all it entailed. But when Assad's barrel bombs were supplemented by modern Russian fighter jets and by the IRGC's financial boost and carte blanche in the region, a sense of utter fear and panic took over Syrians.

By the time Russia's air campaign started at the end of September 2015, claiming it was meant to fight ISIS (which had in fact only been targeted by the global coalition's airstrikes starting in August 2014) but only ever bombing opposition areas outside of the regime's control, Syrians were being pounded from every side. They understood that there was no going back, and that Iran and Russia were here to stay. For the first time, Putin now had a port at his warships' disposal in Tartous, and the Hmeimim airbase on the Mediterranean, with a treaty signed in August 2015 allowing Russia a fifty-year stay, renewable in twenty-five-year segments, becoming an essential base for Russia's military contingent in Syria.

* * *

As of the summer of 2015 and for months on end, Syrians turned to the sea in dinghies and rafts, escaping the hell they had lived and the hell that was yet to come from this coalescence of elements that created the largest wave of refugees since World War II. They were making a last, desperate attempt to find the safety and the dignity denied them in Syria. These were unforgettable days, with a whirlwind of emotions and energies that stayed with us all for a long time, as we watched in real time how the trail of the Syrian tragedy reached Europe.

The EU's Dublin Regulation has stipulated since 1997 that asylum seekers must apply in the EU country they reach first. Of course, this meant countries closest to the EU's borders would struggle more when an influx of refugees occurred, as was the

IT STARTED IN DAMASCUS

case when Syrian refugees headed to Europe in huge numbers. The impact they would have on European politics was to be ground-breaking and long-lasting.

On 27 August 2015, while several European leaders happened to be in Vienna to discuss the refugee crisis in the western Balkans, a gruesome discovery about fifty kilometres away was to trigger some unexpected changes in European attitudes towards refugees, at least at first. In the vicinity of the luxury designer outlet in Parndorf, an abandoned lorry was found on the hard shoulder of the A4 motorway; when police opened the back of the lorry, they found the decomposing bodies of seventy-one refugees who had suffocated to death. Most were Syrian.

The horror of this exploitation of people by smugglers, and the despair leading refugees to accept the most dangerous and demeaning methods, shocked European leaders into action. Germany suspended the Dublin Regulation for Syrians, allowing up to a million refugees to apply for asylum even if they came through another EU country. A few days later, at a press conference in Dresden, German chancellor Angela Merkel commented that Germany was a strong country, adding: 'We managed so much before, we can manage this.' Hungary finally allowed thousands of refugees to leave through Austria, after they had been stuck at Budapest's main train stations for days and forbidden from continuing without an exit visa. Austria opened the border crossing of Nickelsdorf with Hungary, allowing thousands to continue their way westward.

Another death would show just how much people were willing to risk everything to leave home and country. On 2 September, a tiny body was found on a Turkish beach close to a resort in Bodrum: it was that of a little boy lying face down, in his little blue shorts and his dark red t-shirt. Aylan, barely two years old, never even made it across the sea and would have drowned in anonymity but for the tide that washed him back to the shore.

NEW DOMINIONS IN GREATER SYRIA

As so many cried for these lost souls, Assad was still in full killing spree, dropping barrel bombs all over Syria, creating thousands of other Syrian victims who mostly remained nameless, faceless, story-less.

* * *

I had never imagined that one day, in the same city that had witnessed the birth of the JCPOA just weeks earlier, hundreds of thousands of Syrian refugees—and others who rode on the tail of the Syrian tragedy—would pass in search of life, and that I would be there to help welcome many of them in the heart of Vienna, where we now lived. We had seen their tremendous suffering in Syria, their abuse by people who tried to benefit from their plight, their immense fear when they boarded the flimsy boats holding their children tight, their mistreatment by many authorities as they tried to make their way on foot, dreaming of safety.

As news came that refugees were being transported from the Hungarian border to Vienna's main train stations, I rushed there for days in a row, joining many other Austrian, Syrian, and international volunteers who wanted to help people at an incredible juncture in our joint history. On my first day, fifty buses had brought 2,500 people to the station, as cordons of police officers lined the platform, and volunteers guided exhausted people to an area where food and drinks—and another long waiting period—awaited them. A lovely choir of about twenty adults had moved along the platforms, singing inspirational songs to bemused refugees. This was not the kind of welcome they had experienced before, and when Austrian president Heinz Fischer made an unannounced visit as well, thanking officials and volunteers and chatting with some refugees, it was clear that at least ninety-nine percent of them had no idea who he was. Large posters from the City of Vienna told them 'You are safe' in English and in Arabic, and volunteers explained that trains would carry them to

Munich, for free, as most were heading to Germany where they knew they were welcome.

The fear and exhaustion were clearly visible on every face, and many were too overwhelmed to talk. I spent most of my time translating for refugees and various authorities, and bringing several people to the medical area where doctors were treating injuries sustained during the long journey. Along the way, I heard some of their stories.

One morning, I was led to a small Syrian boy who had headaches and had been feverish for several days; his forehead was burning, and I took little Ahmad and his mother Nour to a doctor. As he was being checked, I asked Nour about her own state: she bent her head and wept on my shoulder as she recounted their ordeal from Bab Al Hawa to Vienna—from Assad's bombs to a camp in Turkey, to a terrifying sea crossing, to the long journey through Greece, Macedonia, Serbia, and finally through Hungary, where Nour had broken down and begun to cry.

While volunteers had been humane, selfless, and welcoming everywhere, some authorities had made refugees' lives even more miserable. There was a common denominator to the conversations I had with Syrian refugees that month, as I am sure was the case with most volunteers: it was their shock at the degrading treatment they received from certain authorities in Hungary amid the government's rising anti-immigration policies. Most were shaken to their core and bursting to tell those who would listen, thinking we did not know and that it was not being reported in the media.

I helped a young woman limping on one crutch to the paramedics; she had been pushed to the ground in Hungary and seemed to be in great pain. Dima, however, categorically refused to let the Viennese doctor touch her swollen leg, to his shock. She was still traumatised by the nurses and doctors who she said handled her roughly and rudely, and was only asking for painkillers. After she shared some shocking details with me, showing me bruises on her arms after they woke her up by pinching her, I asked her father to convince her to let the doctor treat her, saying I would be by her side the whole time. He was in his late sixties and trembled with indignation as he gave me details of 'what they did to us in Hungary'—a sentence I heard repeatedly. Dima looked for me half an hour later, still in pain, to tell me her father was now crying; after holding back for so long, he was finally able to break down, in the safety of Vienna.

He was not the only grown man crying. On one side of the platform, I remember how a middle-aged Syrian man tried unsuccessfully to control his tears as he told us how he was separated from his wife and children in the chaos, as they were led into buses. He had lost his phone and could only wait, devastated by the tragedy within the bigger tragedy, the fear of not finding his family after having gotten so far. Save for a few comforting words that were worth absolutely nothing, I could only think of our own impotence in the face of a catastrophe of this magnitude. How many Syrians would be looking for family members across the world in the years to come, just as so many people, Jews in particular, did for years after World War II? Why were we considering ourselves free and progressive civilisations if we allowed entirely man-made displacements of this enormity, again?

While despair was palpable in many refugees, so was a definite sense of resolve in most. One day, two young couples, from Aleppo and from Hama, chatted with me about their plans in Germany. One man was a mechanical engineer, the other a graphic designer, and as their pregnant wives sat by a pillar resting their aching backs, both told me they were eager to settle down, learn German, and start anew. In a world where there are inevitably differences between haves and have-nots, they were clearly closer to the former, of the professional middle class that had turned into the latter when barrel bombs pushed them into exile with only a small bag to their name.

They were like that grandmother from Daraa whose family had no choice but to flee the barrel bombs, her tears beginning to flow as she told me of her concern that one of her disappeared sons would not be able to find them if he ever came out alive. As she spoke, I was moved by her calm grandson of about five or six, standing by her side munching on some peanuts handed out by volunteers. To lighten the mood, I told him that he looked like a bright boy who would learn German quickly: 'You'll see, it will be easy for you and I'm sure you will do well in school.' He nodded in agreement and, as any Syrian would, stretched out his hand and offered me some of his peanuts.

Amidst all the chaos at those train stations was great dignity as well. The dignity of the refugees, who smiled when we welcomed them and who often politely refused to accept offered food, merely asking to be directed to the trains to Munich. The dignity of the children who, when handed chocolate bars and urged to take another, would say 'no thank you, one is enough'. The dignity of the volunteers, who seemed to instinctively know when to circulate, when to initiate contact, and when to stand on the side with trays of warm drinks, small things to eat, and even cigarettes for these people whose anguish they saw and understood.

Each refugee was a story of hardship, of losing a home, of a desperate search for safety and dignity, of hope that the next generation would at least have a chance of a normal life. The one who will stay with me forever is Loulou, a pretty eight-year-old girl from Damascus whose little bag with the few things she had chosen for the escape from home had sunk into the sea during the crossing. She had been in the same clothes for weeks, and was given some old sneakers when her wet ones finally gave out. She was sneezing, exhausted, and waited patiently while her mother Salma recounted their journey to me. Still outraged about what was done to them in Hungary, she told me it had been the first time since they left Damascus that she had nearly regretted leaving.

I felt an immediate attachment to them, perhaps because Loulou was nearly my own daughter's age, and perhaps because Salma was a fellow Damascene with a shared environment and roots, and I arranged to have some clean clothes and a Barbie doll brought to her daughter later that day, just before their train was scheduled to depart for Germany. As I prepared to say goodbye, Salma reached into her handbag and tried to give me the one luxury item still in her possession: a small bag of Arabic coffee, carefully wrapped in plastic. I fought back tears when I realised what she was doing; I knew the emotional value of that tiny item, that little ephemeral piece of home that had travelled so far with them. She was pained when I refused to take it, insisting 'Please, it's from Syria.' I promised to accept her hospitality in their home in Germany one day, safe from the Air Force Intelligence unit that had taken her older son and prompted the family to flee when they managed to get him out.

These were days of humanity and kindness, of positive energy that Syrians had not seen for a long time, and would not see again for a long time. For the next decade or so, unless it was to talk about the refugee crisis and what to do about it, Syrians were mostly forgotten again.

* * *

By 2018, nearly seven million Syrians were now refugees; most were in neighbouring countries that did not want them, the rest in faraway countries that mostly did not want them either. In Jordan and Lebanon, some two million Syrians were relegated to sprawling camps of misery, while over three and a half million in Turkey populated the areas bordering Syria and spread further, turning Istanbul into an unexpected Syrian exile hub. Tolerated at first, they soon became actively opposed and mistreated in some areas, especially in Lebanon where one of the Assad regime's most powerful enablers, Hezbollah, controlled the scene. Meanwhile, an entire generation of Syrian children, some born and raised in camps, was now illiterate, children who would come of age as prisoners of hopelessness—abandoned, depressed, angry, and with nothing to live for or to lose.

Homs had been retaken in 2014 by the regime while the pretend negotiations were taking place in Geneva. With Russia's entry and the bombing of all rebel areas, the next big goal was to retake East Aleppo, whose war of attrition had become known as Syria's Stalingrad. As death and destruction rained on the city, the Russian air force had dropped thousands of leaflets telling people to flee, warning: 'If you do not leave these areas urgently, you will be annihilated. You know that everyone has given up on you. They left you alone to face your doom.' They were absolutely right: Syrians faced their doom alone.

With Russian air support, and Iranian ground forces and allied militias led by IRGC commander Qassem Soleimani, the regime eventually obliterated Aleppo in December 2016, forcibly displacing tens of thousands of Syrians, yet again. They walked out of their devastated neighbourhoods, in silence, dragging the small bags they could carry; like Homsis and other Syrians before them, they were put on buses and driven away from their homes, joining other forcibly displaced people in Idlib. The homes and buildings that had miraculously not turned to rubble were confiscated and distributed to people chosen by Iran.

Assad conducted another significant chemical attack on Khan Shaykhun, in northern Syria, on 4 April 2017. It killed nearly one hundred people and injured over five hundred with toxic gas that included sarin, which was supposed to have disappeared from the Syrian arsenal after the 2013 deal between Obama and Putin. This time, even in the absence of a new red line, it took the US under President Donald Trump just three days to launch fifty-nine Tomahawk missiles on the Shayrat airbase from which the chemical attack had been launched. At that late stage of the conflict, the strikes changed nothing, and Putin did nothing either, especially as he had been notified well ahead of time by Trump so that Russian and Syrian troops would be safely out of the way.

Assad launched chemicals again in April 2018, in Douma, in an attack that experts (including OPCW) said used chlorine gas combined with a nerve agent. It killed nearly fifty and injured hundreds again. One week later, the US, the UK, and France launched targeted strikes on Syrian chemical weapons centres and storage facilities that never seemed to disappear, with or without OPCW. Had this response been given in 2013 by these very same powers, debated Syrians among themselves in the aftermath of the strikes, would we all be where we are today?

Eastern Ghouta, the scene of the first large-scale chemical massacre, had been under siege for years and was the last big thorn in the regime's immediate side. With the help of ferocious and relentless Russian airstrikes and Hezbollah forces on the ground, Assad could claim victory once more in mid-April 2018 and forcibly displace yet more Syrians north.

Russia had developed a penchant for striking not just civilian areas, but specific civilian facilities like hospitals. Between the Syrian and the Russian air forces, numerous hospitals, clinics, and medical facilities were deliberately targeted and bombed. They did not even need to search for the field hospitals that Syrians tried to set up wherever they could: the United Nations gave Russia a list of medical facilities and their positions, aiming at sparing them, and protecting them from the bombs. Instead, the UN's list had condemned them to destruction: Russia converted that restriction list into its to-do list, striking one facility after another with full impunity, destroying over six hundred medical facilities and suffering no consequences despite ample documentation of these war crimes.

As the world sent thoughts and prayers, expressing concern from one massacre to another, Assad and Russia had carpet bombed and destroyed most of Syria, leaving apocalyptic scenes in cities under the rubble, with thousands upon thousands of uncounted bodies yet to be dug out, and over fourteen million Syrians—more than half the population—pushed out of their homes. No other country in the entire world has had over sixty percent of its population displaced, their homes destroyed, for the sake of a man and his clan, and for the imperial designs of his supporters.

Had this violent regime been stopped in its tracks in due time, had powerful democratic leaders confronted its Iranian and Russian enablers, had mass murderers not been appeased, and had Syrians not been left helpless in the face of this abject monstrosity, the world would have been a very different place today.

* * *

Syrians inside and outside the country changed under the force of this unrelenting assault on the very dignity for which they strove. Some were liberated from the shackles of their earlier prohibitions, adopting more liberal stances and stronger confidence in making their opinions matter. Others closed themselves in, nestling into the only codes of conduct and philosophies of life that had held them together when everyone else had ignored their tragedy. Many now found solace only in sacred texts, in the holy books offering the salvation they could never attain at home, in life. As they all changed and discovered those chasms amongst them, so did the world that swayed from the force of this Syrian storm.

The domino effect gained traction as politicians in Europe and beyond liberally helped themselves to this tragedy to score points domestically. One of the first countries to experience a drastic change was Britain. After repeated attempts to gather popular support to leave the European Union, the anti-EU camp received the PR gift of refugees crossing Europe; it gave Leave campaigners leeway in claiming Britain was in danger as UKIP (UK Independence Party) splashed giant posters of the refugees crossing Croatia, carefully zoomed in on groups of young men, captioned 'Breaking Point'. There were many important factors in the Brexit debate, of course, but without Syria, and without the contrived fear that refugees—or migrants as they tend to be called by the Leave camp—like the Syrian ones were going to wreak havoc on British life, the vote might have well gone the other way, giving the 52% to the Remain camp instead.

Even before the Brexit vote, there had been divisions in British politics stemming from the Syrian predicament. Ed Miliband's consequential non-interventionist stance of 2013 after Assad's first large chemical massacre was followed by an even more advantageous Labour position for Assad with the election of Jeremy Corbyn as leader in September 2015, following the defeat of Labour at the general election and the resignation of Miliband. The archetypal anti-imperialist, Corbyn did not speak of Assad's crimes, nor of Russian and Iranian imperialism in the region, their bombings and killings, and their militias roaming the region. While some Labour MPs did vote for measures that Corbyn opposed, such as strikes against ISIS, his leadership cemented Labour's sharp left turn for years, and its detachment from foreign involvement that strayed from hard-left stances.

This may not have been solely because of Syria, but there has been a clear shift from centrist politics to further left or further right in most democratic countries. If the actual presence of refugees was not driving the change to either extreme, the threat of their eventual arrival did, along with the predictable tangent of security concerns touted by many. With the spate of Islamist terror attacks such as those on Bataclan and other Paris sites in 2015, the issues of radicalisation (especially of European-born ISIS sympathisers) became increasingly tied to those of refugees. In both cases, there was a Syrian connection that influenced the harder lines; ironically, the truth was that the more the Assad regime prevailed, the more the number of refugees increased, and the more radicalised cases grew.

Inevitably, refugee-phobia and the more general Islamophobia changed the politics, but not the measures taken to stop people becoming refugees. In Europe, right and far-right parties have gained ground with every election. In Hungary, and in other EU members on migration routes, anti-refugee measures have triggered deep changes that have affected other European countries; in the Schengen area that gave freedom of movement and eliminated borders in twenty-seven European countries, border checks have resurfaced. As right and far-right parties swept up 2024 European Parliament elections, to the delight of Putin who remarked that Europe was defenceless, an increasing number of states started calling for new solutions for Syrians, a euphemism for deportations back to a country they wanted to designate as safe. Everyone wanted the Syrian crisis, as they came to call it, to be over, especially after public opinion had turned against the refugees.

Of course, they were merely following the lead of several Arab countries that took the road to rehabilitating Assad. It went slowly, at first, with the UAE reopening its embassy in Syria in 2018; it took until November 2021 for its foreign minister to be the first senior official to visit Damascus. Other Arabs followed, and in May 2023, Assad was welcomed back to the Arab League Summit in Jeddah, and embassies started opening one after another. The rehabilitation urge was simmering in Europe too; in June 2024, seven EU countries called for a re-evaluation of the situation in Syria that they estimated had considerably evolved,

NEW DOMINIONS IN GREATER SYRIA

to allow for the 'voluntary return' of Syrian refugees. In July 2024, Italy named its first ambassador to Damascus. They were all on a roll, as if nothing had happened.

* * *

There was a lot wrong with the prevailing world order, but a new world order where ideologue, authoritarian, violent regimes are given carte blanche to operate freely, under the convenient concept of sovereignty, is terrifying. It is this collective abdication of responsibility that allowed the Syrian catastrophe to reach such incomprehensible proportions in the first place.

The failure to respond to Putin's annexation of Crimea in 2014, and to his devastating intervention in Syria, encouraged him to invade the rest of Ukraine in 2022 while threatening consequences for those who help his victims, or eliminating those who defy him, assassinating Russian opposition public figures like Alexei Navalny. In turn, the invasion of Ukraine has triggered previously inconceivable consequences: countries that had never imagined belonging to NATO hurried their official applications to join the alliance, afraid of facing an emboldened Russia alone.

The EU arranged to pay Turkey billions to police its own shores and prevent Syrians and other refugees from crossing over—the same Turkey whose requests to join the EU had been rejected, and whose NATO position has allowed it to impose conditions on the countries trying to access it, such as Finland (which joined in 2023) and Sweden (which joined in 2024). Fearing more refugee flows from Israel's war on Gaza after the terror attack of 7 October 2023, the EU made a similar deal with Lebanon, even as Hezbollah's leader Hassan Nasrallah had openly threatened to put Syrians in boats and send them across the Mediterranean; until his last days, he continued to use Syrians as mere pawns in his and Iran's grandiose plans.

IT STARTED IN DAMASCUS

More authoritarian leaders began taking increasingly provocative liberties; to arrest a journalist, Belarus forced a flight of a major European airline to divert to and land in Minsk, a major transgression of international law that leaves people with little recourse. In several regions, the private militias fighting at the behest of authoritarian states are developing their own strong followings and becoming increasingly tempted to act beyond their prescribed role. The case of Yevgeny Prigozhin and the Wagner Group he led, most notoriously in Syria at the height of Russian intervention to rescue Assad, will not be an isolated one; his death in a plane crash in August 2023, shortly after he openly rebelled against Putin, shows how easy it will be for militias and their leaders to develop their own counter agendas, putting numerous parties at risk of unexpected confrontations. They are no less dangerous than ISIS.

We were being dragged into a global abyss by megalomaniacs with immense self-conceit, a complete lack of basic ethics, and incurable myopia, as the devastating images of weeping, terrified, emotionally and physically exhausted children became ominous icons of this early century.

The Syrian regime and its allies were neither stopped nor made to face significant consequences for their genocidal war on civilians; given the magnitude of their crimes, other states have felt freer to act with impunity and ignore pleas for moderation, in offence or in defence, from Gaza and Yemen to Ukraine. Nearly twenty-five years after his enthronement, Bashar Assad had managed to affect most of the regional conflicts and the global crises—not because he was a powerful or brilliant strategist, but because he was left unchallenged as he enjoyed the backing of dangerous authoritarians, whose ideological and imperialistic agendas exceeded even the contemptible greed of the Assad clan.

In this era when the United Nations stopped counting Syrian victims very early on, when the leader of the free world snubbed the cries for help of a people under attack, when strongmen flouted international law and faced minimal consequences, when conspiracy theorists and apologists spread disinformation and dangerous propaganda, when strong democracies ignored their own laws and justified their own inaction, and when the creeping normalisation of war criminals was being allowed for the sake of imagined stability, no one was really safe.

* * *

As Arab states embarked on the resumption of ties with Assad, one of their main conditions had been that he put an end to the production and export of huge quantities of Captagon, a highly addictive amphetamine spreading around the region. Most Syrians knew how heavily the regime itself was implicated in its manufacture and distribution, as was Hezbollah; it did not bode well, we thought, because this was the easiest way to make money for the Assad clan. Captagon was the barrel bomb of drugs: cheap, easy, and quick to make, simple to unleash on a wide area for maximum return.

As we knew he would, Bashar Assad lied his way throughout, enjoying his return to the red carpets of Arab capitals, promising everything and delivering nothing. He treated his Arab counterparts like he treated his people, with disdain, thinking he was smarter than everyone else. He rejected their advice, even though they had committed to investing again in Syria in return for ending the flow of drugs to their people, to their children.

He acted in the same irresponsible way with Putin, who had much less time to devote to Syria after the invasion of Ukraine, and whose patience with the unimpressive Assad was beginning to thin. In several stages over the past years, starting in earnest around 2020, Russian media began publishing scathing analyses and news of the mendacity, corruption, lack of popularity, and incompetence of the petty Syrian dictator. It was clear they were not just approved by Putin, but produced under the Kremlin's explicit guidance.

In 2021, Assad got himself elected to a fourth presidential term, with 95.19%—receiving over fourteen million votes in an area of not even ten million potential voters, in yet another instance of the legendary Assadist maths that fed his giant ego.

When Israel's targeting of Iranian and Lebanese militias began in earnest in 2023 and 2024, Assad did not take it seriously, as usual. He stayed in his corner and acted as if the war on Gaza did not concern him; in fact, he may have even thought all these developments, including the weakening of Hezbollah and Iran, would benefit his regime. He probably thought that Israel had cleared the field for him.

As all this was happening, with normalisation gaining ground and humanitarian aid beginning to shrink, interest in Syria had never been lower. It seemed everyone accepted that it was game over, especially as Gaza was being decimated by Israel and as Lebanon was once more under fire. Syrians were seemingly in a parallel universe, mentioned only in the context of Israeli strikes on Iranian assets, as if nothing about them and their predicament mattered any longer and it had all already been settled.

* * *

In the early fall of 2024, one of my cousins in our building began using a telephone landline that was still in my name; it used to be our internet connection line and had been inactive for years. The next day, the phone on that number rang: it was a security branch officer asking about me, having seen the line in sudden use after all these years. He subjected my cousin to an interrogation about my whereabouts, assuming I had somehow snuck back into the country, incognito. My cousin claimed he did not even know where I was as we were not on speaking terms, and that he used the line without my permission while I was abroad.

NEW DOMINIONS IN GREATER SYRIA

I was surprised that with all the devastation in Syria, security still had time to monitor matters relating to people like us, the dissenting writers and oppositionists whose every word was considered a crime and a reason for arrest.

That phone incident was insignificant compared to the years of messages and threats sent my way, but I felt it was a sign that nothing would change amid news that the regime was requisitioning empty houses to distribute to their loyalists. Even if a general amnesty came years later, I knew the regime reserved its ire for people who wrote and spoke, much more than for those who bore arms. For a public advocate and writer like me, it seemed we were reaching the end of hope.

As it had done for the opposition figures they knew, the regime had rescinded all my rights as a citizen in the second year of the revolution, as if wiping them off a slate. An old family friend who had maintained his close ties to regime security sent my mother a copy from their database of the order for my arrest, should I ever cross a Syrian border. When our friend had asked a high official if he could intercede on my behalf and get my name off this list, the answer was: 'Do not bring her name up to me again, Rime Allaf is a red line.' For over a decade, I had kept that paper inside my expired Syrian passport, in the box with all my precious and important things, expecting they would remain painful mementos of an era when we had dared to dream of having a normal country.

Over the years, several buyers had been interested in our home, but I had always pleaded with my family to wait, not wanting to lose that one place in the world that was always supposed to be there, which my mother had spent so many years making comfortable and beautiful, where my father's presence could still be felt, where my aunts' jasmine vines still climbed over the neighbour's balcony. Absurdly, I held on to an impossible future scenario where I might set foot back home again, to the place where I had started to discover and devour Syria in all its intensity.

IT STARTED IN DAMASCUS

When a buyer approached my cousin again to ask if we would sell, we had another family talk in November 2024. Had the time come to say goodbye to home? My book was already ninety percent written, scheduled for publication in autumn 2025, and while the regime could not possibly take away any more of my rights, it could certainly make my family's life even more difficult with a future sale. What was I still waiting for? Tearing up, I finally told my cousin the words I had refused to say for over a decade: please call the buyer and arrange for the sale.

Two days later, Aleppo fell to the rebels.

15

ON THE WINDING ROAD TO DAMASCUS

There are plot twists you see coming, and others that take you completely by surprise. While weary Syrians were no strangers to shock, most had reached a state of lassitude, of an absence of expectations, not allowing themselves to feel hope any more only to be disappointed again. In November 2024, nobody could have predicted that the regime would crumble the way it did, and that Bashar Assad would not mark his silver jubilee in power.

Stunned people all over the globe wondered how this could have happened so quickly; after all, everyone had been told for years that Assad had won and that European countries were preparing to send refugees back to a safe—or safe enough—country. From that perspective, the regime appeared to have collapsed in ten days, without warning, but while the end felt quick indeed, it did not take ten days to bring Assad down: it took 5,000.

A sequence of decisions had precipitated the end of Assad's brutal reign. Whereas most of the world was in tentative normalisation mode and not paying attention, Russia and Iran were acutely aware of the precariousness of the situation, and both were now disillusioned with a regime they could not save as they struggled with their own battles. Iran was reeling from a crescendo of intensive Israeli attacks on its military assets in the region, and particularly on Hezbollah, the Iranian regime's pride and its most effective paramilitary organisation, responsible for so much wanton violence against Syrians. When Israel assassinated its leader Hassan Nasrallah in September 2024, along with dozens of senior commanders, Hezbollah had been crippled and could also not have significantly helped Assad who, despite Iran's request for Syrian help, had not lifted a finger of support as Israel pounded Lebanon, and Gaza before it, during that period.

Russia's difficulties in Ukraine were compounded by Putin's growing irritation with Assad. In 2020, an agreement between Russia and Turkey had regulated the situation in Idlib province, where hundreds of thousands of Syrians had been forcibly displaced by the regime and its allies. Since then, a modicum of understanding had endured between Putin and Turkish president Erdoğan on several parameters that had turned Idlib into a de-escalation zone, despite sporadic Russian airstrikes and subsequent ones by Assad that violated the deal at a time when Putin wanted to move into a new phase with Turkey.

In the summer of 2024, Erdoğan publicly suggested a meeting with Assad to begin normalising ties; this was a development that Putin welcomed and pushed for, but Assad repeatedly refused his personal entreaty to accept. Despite his over-confident obstinacy, he still expected Russia to step in whenever he needed it, and when he lost Aleppo on 29 November, Assad flew to Moscow to request Russian support and permission for Iranian military flights to land at Hmeimim airbase. Assad told his entourage upon returning to Damascus that Putin had consented; Iranians said they had not received the clearance in question, however, as Assad's head of the media office later divulged. Nevertheless, Assad told his generals support was on the way, instructing them to hold their ground. But they didn't.

ON THE WINDING ROAD TO DAMASCUS

As rebels advanced on Hama after having taken full control of Aleppo, many had expected the arrival of the Russian air force to carry out the usual airstrikes, as it had whenever skirmishes and threats to Assad had emerged. This was no simple skirmish though, and the planes did not come in full force as Assad's army tactically retreated, we were told, to shore up defences further south. On 5 December, rebels liberated Hama and the army retreated further south to Homs, as the Syrian news bubble began to burst anew with excitement and a surge of hope that most had lost a long time ago. By then, we knew who was leading the charge and had managed to unite different armed groups coming from Idlib, and a southern front from Daraa. That fateful week, Putin was in Minsk for the twenty-fifth anniversary of the Union State between Russia and Belarus, where he signed a new security pact with his most dependable ally, President Alexander Lukashenko. Over the course of three days, Bashar Assad put in several calls to the Russian presidency to ask for help again, waiting for Putin to respond. But he didn't.

Logically, a big battle would have to happen around Homs, that most important junction that separated northern and southern Syria, and a key access point in the land supply routes of Iranian arms to Lebanon. Some of the regime's forces barely even tried to confront the rebels, fleeing to the coast instead. On 6 December, the Russian Embassy in Damascus called on its citizens to leave Syria immediately, as Iran began to withdraw military personnel and diplomatic staff as well, including IRGC commander Javad Ghaffari who had been redeployed to Syria just days before. By 7 December, Homs was under rebel control. There was now a direct line to Damascus, the jewel in the crown and the most fortified city in the country for which the regime's top defenders, despite the many desertions over that week, were expected to fight to the death. But they didn't.

As they gradually took over Syrian cities from north to south, rebels had passed by the main jails and freed the detainees, most of them political prisoners, people whose only crimes had been supporting the revolution in word even if not in deed, or who were related to someone guilty of that support. Some women came out with children in tow, not knowing who the fathers were after having been subjected to multiple rapes. Some men had clearly been in jail for much longer, before there even was a revolution; one of them, a 58-year-old Lebanese man released from prison in Hama, had been inside for nearly forty years after his arrest at the age of eighteen at a Syrian army checkpoint in Lebanon. Around one hundred Lebanese detainees with similar stories were freed by the rebels, as were several thousand Syrian men and women who came out dazed, not fully grasping who had liberated them or why.

On the night of 7 to 8 December, glued to our screens, we learned that the rebels had reached Sednaya, a mere thirty kilometres from central Damascus, and were finally heading to the prison that Amnesty International had labelled a human slaughterhouse, the death camp where thousands had gone missing since the 1980s. It was probable, at that point, that nearly all Syrians around the world, and those in the country with functioning electricity, were online together, millions of anxious souls watching events unfold live on every Arabic channel except the regime's, already crying from the force of these emotions and the conviction that this time, against all odds, deliverance was imminent.

At 05:08 Damascus time on 8 December, the opposition channel Syria TV was the first to announce that Bashar Assad had fled. He deserted Syria in the dead of night, as a coward would, without notifying his officers, his government, his supporters, his people. In his final act of sheer spite, before bolting to Russia where Putin granted him asylum on 'humanitarian grounds,' Assad had not even ordered his security forces to stand down, to protect those loyal to him. If he still thought fighting would erupt, he could have done so to save a few lives and spare the world's oldest capital, a small gesture for the good of the nation that would have cost him nothing. But from day one, despite the rave reviews so many had fashioned about him, the emperor had no clothes.

He remained without honour until the end, a self-aggrandising autocrat clinging to the delusion that after him the flood, a scorned man who still hoped for violent clashes between his forces and the rebels, and for his shabiha to still chant and deliver on 'Assad or we burn the country.' His extreme conceit could never entertain the possibility that his own subordinates did not respect him and were not willing anymore to remain pawns just to keep him and his gluttonous family in power. He had been flown into Damascus as an unqualified, unremarkable second choice to take over the reins of power, and he had been flown out of Damascus three decades later as a delusional despot who alienated even his allies after having brought the country to its knees.

While the loss of Hezbollah and other Iranian militias would have weakened the regime if its war on civilians had gone back to sieges and urban combat, it was undoubtedly the absence of the Russian air force that had the biggest impact on the rebels' victory. Russia was no longer fighting Assad's battles while his fate was being decided, and without air superiority, with this sudden de facto no-fly zone for which Syrians had pleaded for so long, the Assad regime could not have defeated the alliance of rebels who had spent the last years reforming, uniting, training, and planning their final offensive.

With Assad gone, the biggest violence Syrians experienced was unexpected and of shocking intensity, but ultimately made them feel they had been right all along in believing that for all its empty rhetoric, Israel had always wanted the regime to maintain power. No sooner had Assad fled than Israel viciously pounded every remaining Syrian military and naval base, frightening and angering Syrians who had barely begun to process the momentous

IT STARTED IN DAMASCUS

collapse of the regime. Israel struck more than 480 sites across the country and greedily took advantage of Syrians' chaotic circumstances to invade and occupy even more of the Golan Heights.

* * *

Despite these terrorising airstrikes at this most critical juncture in their history, Syrians had never felt such collective elation. Years of stagnation ended suddenly, bringing action and options, and many things were happening all at once. Traffic jams blocked the entry points into Syria from Turkey and from Lebanon, as tens of thousands, many on foot, rushed back home following Assad's flight. People gathered in every square and at every corner, congratulating each other on their newly found freedom and tearing down every poster of Assad they came across. Others happily smashed and destroyed the statues of Hafez and his son Bassel around the country, bringing down the enormous ugly structures that had towered over Syrians for decades.

Teams of youngsters wearing rubber gloves were seen roaming their neighbourhoods armed with brooms and trash bags, sweeping and cleaning their streets and parks, some even repainting benches, all spontaneously volunteering to beautify and reclaim their public spaces. Others stood in the place of police in areas with defective traffic lights, regulating circulation to keep the flow going and the people safe. Suddenly, for the first time ever, this had become their country.

On the first Friday after liberation, and the first free Friday since the Baath had taken power in 1963, every square in Syria's cities was taken over by the biggest crowds ever seen in the country; people were singing, cheering, rejoicing despite every problem they knew they still had to face. Now that the biggest hurdle was gone, what would follow the 'eternal' that had ended after five decades? There was no precedent in the region for how to proceed after the escape of the upper ranks of a criminal gang, and the disappearance of many of its heavily armed lower ranks, seen removing their uniforms as they ran into hiding in civilian clothes and melted into the population. Moreover, the way it happened added worrying dimensions to these celebrations: it was not clear yet if—or how—the rebels who had liberated Syria would be a part of its future leadership, if not the entire leadership in itself.

At the same time, there were many priorities to deal with at an existential level, and Syrians were overwhelmed by the enormity of the devastation the regime had left behind, discovering more layers of the depravity of the Assad regime.

They discovered the Captagon warehouses and the huge amounts the regime stored, even in the personal property of Maher Assad, where shipments were being readied with the drug hidden in crates of fake fruit, among other methods, ready to flood regional markets despite Arab countries' repeated demands that Assad put a stop to it—and his promise to do so.

They discovered the vast network of wide, high-ceilinged, well-lit and ventilated underground tunnels deep under the streets darkened by regime negligence, tunnels through which large trucks transported drugs, weapons, gold, or anything or anyone the Assads wanted. Fully equipped with powerful telecommunications and bunkers, they connected several Assad properties and allowed a quick and safe escape for the president and his family who, despite their legions of armed guards and despite always receiving nearly one hundred percent of the people's votes, did not seem to feel secure.

They discovered massive stashes of files in every intelligence branch and every Baath office with documents that would not seem out of place in Orwell's Oceania, exposing how most citizens in Assad's Syria had neither freedom nor a right to privacy, their words and movements documented by the army of informants who had helped enable the regime's omnipresence.

IT STARTED IN DAMASCUS

They discovered the obscene wealth of a president the media had portrayed as living a simple life, with the hundreds of cars in his and his brother Maher's massive personal garages filmed for all to see, including rare editions and old-timers worth fortunes. They saw for the first time the extensive Assad property in Latakia, with a commanding view over the shore and long stretches of beaches that had been forbidden to Syrians, so well hidden they could not even be seen from afar.

As all the known prisons had been opened and every prisoner had been released, the scenes in Sednaya jail in particular shocked everyone well beyond Syria. The conditions in which prisoners were kept were so horrific they beggared belief, and many were still missing after every cell was forced open, turning the attention of experts to presumed mass graves they would try to locate. Hundreds of family members who had waited for their loved ones were devastated anew when they did not walk out like others; their anger at the international abandonment of the disappeared and the detainees erupted when UN Special Envoy for Syria Geir Pedersen visited the prison a few days after Assad's escape. As distraught relatives shouted at his team that they had done nothing to help liberate detainees all these years, one shrieked in anguish as they drove off: 'After what have you come, for what? Leave, we don't want you anymore.'

The distrust of the UN and its perceived history of appeasement of the regime also came from the rebels who had turned overnight into rulers. Ahmad Sharaa, the leader of Hayat Tahrir Al Sham which had steered the final offensive on the regime, said that Resolution 2254, passed by the Security Council exactly nine years prior, was now obsolete as it called for a negotiated transition with the regime, adding that the UN had not managed to liberate a single prisoner in that period. For the new authority, the resolution's irrelevance, from their perspective, conveniently rendered the opposition's negotiating committee and its work on a new constitution immaterial as well; for the Coalition that had expected most of its top brass to be in charge, this was uncharted territory.

* * *

Assad had not even been gone a day when several host countries announced a pause in the processing of Syrian asylum seekers' applications; these included Britain, France, Germany, Italy, Sweden, Denmark, and Norway. Others, like Austria, went even further, declaring that deportation plans were being drawn to return Syrian refugees at the earliest opportunity, even offering some money to those who volunteered to go first. The question of where they would go when their homes were piles of rubble, and what they would do when ninety percent of the population in Syria was itself struggling without electricity, water, and sufficient food were not broached by nations who just wanted to get rid of them.

For most mainstream media, the focus was often less on the fall of the vicious Assad regime, and more on the fact that the victorious rebels were the Islamist ones; while both issues were highly news-worthy, glossing over the staggering impact of the Assads on Syria for half a century and on the world so quickly seemed to be, in itself, commentary rather than news.

After a live interview I gave to one of the biggest networks the day after Assad fled, I watched the clip they sent me: for nearly the entire length of an interview of over six minutes, it quoted a single one of Sharaa's comments in bold, all caps, on this being a victory for the Islamic nation, a comment he had made after prayers as he spoke inside the Umayyad Mosque. Over the next weeks, media asked me and others more for comments and elaborations on the Islamic dimensions than on the ruination left by Assad, the regime forces in hiding, the economic devastation they left, or the continuing search for disappeared Syrians, all of which I tried to bring up in my responses.

IT STARTED IN DAMASCUS

On social media, many reactions to Assad's flight were jarring, with numerous voices calling for the swift return of all refugees to Syria, especially after Syrians had celebrated the regime's end in various cities around the world. These were symptoms of great antagonism resulting not just from the presence of Syrians in several countries, but also from more than thirteen years of misinformation and incitement on the Syrian issue, leading to a rise in anti-refugee rhetoric that damaged European cooperation and reinstated border controls, and to voting more far-right parties into European seats of power.

Many berated Syrians for celebrating while Israel was bombing the country and mocked the rebels for not immediately responding. Such reactions came mostly from ideologues who had no other parameter through which to understand Syria, for whom Syria only ever existed as a geopolitical asset, a necessary component of the so-called resistance axis, its people only visible and worthy of care when they toed the line. Predictably, supporters of Hezbollah and the Iranian regime, whose own Islamism was seemingly tolerable, showed Syrians nothing but contempt for their happiness at the regime's demise. Did Syrians not know, went the livid rants, that the replacement to Assad was a known Islamist group? They knew very well, actually, and hardly needed lectures on their own country from non-Syrians, after everything they had been put through.

* * *

It became quickly clear that Commander Ahmad Sharaa, as he was addressed in the weeks following Assad's escape, was personally taking the reins of power with the acquiescence, if not full support at first, of many in and outside Syria. Sharaa, then using his nom de guerre Abu Muhammad Al Jolani, had formed and led the jihadist Al Nusra Front in early 2012, when the regime's severe repression of the Syrian Revolution was nearing the end of its first year. By April 2013, Al Nusra had declared itself to be an affiliate of Al Qaeda, a connection they renounced in mid-2016 before forming Hayat Tahrir Al Sham (HTS) with several other factions in 2017.

Seven years before toppling the regime, HTS settled as the governing body of Idlib. Many Syrians who were involved in civil society activities in the area had come to know their governing style; services ran well, relative to anything else in the country, business was good and the economy was free, but there was no question about the strictness of the Islamic interpretation of the law. While Idlib was already more conservative than several other provinces, women were expected to adhere to strict dress codes that went well beyond the headscarf. That is but one of the reasons why the prospect of HTS in power worried many Syrians.

Sharaa indicated he knew that what had worked in Idlib would not be well received throughout the country, issuing an early statement that no dress codes would be imposed; while reassuring the people, he was also projecting himself as a national leader, one who did not shy away from mentioning his past Al Qaeda years, and from defending the evolution in his thinking and behaviour.

Despite infractions by some fighters and the holier-than-thou individuals who tried preaching to unreceptive civilians, most of his fighters were Syrians who knew the makeup of the country. Many were young men who had been forcibly displaced by the Assad regime and its allies, and even those who left as children returned as euphoric adults to their cities and provinces around the country. Their positive energy was palpable, a new generation that seemed to be less of an ideological or religious persuasion and more of a patriotic one. Most of those we saw in Syria's streets in that initial period were smiling and taking selfies with pretty girls and cheerful people. Above all, they seemed well trained and disciplined, determined to be a part of the country they had dreamt of having.

Still, given his known past, the reception Sharaa got in the immediate aftermath of the regime's fall was remarkable, and his surprising popularity only increased in the first months as people observed him and heard him speak in meetings. His first public appearance in Damascus on the day Assad fled had been a PR success heavy on symbolism, projecting a victorious yet wholesome image. Driving slowly through a dense crowd that thinned as bodyguards secured a passage for him, Sharaa emerged from his car and entered Umayyad Mosque to applause and cheers, as if he, personally, was the long-awaited liberator. As he spoke to the assembled, his photographer caught several poses that captured a charismatic leadership vibe; it would be one of the last times we would see him in military uniform.

In a whirlwind of activity, the regional and international officials who had just weeks before touted normalisation with Bashar Assad, from afar, rushed to Syria to meet with Ahmad Sharaa and establish their positions vis-à-vis his governance. It went much better than most of us had expected. With each successive visit, Syrians understood that one of Sharaa's first priorities was to reassure them that Syria would no longer be a source of trouble, and that Syrians wanted to spend the next years rebuilding their country. For that to happen, sanctions that had been imposed on the Assad's regime for its torture and killings had to be lifted, because the conditions no longer applied after his escape.

Sharaa felt comfortable enough to give interviews to Arab and Western media. In that introductory phase, he also made a point of meeting with large groups of Syrians, including those living in Europe and America, explaining his interim government's vision and responding to questions, as related by many. He also demonstrated a keen understanding of the power of social media by welcoming a variety of vloggers and influencers; they produced spontaneous and longer polished content, giving a fresh perspective on Syrians to an audience not used to seeing them in a positive light.

* * *

From a political and a communications perspective, this did not seem to be a man who was playing it by ear, but someone who knew what challenges faced him, especially as Syrians' tongues had been unleashed since the revolution. People have been open, forthcoming, critical, and complimentary as well, expecting that Syria could never again be a place where their safety was contingent on the praise of a leader they did not choose.

There were certainly areas of disconnect between the authorities and the population from the beginning. On one hand, people understood that international connections mattered not only for the acceptance of Sharaa, which seemed to be the case judging by the initial roster of foreign dignitaries, but also for the lifting of sanctions that had been imposed on the Assad regime. On the other, everyone was quickly frustrated by the opaque and irregular communication style, and the absence of a direct line with a population demanding to be informed promptly through official channels about the numerous decisions being made.

People quickly tired of having to decipher and interpret messages received sporadically from various governing sources and insiders, and from rumours circulating on media. Sharaa seemed to be managing the dissemination of information, delaying the appointment of a spokesperson, even though the demand from the public for clear statements about events and developments in everything that touched them had been strong. For instance, they wanted explanations on why certain Assad regime officials had been arrested and others had been let go despite their documented crimes as senior officers. Likewise, several of the

IT STARTED IN DAMASCUS

Assad regime's businessmen turned warlords were allowed to walk free. Who made the decisions to let them go, and why? Such actions do not fit any understanding of transitional justice, nor Syrian expectations.

More than ever, people wanted to be involved at every level of their country, expecting to play a larger advisory and decision-making role. They felt a touted national dialogue should be a long process allowing the widest possible consultations on a national level, not simply an event decided by a few who invite token representatives. There had been little support for such a strongly centralised process and a lack of diversity in a governing capacity or in a decision-making process. In the long run, this was not sustainable.

After years of stagnation, events started happening faster than we could follow. The Conference on National Dialogue that had been widely expected to become a protracted consultative process was convened hastily with about one thousand Syrians invited, not leaving time for many participants (whose invitation criteria remained a mystery) to travel to Damascus to attend. It lasted only a few hours, with attendees divided into large groups to discuss major transitional issues, ending with a closing statement to which few participants would have contributed. For many, this event was considered to be just another display of form over content that ignored their wish to participate in moulding their country's future.

This was followed by a Constitutional Declaration that determined the law of the land for a period of five years, drawn up by a committee of seven Syrians appointed by Sharaa. They confirmed Islamic law as the main source of jurisdiction, and placed most decisions in the sole hands of Sharaa; he would be appointing members of parliament and judges, putting him at the helm of the executive, the legislative, and the judiciary branches with no separation of powers. On 29 January, he was named president by HTS in its last act before dissolving itself and joining the Syrian army.

Sharaa's focus on stabilising the country was receiving outside support, including from various European countries which had taken rapid decisions to start lifting their sanctions, such as Britain and Germany. In late February, Abdullah Ocalan announced from his jail in Turkey that the PKK was dissolving itself, in a clear indication that President Erdoğan had intervened and offered Ocalan a way out. This was the precursor to the agreement between Sharaa's government and the Syrian Democratic Forces and their Kurdish leader Mazloum Abdi, who agreed to integrate their forces into the Syrian army.

On 7 May 2025, Sharaa headed to Paris at the invitation of French president Emmanuel Macron, the first Western leader to meet with the Syrian president and to call for the full lifting of sanctions. One week later, Sharaa met with President Donald Trump in Saudi Arabia, leading the US president to declare he was going to order the lifting of sanctions to give Syrians a chance. Syrians marvelled at how this could have happened so fast when Sharaa's predecessor had spent twenty-four years in power without managing to meet a single US president.

This meeting happened under the auspices of Saudi Crown Prince Mohammad Bin Salman, and through the combined efforts of several Gulf countries (especially Qatar and the UAE) to play a leading role in rebuilding Syria. While most of these countries had moved to normalise with Assad, the impetus towards the new Syrian state was of another level of vitality altogether. This had encouraged Syrians inside and outside the country, and not a day now passed without a major initiative and investment being prepared in Syria.

Many inside Syria wondered why all these countries were suddenly being so nice to Syria, and so generous, with Saudi Arabia and Qatar having committed to paying Syria's external debt and public sector employees' salaries, and to bringing electricity to the country, for instance. Nothing is free, warned others. Indeed, but the Syrian Revolution and its repression have cost the region and the world much more than that. I would venture that like most Syrians themselves, Arab and Western countries who have engaged with Sharaa see potential for the future. When Hafez Assad came to power in 1970, nobody predicted just how extreme his metamorphosis would be, and how much trouble it would bring the region—let alone the Syrians—for the next half century. In Sharaa's case, many are betting that the transformation has already happened, in reverse, and that he had been retracing his steps back gradually to the pragmatic, conciliatory persona of his youth.

The Arab states had an additional premise to consider, especially those in the Gulf. They knew, from their own populations, that the appeal of a comfortable and dignified life in economic and socio-cultural terms had been a good harbinger of social peace, one that could lower the burning desire for the full democracy that Arab Spring energy had spread. It is likely that Sharaa's commitment to rebuilding country, economy, and society while keeping democratic ideals on the back burner will buy him time as the region tries to move past the era of revolutions, even though the revolutionaries who demanded democracy and its related freedoms will not settle for less so easily.

Syrians noticed, in the first months of his leadership, that some qualities seemed to distinguish Sharaa. While he clearly makes important decisions unilaterally, and while he has a close circle of advisors holding high positions, such as the minister of foreign affairs, he is someone who listens and who takes notes, always with a pen and notebook in hand during his meetings with peers or with subordinates. This is not an image Syrians were accustomed to seeing, and they found it refreshing to have a leader who does not pretend he knows everything.

ON THE WINDING ROAD TO DAMASCUS

The government he named on 29 March 2025 has satisfied most Syrians as they recognised respected names who have proven their competence in the private sector, but also who already served in Syria previously. Having appointed no prime minister, a detail which implies his involvement in governing will be a full one, Sharaa is betting his personal leadership will be a positive factor in keeping potential problems under control, as he keeps a number of ministers from the same ideological and cultural background under his wing.

The first few months were not all rosy, however, and two major issues shook Syrians' faith in the future. The first was Israeli interference in Syrian dynamics, its encroachment on Syrian land, its regular bombing campaign, and its claim that the new Syrian government was targeting and killing Druze which Israel has declared it will protect. The second was the danger of regime forces remnants, scattered around the country, armed and angry, encouraged by Iran to retake what they did not fight for in December 2024. Various groups have laid ambushes on Syrian security forces, killing and triggering a massive response by armed forces and volunteers, leading to a massacre of hundreds of people in mostly Alawi areas. This has greatly demoralised Syrian society, worried that continued incitement will lead to further killings and sectarian strife, especially in the absence of economic stability.

* * *

Democracy is not on the cards for Syrians' immediate future, and that is not necessarily a bad thing for a country with more than half the population displaced internally or abroad for the better part of the fourteen years preceding the Assad regime's collapse. Until these Syrians can return to Syria, with a home and a basic livelihood, elections would be unrepresentative and unjust. Sharaa has mentioned the need for a census, a logical requirement after a catastrophe of this magnitude; there are Syrians around the world who do not even exist legally, born in refugee camps, some of them nearing adulthood. There are also many Syrians whose deaths have not been officially documented, or who have not yet been found.

Even if these logistics were to be resolved quickly, Syrians need time to create a true political process and develop the political parties that the Assads banned for fifty-four years, disseminating their ideas, manifestos, and programmes to engaged Syrians. What would elections achieve for Syrians who do not know each other in a political sense, apart from offering a performance that would only give the illusion of a genuine process? Building a democratic and participatory environment is as important for Syrians' future as the physical reconstruction of the country is, this quest will require support on several levels.

As they work towards these goals, new factors will complicate the process; not all Syrians who return have had the same kind of experience, and their expectations and positions on the pyramid of needs will be quite different. They must all find their place back home and enjoy the same rights and the same privileges—even as they are given different levels of support at first.

Some Syrians crossed the dangerous sea and endured degrading treatment as they sought asylum, others had easier transits via official refugee programmes. Some refugees have been in miserable camps in countries that imposed curfews and begrudged their very existence; others managed to make a new life, building their skills and advancing their education, often becoming fully functional members of society and professionals in their fields. Some people will come back bilingual, with a solid education, technical skills, and valuable professional knowhow; others will be practically illiterate and unable to find jobs to sustain them.

Likewise, Syrians who stayed home are not all the same either. Some lived in relatively comfortable circumstances, managing to secure a decent standard of living in calm neighbourhoods; many others lived in derelict areas not served by basic services, struggling to make ends meet, at the mercy of the violence and greed of warlords, gangs, and regime operatives. Like the poorer Syrians who, in the last years of Assad's first decade, watched the chasm grow between them and the velvet society, they do not have the same background nor the same outlook, and will probably not have similar politics.

But even if it were not for these experiential differences, even if, in a parallel universe, Assad had delivered on his endless claims of reform at some point in his first ten years of power and they had not gone through hell and back, Syrians would still be divided and want different things—just like every other people in the world.

Some want modernity and technology in everything; others want to hold on to traditional ways of doing things because they worked fine in their childhoods. Some are deeply religious, observant, and like to see their faith reflected in public life; others are less so, living a more secular life while celebrating the religious holidays and adopting various traditions. Some think faith should guide legislation, believing that divine laws outrank any other considerations; others believe there must be a separation of state and religion, confident that our civilisation can provide the morality and justice we all want. Some swear the way forward is imposed secularism; others point to the place and the placement of God in many democratic countries, such as in US official and public life, in its White House Faith Office, and in its 'In God We Trust' inscription on coins and bills. Some want clerics of any religion to remain outside the political realm; others insist they are as entitled as others to join it, pointing to the Anglican prayers that start the day at Westminster, and the Lords Spiritual bishops in the House of Lords.

Some people are accepting of extended personal freedoms; others believe these negatively affect society and infringe on their right to be spared such an environment. Some demand that women play a leading role in governance and public life; others insist society must honour a woman's role revolving around her home, her husband, her children, and that she should be supported and respected in that capacity. Some would like to push for free enterprise and a limitation of the state's involvement in a social context; others think social welfare is a necessary component of life in a compassionate society. Some want everyone to have the freedom to say anything they want; others maintain there are red lines that no one should cross.

In short, Syrians are exactly like every other society in the world and will argue about politics, the economy, education, public health, climate change, gender equality, and a million other things. One day, they will be able to vote, and they will be able to agree or disagree as long as the voice of each one of them is equal to the other. After everything they have gone through, one person, one respected vote is the minimum acceptable. And like every society in the world, they might elect admirable figures at times, and detestable ones at others.

* * *

Knowing how Syrians got to where they are today is a prerequisite to understanding what they are willing to accept and what they are willing to overlook. If you were to take out a map and point at geographical areas with tired old labels as you began an analysis of Syria, you would be adopting a misleading and quasi-irrelevant perspective that would tell your audience nothing of value about the Syrians of today.

Yet, this is still the reductive method of an assortment of non-Syrian professors, lecturers, historians, and even journalists who paint a picture of Syria with monolithic blocs of sects, ethnic groups, and religions, each with distinct historical grievances and aspirations. You would think they were just coming out of the

ON THE WINDING ROAD TO DAMASCUS

Mandate era or, even worse, the Sykes-Picot negotiations chambers. Syrians today would not explain their country with such basic generalisations, and it is high time to shun superficial approaches that show complete detachment from the people who do not see themselves in these old one-dimensional designations.

It has been one hundred years since the Great Syrian Revolt of 1925. In essence, that revolt did not just repudiate the colonialist prism that divided Syria into statelets according to sectarian or ethnic identities; it also staked the claim and the aspiration that Syrians were Syrians first and foremost. If we are going to oversimplify a particular element in Syrians' identity, let it be that one, that insistence of many Syrians throughout history to be Syrian, and that refusal to be defined by orientalist labels meant to divide them and sort them into manageable colonial assets.

One century after the Great Revolt, the Syrian Revolution brought an outburst of free speech, creating open forums that tell us again and again what Syrians want on that pyramid of needs. What is not on that pyramid is a Muslim–Christian, or a Sunni–Alawi divide, despite the media headlines and the incitement that some parties still attempt. Granted, every one of these sub-groups suffers from a scattering of loud, hardcore separatists, in the mental if not physical sense, who view the country as one of majorities and minorities and sectarian prisms—just like the non-Syrians holding that outdated map—and who have never had the opportunity to live as citizens and compatriots with equality of rights and equality of duties.

The Assad regime's propaganda about its role in protecting minorities obscenely implied that before Hafez's coup, minorities needed protecting from a dangerous majority. But countries with far more complicated histories than Syria's do not speak of minorities or majorities; they speak of citizens, all equal under the rule of law, the very citizens that Syrians have been clamouring to become for years. The truth is that like many other societies, Syrians are divided by lifestyle choices, by social class, and by numerous other sociodemographic factors about which the old maps say nothing. They do not need an inclusive government where there are token representatives of every section of society, but a genuine inclusive society where the only identity that carries weight legally is that of citizen.

Many Syrians believe that the revolution is not yet over, despite Assad's escape. They will be waiting to reach this desired state of equality and laws that protect personal liberties, including freedom of speech. They will be opposing other Syrians who think that the revolution is over just because Assad is gone, and they will be opposing others who welcome the prospect of a conservative government and a more visible role for religion. And like with every society that has had to argue and climb its way to democracy, the coming period in Syria will not necessarily be calm as they seek their peace, knowing that peace without justice is not peace, and that justice without accountability is not justice.

* * *

We sometimes find comfort in the strangest rituals, even those we once found harsh in a previous era of our life. A consequence of maturity, perhaps, it comes with the acceptance of a community, a heritage that we initially did not mean to appreciate.

I had the misfortune of experiencing my first Syrian mourning ritual with the death of my father. Desperate for my own time and space to grieve, I was instead thrust into a highly regulated process that took precedence over personal wishes as the larger family guided us through the difficult days and the hundreds of visitors that would come. I found the customs archaic, strict, and unsuited to our modern life, so cruel in their immediacy that allows one no chance to absorb the shock. Muslims, like Jews, bury their dead as soon they can, sometimes hours after someone's passing. In our culture, the departed are honoured with a fast burial immediately followed by the condolences process, announced in notices plastered on walls, lamp posts, and doors that people will stop to read in the neighbourhoods where the deceased and the family would be known.

Damascus still maintained traditions not observed in other cities, with a ladies' *asrieh*, named for the afternoon time in which it is held, taking place three days in a row. Dressed in black with a flimsy white scarf worn loosely over the hair and falling around the shoulders, the women of the family sit at the head of the reception room across from a small settee or a couple of armchairs reserved for the condolers. Outside the room, a bevy of relatives and friends organise the traffic, offering bitter coffee and cold water with a touch of orange blossom, managing the bulk of the process to support the main mourners.

Ladies calling on the family will enter the lounge alone or in pairs as everyone stands up, and they all sit down at the same time just long enough to say a short silent prayer for the deceased, lasting less than a minute. As they begin to stand up, so do all the women in the family again until the condolers have left. For the ladies paying their respects, the entire visit takes just a few minutes; for the women in the bereaved family, this can go on for several exhausting hours if they have a large social circle.

After my traumatic experience being on the receiving end of interminable condolences for my father in this manner, I always felt anxious when paying similar condolence calls with my mother or a relative. One day, I found myself having to do it alone, and as I sat down, I made eye contact with one of the family mourners; in a few seconds, I saw a world of appreciation in her teary eyes, an expression of comfort in her kind face that showed, despite her sadness, the strength and relief she felt through our brief interludes, paying our respect and offering our sympathy silently. The most unexpected feeling of calm and serenity overtook me as I said my prayer sitting across from these grieving ladies. As I stood up again and they all followed suit, as per the custom, I felt I had become a true Damascene lady at that very moment—not for doing the social duty that I had done many times before, but for finally valuing the significance of these gestures in our empathic society.

That moment would replay in my mind as bereavements multiplied across Syria as of 2011. Without being able to carry out their most basic mourning processes, without the physical and temporal space to hold their rituals amidst so much death and destruction, Syrians were rushed into brutal goodbyes and the pain of not honouring their dead properly, as they deserved, as is mandated by their traditions. They did not receive the condolences of their community in the way they should have, nor hear the consoling words we often say as we part: 'May this be the end of your sorrows.'

As they shifted timelines in December 2024 and embarked on a new era, I felt more than ever that Syrians were still waiting to be offered condolences on their great collective loss. It will probably take years for their nation to get closure after this long difficult journey, but it would mean the world to so many of them to hear 'may this be the end of your sorrows' from people who had not yet understood their distress.

The collective Syrian spirit is still being crushed as the country tries to emerge from the ravages of Assadism and its remaining enablers, from the expansionist Israeli aggressions, and from the multitude of domestic disagreements and the challenges of transitioning into a governing system that satisfies a demanding population. As the Syrian people prepare to rebuild their lives and their country, this world must decide where it now stands, and whether it really believes its own touted declaration that all human beings are born free and equal in dignity and rights.

* * *

ON THE WINDING ROAD TO DAMASCUS

As eternal lovers of stories about people and places that touch them, Syrians have entertained numerous myths about Mount Qasioun, overlooking Damascus. One is that Adam, the first man for Abrahamic religions, lived in one of its caves that people still visit to this day. Another follows with the reason for the reddish hue in Qasioun's soil, saying it became stained with the blood of Abel when he was killed by his brother Cain. My personal favourite legend involving the mountain is a gentler one, however, a tale of foretold splendour relating that Prophet Muhammad, the founder of Islam, came upon Mount Qasioun during one of his travels. From its top, he looked admiringly at Damascus, so taken by its serene beauty that he refused to come down and walk through one of the city's gates, because he knew that man can only enter paradise once.

Damascus would blossom after the Prophet's death when it became the capital of the Umayyad Empire in 661, an empire that for centuries spread its magnificent culture and architecture, and its science and learning, all the way to Andalusia on one side of the world to India on the other. Since then, many have entered Damascus and Bilad Al Sham, the Lands of the Levant, from the savage Tamerlane to the grandiose but ruthless Ottomans who ruled it for four hundred years. They were followed by the French Mandate which managed, in less than three decades, to plant into a smaller Syrian state the seeds of divisions. These separatist concepts would be exploited by those seeking further partitions, ending with the absolute devastation brought by an insatiable clan and its pyramid of abusive governance for half a century, even as their celebrated distant past reminded them of what their nation was supposed to become.

The Syrian Revolution reshaped our world on many levels. It reshaped our small Syrian realm when unprecedented cruelty answered calls for dignity, and global indifference abandoned us to a tsunami of grief that engulfed everything and everyone we cherished. It reshaped our region, scattering millions seeking refuge and safety, shaking the Middle East's balance with a proliferation of militias and drugs. It reshaped our entire world with the appeasement of bullies, the collapse of post-Cold War alliances, and the success of political opportunists that have weakened the pan-European unity that gave security and opportunity to millions.

Today, much of that world can be reshaped into form again if the spirit of the long Syrian Revolution guides justice and normal reconciliations, and if a more engaged global community helps redress the balance.

Syrians have moved heaven and earth to survive the calamities imposed on them. A quarter of a century after their hope started to grow, the time has come to lift them up so they can thrive, because their destiny is to complete what started in Damascus.

ACKNOWLEDGEMENTS

My heartfelt thanks go first to my literary agent, Andrew Gordon, who believed in this book when many thought the subject of Syria was a thing of the past. His expert guidance and insight helped me develop *It Started in Damascus* into the solid proposal that shaped the final book. I am also grateful to David Evans and the larger team at David Higham Associates.

Thank you to everyone at Hurst Publishers for making this book a reality, and for their scheduling flexibility when the Syrian regime collapsed in December 2024 just as I was about to finalise the last two chapters. I appreciate the support from director Michael Dwyer, book editor Alice Clarke, copyeditor Tom Feltham, Daisy Leitch and Letty Allen in production, and the press and publicity team of Kathleen May, Rubi Kumari, Raminta Uselytė, and Jess Winstanley.

There are many people whose collegiality and friendship continued beyond our periods of collaboration, and who have been part of my professional development over the years, particularly the following:

Dr Rosemary Hollis played a big role in my world and my life for the better part of two decades as a mentor, a colleague, and a friend. Rosy brought me into Chatham House soon after my move to London, and it was my honour and privilege to be part

ACKNOWLEDGEMENTS

of the Middle East and North Africa team she led. I fondly remember my work with numerous colleagues in the institute, foremost of which Nadim Shehadi, Yossi Mekelberg, Robert Lowe, and Keith Burnet.

Hanna Anbar, my editor at Lebanon's *The Daily Star* that was twinned at the time with *The International Herald Tribune*, guided me through the craft of newspaper writing when I first began to publish opinion pieces and analysis on the region. *Syria Today*'s publisher Abdul Ghani Attar and editor Francesca de Châtel likewise carried my monthly columns, often social commentaries strewn with references to the larger Syrian context, until my regime ban in 2009.

With my companions on the board of directors of The Day After (TDA), I shared days and nights of discussions, dreams, and arguments from our 'kitchen cabinet' created as the Syrian Revolution picked up pace. We held on to the ideal and to the workable framework for democratic transition in Syria, through one project after another with TDA's able and dedicated team.

I have collaborated with many Syrian friends and peers over the years, before the revolution and after; they include Ayman Asfari and many in the political opposition, and in the academic and civil society realm. But how to acknowledge the effect of an entire people on our common resolve during the most difficult periods? Their courage and resilience convinced us that if they had not given up, neither could we.

They include the White Helmets and all the other humanitarians, nurses, and doctors, and the anonymous Syrians who risked their lives trying to alleviate suffering, feed and help others at home and in exile. They include the national figures who defected knowing the price they would pay, such as Muhammad Faris, the only Syrian astronaut who went to space and whose enlightened vision could not fathom the violence unleashed on his people.

They include children whose cries were unheard, such as the shocked small boy in an ambulance looking at his dusty wounds

ACKNOWLEDGEMENTS

without uttering a sound, or the injured little girl lying on the floor of a makeshift clinic, clenching in her fist a piece of bread soaked in blood, still hungry after an airstrike on a besieged area.

My inspiration was fuelled by exceptional strong will too, seen in the young couple being forcibly displaced but pausing to write on a wall: 'to the one who shared my life during the siege, I love you.' And it was manifest in a private moment, caught by a photographer at Budapest's main train station, of a young refugee couple inside a flimsy tent, momentarily oblivious to the despair outside as they kissed passionately.

This Syrian yearning for life never abated nor ceased to motivate me as I wrote. Throughout, I had the emotional, psychological, and material support of my mother and daughter, to whom I am eternally grateful.

INDEX

à la Nasser, 12, 34
Abbasid Dynasty, 99
Abbott, Diane, 275
Abdelwahab, Mohammad Ahmad, 226
Abed Street, 71
Abel Majid, Bassam, 195
Abou Fares, 149–54
Abou Roummaneh Avenue, 5, 7, 34
Abou Roummaneh, 62, 64, 120
'active citizenship', 212
AdDomari (newspaper), 162–3
Addounia Television, 255–6
Affordable Care Act (Obamacare), 282
Afghanistan, 108
Agreement of Disengagement, 35
Aicha, 7
Aiki Lab, 223
Air Force Command, 150
Aïshti, 182
Akhras, Dr Fawaz, 108

Al Askari Mosque (Samarra), bombing of, 199
Al Baath (newspaper), 17
Al Bouti, Sheikh Muhammad, 265
Al Darwishiah Mosque, 205
Al Furat Petroleum Company, 120
Al Hayat (Lebanese newspaper), 100
Al Iktissadiah, 163
Al Iqtissadiya, 196
Al Jader, Youssef, 226
Al Jazeera (Arabic channel), 102, 233–4, 236, 256, 257
Al Kawakibi Forum in Aleppo, 101
Al Khatib, Mouaz, 272
Al Malki Avenue, 15
Al Omari Mosque, 215, 216
Al Qaeda, 246, 253
Al Rashid, Haroun, 99
Al Rawda Café, 71–2
Al Reem (belonging to Khaddam's daughter), 120

INDEX

Al Saleh, Abdul Qader (Hajji Marea), 226–7
Al Thawrah (The Revolution), 17
Al Watan, 196
Alawis, 41, 47, 264
Albright, Madeleine, 24
Aleppines, 142
Aleppo Artillery School, 45
Aleppo, 9, 45
   fall of, 305
   Russian air campaigns on, 274, 294
Alexandretta, 90
Ali, Hatem, 165
Allaf family, 7
Amal Movement, 41
America, 23
Amina, 7
Amiralay, Omar, 154, 166
Amman, 21, 63
Ammar Headquarters, 283
Amnesty International, 204, 308
Anjar, 174
Annan, Kofi, 22
anti-Assad conspiracy, 255
anti-Assad, 263
anti-Lebanese measures, 181–3
anti-Syrian sentiment, 178
Arab League Summit (Jeddah, May 2023), 298
Arab League Summit (Mar 2013), 272
Arab League, 235–6, 239
Arab Spring, 104, 205–6, 211–13
Arabism, 56

Arab–Israeli conflict, 73, 83
Arab-Kurdish opposition, 221–2
Arafat, Yasser, 22, 89
Arar, Maher, 107
Asaad, Riad, 225
Asharq Alawsat (pan-Arab newspaper), 104, 211
Asmar, Aziz, 276
Assad clan, 6, 118–19, 120, 137–8
Assad Library, 15
Assad regime, 29, 33
Assad, Asma, 195, 212
Assad, Bashar, xi, xii, 6, 10, 16–17, 19–21, 24, 26, 27, 47, 98–9, 106, 107–8, 125, 127, 132, 138, 172, 173
   appointed Ghazaleh, 174
   ceasefire speech, 185–6
   descriptions of Assad in Western media, 258–61
   economic and administrative reform, 128–30
   economic reforms and mismanagement (2007), 196–9
   'exclusive' interviews, 260–5
   fled, 308–9, 313–14
   fourth presidential term, 302
   Iraqis refugees' management, 199–202
   Israel's violation, 108–11
   lost Aleppo, 306
   mini summit with the emir of Qatar and Sarkozy, 194
   monopoly, 119–21
   new cabinet, 210

INDEX

New York UN World Summit (2005), 194
Paris visit (2008), 192–3
PR machine, 100–5
Qatar as ally of, 233–4
Rami's development, 125–8
re-elected (2007), 195
siege, imposition of (Apr 2011), 219
Sleiman, meeting with, 192–3
Syrians' Arab Spring and responses, 215–17
tenth year in power, celebration, 203
Turkey and, 234–5
Wall Street Journal interview, 212
See also Baath Party
Assad, Bassel, 9, 26, 47, 87, 88, 132, 169
Assad, Hafez, xi, 12, 16, 26, 29, 34, 36, 46–7, 54, 68, 86, 91, 172, 174, 248, 259, 310, 320
death of, 3–5
funeral, 12–13
and Hussein, 76–9
Israel's violation, 108–11
Kuwait liberation, 79–80
monopoly, 119–21
relations with Iran, 284
Sheikho on, 10–11
Syrian education, 54–7
Turkey, 89–90
See also Bush, George H. W.; Syria
Assad, Maher, 311–12
Assad, Rifat, 17, 42–6, 68, 87
Assads official two-day visit to Paris, 203–4
Association Agreement, 111–12
Asterix (comic series), 227
Atassi, Nureddin, 33
Atassi, Suheir, 101
Attieh, Rouwaida, 174, 175
Austria, 288
Avenue Foch, 17
Aziz, Omar, 222–3

Baath Party Congress, Tenth (June 2005), 180
Baath Party, xii, 6, 12, 36, 41, 54–5, 57, 111, 122, 129, 154, 310, 311
Baath Vanguards, 55
Baathification, 111
Baathism, 57, 77, 181
Baathist coup (1963), 32
Bab Al Hara, 158
Baba Amr (Homs), siege of, 236–8
Baba Amr assault, 229
Bahsa, 134
Baker, James, 80
Ban Ki-moon, 240, 270
Barcelona, 255
Basij, 283
Bayada Martyrs Battalion, 230
BBC World Service, 73–4, 112
Beirut, 63, 129
Beirut–Damascus/Damascus–

337

INDEX

Beirut Declaration (May 2006), 184, 195
Belarus, 300
Bellingcat, 277
Ben Ali, Zein Al Abidine, 217
Bena Properties, 126
Berri, Nabih, 88
Big Brother, 31, 132
Big Dreams, 166
Bilal, Mohsen, 202
Black Lives Matter, 276
Blair, Tony, 108
Blinken, Antony, 251–2
Bosnia and Herzegovina, 274
boutiques, 197–8
Bouvier, Edith, 238
Breaking Bones (drama), 165
Brexit, 297
Britain, 22
British Syrian Society, 108–9
Bucharest, 36
Build-Operate-Transfer (BOT), 123
Bush House, 73–4
Bush, George H. W., 35, 78, 80, 82, 83, 106–7, 110, 194

Caesar Syria Civilian Protection Act, 251
Cameron, David, 244, 245, 278, 279
Camp David Accords (1978), 79
Canada, 69
Captagon, 301, 311
Carazon, Diana, 174, 175

Carter, Jimmy, 35
Ceaușescu, Nicolae, 36, 76
Central Bank of Syria, 58
Central Committee of the National Command, 6
Cham Holding, 126, 129
Cham Wings, 126
Channel One, 74
Channel Two, 74
Chatham House, 112, 189, 190
Cheers, 156
Cherbaji, Maan, 221
Chirac, Jacques, 21, 186
Chomsky, Noam, 277
Christians, 105, 143
Christopher, Warren, 89
Chtaura, 179
City of Jasmine, 95
Clinton, Bill, 23–4, 28, 87, 89
Clock Tower Square, Homs, 229
CNN, 18–19
Colvin, Marie, 237, 238
Committees for the Revival of Civil Society, 101
Conference on National Dialogue, 318
Conroy, Paul, 238
Constitutional Declaration, 318
consumerism, 167
Cook, Robin, 22
Cooper, Anderson, 237–8
Corbyn, Jeremy, 297
Corrective Movement, 54–5, 60
Creeping Assadisation, 36–7
Crimea, annexation of, 286, 299

INDEX

Croatia, 297
Czechoslovakia, 76

Damascus Bridge Club, 9
Damascus International Airport, 18, 81–2, 87, 121
Damascus Spring (2000–01), xii, 112, 163–4
Damascus University, 104
Damask Rose, 95
Daraa, 214–15, 216, 218, 219, 229
Daraya, 221, 240
Davutoğlu, Ahmet, 234, 235
de Cuéllar, Javier Pérez, 81
de la Croix, Agnes Mariam, 237
de Mistura, Staffan, 274
Decree 50, 160–2
Defence Brigades, 42, 43–4, 46
Demirel, Suleiman, 90
Denmark, 51
Disengagement Agreement, 105
Doha Agreement, 186
Doha Debates programme, 112
Dorchester, 109
Douba, Ali, 53
Douma chemical attack, 295
Duma, 22

Eastern Europe, 75, 84
Economic Tuesday, 103
Economist, The (News journal), 152, 153
Egypt, 22, 33, 79, 90, 206, 213, 217
Eighth Congress, 5–6

Eighth Gate, 126
El Al flight, 69
11 September attacks, 106–8, 174
    See also Hussein, Saddam; United States (US)
Elysée Palace, 21
Emergency Law, 12
Erdoğan, Recep Tayyip, 234, 306, 319
EU Association Agreement, 181
Euphrates river, 37
Europe, 53
European Union (EU), 22, 75, 111–12, 281, 297
    Dublin Regulation, 287–8
Express Attack, 237

Facebook, 212, 214, 224, 241, 276
Fairuz, 95
Fares, Raed, 227
fatwa (religious ruling), 41
Ferzat, Ali, 162
Field Marshal, 27
Fijeh, 38
Finland, 299
Fischer, Heinz, 289
Flood in Baath Country, A (Amiralay), 154
Floyd, George, killing of, 276
Floyd, Pink, 276
forced displacement, 252–3
Ford, Gerald, 35
Foreign Policy (magazine), 223
Four Seasons Hotel, 198, 274
Four Seasons, The, 165

INDEX

France, 21, 63, 90, 171, 176, 177, 186, 244, 246, 295
National Day, 192
Free Syrian Army (FSA), 225–6, 229, 240, 247
French Mandate, 11, 33, 158
Friends of Syria Group, 270
Future Television Network, 174

Gdansk shipyard, 75
General Organisation of Tobacco, 119
Geneva Communiqué, 269–71, 273
Geneva, 23, 35, 73, 78, 81
Georges-Picot, François, 3–5, 284
Germany, 288, 290, 292, 293
Germany, 63
'Ghadan Naltaki' (We Meet Tomorrow), 74
Ghaffari, Javad, 307
Ghazaleh, Rustom, 174, 214–15
Ghosh, Bobby, 262
Ghouta, 246, 252, 271
  Russian air campaigns on, 274
  siege of, 243, 244, 295
Gilligan, Andrew, 260
Global March for Syria, 258
Globe and Mail, The (Canadian news site), 134
Golan Heights, 32, 35, 37, 77, 82, 105
'The Golden Knight', 87
Gorbachev, Mikhail, 75, 83
GOTA (General Organisation for Trade and Distribution), 121–2

Great Syrian Revolt (1925), 325
Great Umayyad Mosque, 97, 105
Greater Syria, 56
Greek Orthodox church, 106

Haddad, Saad, 172
Hafez Assad Mosque, 97
Haidar, Ali, 53
Haines, David, 278
Hama massacre (1982), 32, 76, 236
Hama, 32, 46, 143, 218, 258, 307
Hamada, Wael, 228
Hamidiyeh Souk, 44, 145–6
Hammadi, Nazim, 228
Hariri, Rafic, 88, 176, 179
  assassination of, 177
  Mehlis report, 184
  Saudi citizenship, 185
Harmoush, Hussein, 225
Hassan Al Banna, 41
Hassan, Jordanian Crown Prince, 87–8
Hauran, 214
Havana, 71–2
Havel, Václav, 76
Hayat Tahrir Al Sham (HTS), 312, 315
Head of Presidential Security, 87
Heathrow Airport, 69
Hennawi, Rami, 223
Hersh, Seymour, 276–7
Hezbollah, 172, 173, 178, 186, 277, 278, 283, 295, 301, 306, 309, 314
Israeli soldiers, killing of, 185

340

INDEX

took over Beirut (2008), 186
Hindawi Affair, 79
Hollande, François, 246
Homeland (1979), 156
Homs, 252, 271, 294, 307
   protests in, 229–30
Homsi, Mamoun, 124
Houla, 239
'Houna London' (Here is London), 73–4, 84
House of Commons, 245
Hrawi, President Elias, 88
Human Rights Watch, 204, 219
Hungary, 75, 288, 290, 293, 298
Hürriyet (newspaper), 235
Hussein, Saddam, 69, 76, 107, 109, 162–3, 282
   See also Assad, Hafez

Ibrahim Hanano Street, 15
Ibrahim, Dr Saad Eddin, 112
Idlib, 315
Infantry Academy, 226, 227
Iniesta, Andrés, 255
Institute for Strategic Dialogue, 277
Intercontinental Hotel, Geneva, 269
International Damascus Fair, 14–15
Investcom, 124
Iran, 24, 41, 77, 248, 249–50, 275, 283–4, 302, 305–6, 321
   economic influence in Syria, 285
   JCPOA and, 281–2

Iran–Iraq war, 79, 185
Iraq, invasion of, 176, 282
Iraq, xii, 33, 69, 76, 77, 89–90, 107–8, 111, 112, 118, 169
ISIS (Islamic State of Iraq and Syria), 228, 253, 278, 279, 287
Islam, 143
Islamic revolution, 77
Islamic Shia, 41
Islamophobia, 298
Israel, 178, 309–10, 314
   interference in Syrian dynamics, 321
   occupation of southern Lebanon, 172
   7 October 2023 attack, 299
   targeting of Iranian and Lebanese militias, 302
   war on Gaza, 299, 302
Israel, 19, 20, 23, 32, 33–4, 52, 77, 79, 83, 89, 105–6
It Is Not a Mirage (series), 158
Italy, 299

Jabal Al Zawiya, 239
Jackson, Jesse, 24
Jacquier, Gilles, 237, 238
Jadid, Salah, 33
Jamal Atassi Forum for Democratic Dialogue, 101
Jarba, Ahmad, 249
Jaruzelski, General Wojciech, 75
Jerusalem, 106
Jneed, Hamood, 227
Jobs, Steve, 135

INDEX

Joint Comprehensive Plan of Action (JCPOA), 281, 289
Jordan, 23, 33, 89, 169, 175, 293
Jordanian army, 175

Kafranbel Media Centre, 227
Kafranbel, 164, 227
Kalashnikovs, 4, 27
Kanaan, Ghazi, 173, 174, 184
Karm El Zeytoun, 239
Kassir, Samir, 178
Kerry, John, 284
Khaddam, Abdul Halim, 104–5, 120, 173
   on Bashar, 184
Khalil, Samira, 220
Khan Shaykhun chemical attack, 276, 294–5
Khan, Abbas, 278–9
Khartabil, Bassel, 223
Khatami, Mohammad, 24
Khatib, Hamza, 219–20
Khouli, Mohamed, 5
Khuzestan, 283
Kilo, Michel, 101
Kim Il-Sung, 36
Kim Jong-un, 260
King Faisal of Saudi Arabia, 33
King Hassan of Morocco, 21, 22, 23
King Hussein of Jordan, 20–1, 22, 23, 35, 39
Kissinger, Henry, 33–5, 105
Klein, Joe, 262
Kouchner, Bernard, 186

Kurdistan Workers' Party (PKK), 90
Kuwait, 33, 35, 76–9, 83, 86, 89, 111
Kuwait, invasion of, 168

La Noisette, 121
Lahoud, Emile, 176, 177
Laique, École, 171
Lamia, 67
Latakia Airport, 88
Latakia, 246
Lebanese civil war, end of, 173
Lebanon, xii, 19, 22, 31, 38, 41–2, 61, 80, 86, 102, 110, 112
   demanding the withdrawal of Syrian troops, 179
   Rami trip, 122
   refugee crisis, 293, 294
   Syria's detachment from, 181–2
   Syrian presence in, 167–70
   Syrian workers in, 169–70
Lèse-majesté, 138
Libya, 77, 206, 213
Liwa Al Tawhid, 226
Local Coordination Committees (LCCs), 222, 241, 274
London, 69, 73–4, 88, 117
Los Angeles Times (newspaper), 19
Los Angeles, 130
Lukashenko, Alexander, 307

maamoul, 170
Mac, Daniel, 130
Machiavellian, 54

INDEX

Macron, Emmanuel, 319
Madrid Peace Conference, 82, 83
Madrid, 83–4, 89
Maghout, Muhammad Al, 156
Makhlouf, Ali, 130
Makhlouf, Mohammad, 119–20
Makhlouf, Rami, 113, 116, 117–19, 121–2, 126, 129, 163, 175, 203
   businessman, 121–5
   development, 125–8
   monopoly, 119–21
Malek, Anwar, 236
Malki neighbourhoods, 4
Malki, 121
Mamlouk, Ali, 188–92, 193, 196, 202
man-portable air-defence systems (MANPADS), 247
Maronite Christian groups, 39
Masharqa, Zouheir, 21
Matar, Ghiath, 221
McCain, John, 249
Mecca, 78
Mehlis, Detlev, 184
Meridien Hotel, 67
Merkel, Angela, 288
Messi, Lionel, 255
Mezzeh neighbourhood, 5
Mezzeh, 7–8, 121, 141
Midan, 257
middle class, 197
Middle East, 34, 83, 107, 111
Miliband, Ed, 244, 245, 297
Military Hospital, 13

Milk Statement, 219
million-strong march, 257–8
Minnesota, 23
Miro, Mustafa, 162
Mirrors (television series), 156
Mohammad Bin Salman, Saudi Crown Prince, 319
Morocco, 23, 33
Mossad, 4
Mousa Sadr, Imam, 41
'Mr Five Percent', 119
Mubarak of Egypt, 90, 112
Mubarak, Hosni, 22, 87–8, 217
Mufleh, 122
Muhajireen neighbourhoods, 4, 43
Muhammad, Prophet, 329
Muhanna, Ghassan, 120
Muslim Brothers (MB), 41–2
Muslims, 40, 105, 143
My Lai massacre (1968), 277

Najib, Atef, 214, 215
Nasrallah, Hassan, 185, 299, 306
Nasser, Gamal Abdel, 12, 20, 34, 112
National Coalition of Syrian Revolution and Opposition Forces, 247–9, 269, 270, 272, 273
National Dialogue Forum, 101
Nationalism (Qawmieh), 56
NATO (North Atlantic Treaty Organization), 275, 277, 299
Navalny, Alexei, 299
Neighbourhood Gate, The (series), 158

INDEX

New York Times, The (newspaper), 265
New York UN World Summit (2005), 194
New York, 73, 81, 107, 110
Ninth Baath Party Congress, 27
Ninth Baath Party Regional Congress, 5
Nixon, Richard, 33–4, 105
No-Fly Zone, 247
Nora, 5
North Korea, 9, 23, 36, 37
Norway, 89

Obama, Barack, 194–5, 242–3, 245, 246, 250 1, 254, 268, 272, 282, 294
  foreign policy, 248, 249–50
Ocalan, Abdullah, 69, 90, 218, 319
Ochlik, Rémi, 238
October Village (1973), 156
October War, 34
Olmert, Ehud, 192
OPEC, 33
Operation Desert Shield, 78
Operation Desert Storm, 78–9
Orascom Telecom, 122, 123–4
Organisation for the Prohibition of Chemical Weapons (OPCW), 246, 277, 287
Orient Club, 34
Oslo Accords, 89
Ottoman Empire, 158

P5+1, 281

Palacio de Oriente, 83
Palestine Liberation Organisation (PLO), 39, 42, 89
Palestinian refugees, 179–80
Palestinians, 277–8
Palmyra Prison, 46
Paolo, Father, 228
Paris, 120–1
Paul II, Pope John, 105
Pedersen, Geir, 312
Pelosi, Nancy, 249
PKK, 222, 319
Pocket World in Figures, 152
Poiron, Caroline, 237
poverty, 197
pre-YouTube, 9
Prigozhin, Yevgeny, 300
Primakov, Yevgeny, 22
privileged classes, 171
Prodi, Romano, 22
'pro-Syria', 277
protests (Damascus, 17 Feb 2011), 205–6, 213
Putin, Vladimir, 22, 245, 246–7, 285–6, 295, 298, 301, 302, 306
Putin-Medvedev-style agreement, 272–3
PYD, 222
Pyongyang Times (newspaper), 38
Pyongyang, 36

Qabbani, Nizar, 13, 165
Qaddafi, Muammar, 41, 77
Qardaha, 87
Qatar, 186, 194, 233, 257, 319–20

INDEX

Qubaysi, Mounira Al, 143
Qubaysiat, 143
Qubeir, 239, 240
Quneitra, 105–6
Quran, 143
Quwatli, Shukri, 33

Rabat, 21
'Rabin Deposit', 89
Rabin, Yitzhak, 89
Radio Fresh, 227
Radio Monte Carlo, 73
Ramak, 182, 121–2
Real Estate Bank of Syria, 119–20
refugee crisis, 287–94, 322
Reporters Without Borders, 203–4
Republican Guard, 87
Resolution 1441, 109
Return to Homs (film), 230
Revolution for Dignity, 286
Revolutionary Youth, 55, 56
Rice, Susan, 250
Romania, 76
Rubio, Marco, 249
Russia, 21, 22, 269, 275, 285–7, 295, 305–6
   air campaign, 287

Sabboura, 142
Sadat, Anwar, 35
Saint John the Baptist, 105
Saleh, Habib, 101
Salhieh Nights (series), 158
Salhieh shopping street, 43

Salhieh, 71
Samaha, Michel, 193
Sami, 3, 4
Sankar, Omar, 125
Sarkozy, Nicolas, 186, 194, 204
Sarout, Abdel Basset, 229–30
Saudi Arabia, 22, 33, 79, 90, 185, 234, 319–20
Sawiris, Naguib, 122
Seale, Patrick, 20
Secretary General of the United Nations, 81
Security Council Resolution 425, 172, 178
Security Council Resolution 1511, 110
Security Council Resolution 1559, 176–7, 178
Sednaya, 308, 312
Seif, Riad, 101, 124
Seleznyov, Gennady, 22
Seven Fountains Square, 58
Shaban, Bouthaina, 211, 215–16, 246
shabiha, 239–40
Sharaa, Ahmad, 312, 313–14, 316–17, 318–19
   Paris visit, 319
   stabilisation efforts, 319
   Trump and, 319
Sharaa, Farouk, 81–2, 89
Sharon, Ariel, 106
Shebaa Farms, 173
Shehadeh, Bassel, 222, 228
Sheikh Saad market street, 98

INDEX

Sheikho, Marwan, 10
Sheraton Hotel nightclub, 51
Shia Islam, 41
'Shiification', 284
Shishakli, Adib, 38
Shukri Quwatli Street, 14–15
Sibai, Mustafa, 41
Siniora, Fouad, 186
Six Day War (1967), 32
Sleiman, Michel, 192–3
'social market economy', 181
social media platforms, access to, 212
Socialist Arab Baath Party, 55
Socialist Baath Party, 39
Soleimani, Qassem, 285, 294
Solidarność movement, 75
South Lebanon Army, 172
Soviet Bloc, 75
Soviet Union, 20, 73, 75–6
Spain, 106
Spotlight (series), 155, 157
'Statement of the 1,000', 103
Stop the War Coalition (StWC), 275
Suleiman, Fadwa, 229
Sunni Muslim, 40–1
SuperStar programme, 174–6
Supreme Islamic Shia Council, 41
Sweden, 299
Switzerland, 31
Sykes, Mark, 284
Syria Accountability and Lebanese Sovereignty Restoration Act (SALSA), 110

Syria Times (newspaper), 38
Syria Today, 202
Syria TV, 308
Syria, xi, xiii, 11–12, 29, 34, 90
  Assad and Hussein, 76–9
  Assad's funeral, 12–13
  banana shortage, 60–3
  Clinton, relations with, 23
  drama industry, 154–60
  economic and administrative reform, 128–30
  education, 54–7
  gender, 142–6
  Israel's violation, 108–11
  mobile phones, 146–7
  monopoly, 119–21
  news on, 18–19
  party leadership, 6
  Rami's development, 125–8
  Rami's involvement, 117–19
  scholars, 20
  troops, 42–5
Syrian Airlines, 122, 126
Syrian Arab Airlines, 69
Syrian Armed Forces, 27
Syrian Central Bank, 59
Syrian Computer Society, 87, 132–3
Syrian Jews, 87
Syrian military checkpoints, 169
Syrian Ministry of Foreign Affairs, 80
Syrian National Council, 234
Syrian Network for Human Rights, 252

INDEX

Syrian Pearl Airlines, 126
Syrian Revolution, 164
Syrian Treasury, 119
Syrian TV, 23–4, 136
Syrian–Arab relations, 185
Syrian-Egyptian war, 32
Syrian–Iraqi border, 110
Syrian–Israeli border, 35
Syrian–Israeli peace treaty, 89
'Syrians' Arab Spring, 205–6, 213–31
  Al Jazeera, 233–4
  Arab League actions, 235–6, 237
  Assad regime's systematic responses to, 218–19
  Assad speech, 216–17
  Aziz, torture of, 222–3
  Casual Bystander stories, 265–6
  chemical weapons usage, 239, 242–3, 244–7, 252, 285
  coastal area of Tartous, targeting, 240
  Day of Rage, 214
  death rate, 241–2, 274
  defections in the ranks of regime forces, 225–7
  diplomatic action, 233
  first weeks of, 217
  Ghouta, siege of, 243, 244
  Hamza's torture and death, 219–20
  Human Rights Watch report, 219
  Khartabil, arrest of, 223
  mass slaughtering, 238–41
  massacre in Homs, 229–30
  Milk Statement, 219
  Obama's calculus, 242–3
  peaceful demonstrators, killing of, 220–4
  religious terms, 267–8
  schoolboys, arrested, 214
  Shehadeh, arrest of, 222
  siege, imposition of (Apr 2011), 219
  Syrians' filming skills, 266–7, 268
  Syrians' online skills, 224
  Tammo, assassination of, 221
Syrian–Saudi cooperation, 173
Syriatel, 122–4, 175

Taeb, Mehdi, 283
Tahrir Square, 217
Taif Accord, 172–3
Tammo, Michal, 101, 221
Tartous Forum for National Democratic Dialogue, 101
Tartous, coastal area of, 240
Thatcher, Margaret, 69
Thatcherism, 117
Time (magazine), 262
Time International, 262
Times, The, 238
Tishreen (newspaper), 17, 162–3
Tishreen Park, 203
Tlass, Firas, 121
Tlass, Mustafa, 16–17, 52, 120
tourism industry, 198

INDEX

Treaty of Maastricht (1992), 75
Truman Show, 253
Trump, Donald, 251, 295, 319
Tueni, Gebran, 178
Tunisia, 204, 206, 213
Turkey, 90, 169, 234–5, 293, 299
Turkish army, 218
Twitter, 212

UAE, 298
UEFA, 255
UK (United Kingdom), 108, 110
   response to the chemical massacre, 244–5
Ukraine, 286
Ukraine, invasion of, 299
Umayyad Empire, 106
Umayyad Square, 14–15, 27, 198, 199, 329
UN Security Council Resolution 2254, 312
UNHCR, 200, 201
Union for the Mediterranean, 192
United Arab Republic, 34
United Nations (UN), 21, 46, 81, 239, 240, 274–5, 295–6, 300–1
United Nations Security Council, 111
United States (US), 20, 23, 24, 31, 35, 69, 73, 176, 244, 275
   Assad and Hussein, 76–9
   11 September 2001,
   new ambassador to Damascus, 195
   response to Khan Shaykhun chemical attack, 276
   targeted strikes on Syrian chemical weapons centres, 295
   terror attack of, 106–8
UNRWA, 278
UNSC Resolution 1483, 110
upper classes, 170–1
US–Syrian understanding, 168

Valentine's Day (2005), 172
Vanguards (the party's student wing), 43
Velvet Revolution, 76
Vienna, 81, 84, 288, 289–90
Villa Moda Emporium, 183
Violations Documentation Center, Douma, 228
Vogue, 212
Voice of America, 73

Wagner Group, 300
Wajiha, 7
Waldheim, Kurt, 81
Wałęsa, Lech, 75
Wall Street Journal, 212
'war on terror', 106–7
Washington, D.C., 24, 35, 84, 107
Watergate scandal, 34
Waters, Roger, 276
West Berlin, 75
White Helmets, 276
White House, 89
World War II, 75, 158

Y2K, 131

INDEX

Yaffour, 142
Yafi family, 170–1
Yafour Complex, 126
Yanukovych, Viktor, 194, 286
Yarmouk refugee camp, 278
YouTube, 212, 224

Zaitouneh, Razan, 228
Zakani, Ali Reza, 283
Zarif, Javad, 281
Zein, Melhem, 174, 175
Ziad, 72
Zoubi, Mahmoud, 121–2